CHRISTIANITY

IN

WORLD PERSPECTIVE

by

KENNETH CRAGG

LONDON
LUTTERWORTH PRESS

First published 1968

COPYRIGHT © 1968 KENNETH CRAGG

Second impression 1969

LONDON

Lutterworth Press, 4 Bouverie Street, E.C.4.

AUSTRALIA and NEW ZEALAND

J. H. Morgan, Lane Centre, 325 Flinders Lane,
Melbourne, Australia

G. S. Cook, P.O. Box A351, Sydney South,
N.S.W., Australia

R. H. Horwood, 75 Kitchener Road, Milford, Auckland,
New Zealand

CANADA

G. R. Welch Co. Ltd., 222 Evans Avenue, Toronto

CARIBBEAN

K. Jackson Marshall, P.O. Box 420, Barbados,
British West Indies

FAR EAST

Graham Brash Ltd., Prinsep House, 36c Prinsep Street,
Singapore 7

M. Graham Brash & Son, F-1, 12th floor, Mirador Mansions,
58 Nathan Rd, Kowloon, Hong Kong

INDIA

Christian Literature Society, P.O. Box 501, Park Town, Madras
Tract and Book Society, South Street, Bangalore,
Wesley Press and Publishing House, Mysore

S. AFRICA

J. R. Dorman, P.O. Box 5532, Johannesburg

ZAMBIA

United Society for Christian Literature, 3 Cairo Road,
Lusaka, and P.O. Box 274, Kitwe, Zambia

This book is published in the U.S.A. by Oxford University Press, New York

7188 1357 X

Printed in Great Britain by
The Camelot Press Ltd., London and Southampton

To
the brethren of
St. Augustine's College,
Canterbury,
from many lands,
1960-1967,
a Warden's grateful salute

"Ah, when to the heart of man
Was it ever less than a treason
To yield . . . and accept the end
Of a love or a season?"

CONTENTS

PREFACE

THE CHAPTERS of this book present, after further reflection, the substance of eight Lectures delivered, by invitation of the Faculty of Divinity, in the University of Cambridge, during the eight weeks of the Michaelmas Term of 1966. Through two earlier autumns Canon M. A. C. Warren had presented studies, subsequently published as *The Missionary Movement from Britain in Modern History*, and *Social History and Christian Mission* (London, S.C.M. Press, 1965 and 1966). I must record my deep gratitude for the privilege of the opportunity and the honour of the sequence.

Through work at the Central College of the Anglican Communion at Canterbury, and from other causes, I had for some years been impressed with the consequences of the contrast between nineteenth-century Christian mission in the world and the apostolic precedents in the first century. Not the least of these was the marked dominance of western cultural forms and assumptions in the whole context of Christian thought, worship, custom and practice among the nations of the Gospel's dispersion. The geographical universality of the Church, or nearly so, had been achieved only in the context of a deep cultural partiality.

How might a will to genuine and reciprocal diversity within the one faith of Christ undo this heavy western bias of its modern history? How might 'Englishness' be transcended, as 'Jewishness' first had been, in the true fullness and freedom of the Holy Spirit?

This is the 'perspective' meant in the title. What follows here is no more than an essay. It aims only to illustrate what an answer might involve in three areas where it must be given, namely in relation to the Jewish, the Islamic and the African, with some reference also to the secular temper.

These, it is realized, do not make a 'world perspective' except as samples of a much wider duty. My silences may at least help to atone for my temerity.

The ascription, with acknowledgements to Robert Frost, combines with acquiescent sorrow a warm gratitude.

Canterbury, 1967   KENNETH CRAGG

ACKNOWLEDGEMENTS

Authority to quote from the works named is hereby acknowledged to the Publishers indicated:

Cambridge University Press: *My Life* by Ahmadu Bello.

Cassell & Co.: *Broken Images* from *Collected Poems* by Robert Graves.

Chatto & Windus Ltd.: *The Lost World of the Kalahari* by Laurens Van Der Post.

William Collins Sons & Co. Ltd.: *Brief Authority* by Charles Hooper; *Letters from a Traveller* by Teilhard de Chardin.

Faber & Faber Ltd.: *The African Image* by Ezekiel Mhpahlele; *Markings* by Dag Hammarksjold.

Victor Gollancz Ltd.: *Black Mother* by Basil Davidson.

Grossman Publishers Inc.: *The Colonizer and the Colonized* by Albert Memmi (an Orion Press book distributed by Grossman Publishers).

William Heinemann Ltd.: *Arrow of God* and *Things Fall Apart*, both by Chinua Achebe.

Hogarth Press Ltd.: *The Dark Eye in Africa* by Laurens Van Der Post; *Turbott Wolfe* by William Plomer.

Longmans, Green & Co. Ltd.: *A Humanist in Africa* by Kenneth Kaunda.

Melbourne University Press: *Mamre: Essays in Religion* by M. Buber.

Thomas Nelson & Sons Ltd.: *Autobiography* of Kwame Nkrumah.

Overseas Missionary Fellowship: *The Weathercock's Reward* by D. Bentley Taylor.

Présence Africaine: *Bantu Philosophy*.

Routledge & Kegan Paul Ltd.: *Child of Two Worlds* by Mugo Gatheru.

Seabury Press: *Conflicting Images of Man* by W. Nicholls.

S.C.M. Press: *The Primal Vision* by John V. Taylor.

Society for Promoting Christian Knowledge: *Pastor on the Nile* by H. C. Jackson.

Union Seminary Quarterly Review: *No Religion is an Island* by A. Heschel.

"The Church is no island, entire unto itself . . . every man's need diminishes me, as every man's life increases me: for I am involved in mankind. Therefore, send to know for whom the temple waits, for whom the drum beats, for whom the muezzin calls, for whom the silence speaks—it is for thee."

CHAPTER ONE

NINETEENTH-CENTURY MISSION
IN
TWENTIETH-CENTURY PERSPECTIVE

'Tell me whose men ye are' says he,
'Or whose men that ye be;
Who gave you leave in this Cheviot chase
In the spite of mine and of me?'

THE question is as old as the families and nations of mankind and their territorial stakes and frontiers. It fits well enough the whole nineteenth-century penetration of the rest of humanity by white empire and by western Christianity.

Those Percies of Northumberland who invaded the border lands of the Douglas clan, as the *Ballad of Chevy Chase* records with a grim gaiety, have a family chapel on their ancestral estate, lined with tablets and brasses that celebrate their worthies of many generations, victims of strife or builders of power. A visitor there, turning from a perusal of these proud monuments to the business of Divine worship, observed wittily to himself that the familiar clause of the Prayer Book might well have begun "Almighty and most Perciful God".

"Whose men are ye?" "In the spite of mine and of me?" Though quoted remotely from a medieval source, the question and the protest so plainly characterize the issues that occupy the chapters of this book. Modern times have witnessed a wide expansion of the Christian Church across many frontiers into most of the cultures and societies of the world. For all its continuing frailty and fragmentation, Christianity intends and embraces the human whole. But this modern extension of the Christian name and presence has been largely dominated by one culture and derives from one hemisphere. For all its inclusive impulse it is seen by most of

13

the world as the perquisite of western proprietors. Their near monopoly in its expression and theology, their weight of numbers and tradition, compromise its true dimensions in humanity.

By the same token, it has often seemed, in its coming, an intruder and an alien, a presence disruptive of existing societies and ancestral cults, a trespasser among historic faiths and the communities they have begotten. Its quality as possessed, in the main, by western servants has induced a defensiveness against it and inspired the conviction that this ubiquitous and intrusive Christianity, for all its panoply of love and compassion, is a venture "in the spite of mine and of me", of us and ours. Men in their cultures have rallied in the re-assertion of themselves or hesitated, in wistful or dubious uncertainty, to know whether the Christian promise of the human unity in Christ would, or could, surmount the paradox of its highly partial custody in modern history. "The Holy Spirit and us . . ." the apostles said, in a notable communiqué from their Council in Jerusalem, according to Acts 15. "Christ and ourselves" is the much more problematic association with which the contemporary Church addresses the human community from its mainly western capitals.

The immediate purpose is not to retell the history of modern missionary ventures[1] but to take the measure of this fact that its universal impulse has been articulate and operative in circumstances of strong particularism. "The voice is the voice of Jacob: but the hands are the hands of Esau." The solidarity of all men as a conviction in Christ is proclaimed and propagated so as to enfold "the ends of the earth". Yet the agencies which are the condition of that enterprise carry so markedly the fashion of their origin in one-quarter of the world—the Lord of all humanity in the serving company of some of them. "No doubt the God that Fr. Labbat revealed to my ancestors is also the God of the

---

[1] Admirably done by Max Warren, *The Missionary Movement from Britain in Modern History*, London, 1965, and Stephen C. Neill, *A History of Christian Missions*, London, 1964.

towards universality discernible in certain Greek cults and in Stoicism were thus powerfully actualized in Christianity, by dint, too, of the generous impulses of Jewry towards the Gentiles symbolized in the Septuagint. These were all the more energetically accomplished in the Church by reason of its liberation from the hesitancies by which Judaism had been inhibited from the decisive implementation of the human unity implicit in Biblical monotheism. Now in Christ there was neither Jew nor Greek, neither bond nor free: all were children of God by faith in Christ Jesus.

Deferring a more adequate account of the sources and sinews of the New Testament "will for the world", the immediate point is to see the great expansion of nineteenth-century Christianity as moving in the same obligation and in the vigour of the same compulsion. The critical assessments to come do not obscure or question that essential obedience and its rich outpouring of personal devotion. There can be no right concern, as ours here, with a falling short of world perspective in terms of theology and culture, except in generous salute to a heroic attainment of it in respect of adventure and of travail. There have been few sustained movements in history more consistently given to ministry, more zealous in compassion, more generous with advantage, more unstinted in quality, than the initiatives of Christianity towards "the stranger beyond its gates" in the nineteenth-century. In the end, it is by its own, and not some external, insight that its compromises and failures are to be discerned and reproached.

Furthermore, it is only in the light of subsequent experience and the vantage of time that different criteria emerge to its judgement. There was a near inevitability about many of the conditions of mind or circumstance within which it proceeded. It is in some measure because of its achievements that attitudes of greater hospitality to culture, bolder and deeper relationships in encounter and communication, not to say energized sources of articulate resistance to its Gospel, have become practicable. It is futile to apply considerations founded on twentieth-century situations to nineteenth-

coloured people", writes M. Capecia, poet of Martinique, "but He is still white".[1] For all its will to comprehend mankind in equal standing in the Gospel and in a single reconciliation, there was inseparable from that Gospel's nineteenth-century custody a priority of position for those addressing over those addressed. The welcome Godward was also an entering into relation, as it were, with His elder brethren. These, in offering what was God's, were purveying what was theirs. Possessiveness on the one hand and indebtedness on the other were accentuated by a variety of sharpening factors to which the relationships were liable. Thus the faith of Christ was somehow reserved even while it was given: it belonged to its bearers in the very act of being opened to its hearers. The very communication tended to be an exercise in retention. The freeing of men by the Gospel was at the same time a binding of them to a fashion of its corporate expression congenial to those who brought it. Thus what was universal in its motive and meaning was at the same time culturally 'partialized' in its form and sequel. The legacies of this paradox are with us still.

It may be argued that this situation is inescapable: the learner is always dependent on the teacher, the 'missioned' on the missionary. Is it not the same shape of things which the New Testament captures in the words of the First Epistle of St. John: "That which we have seen and heard declare we unto you, that you also may have fellowship with us: and truly our fellowship is with the Father and with His Son, Jesus Christ" (1: 3). Here, too, is the original message and the prior people: hearing the one means recruiting to the other. Yet somehow the Church of the Apostles and their immediate successors seem far more surely to have attained a unity of heart within the relationship of preaching and receiving than has been the case with their modern counterparts. The telling and the taking were then far nearer to their proper quality as a transaction of equals in the very nature of the grace of God.

The New Testament translation of particularity into

[1] *Je Suis Martiniquaise*, Paris, 1948, p. 65.

universality, with its decisive precedents and inner tensions, is the theme of chapter 2. We may best broach the nineteenth-century contrasts by first bringing into one focus the authority under which all other criteria of judgement and comparison must proceed. We state it with an eloquent simplicity in the phrase of the Nicene Creed: "Who for us men and for our salvation came . . ." The neighbourhood of man is constituted in the Saviourhood of God: the unity of humanity is postulated in the Incarnation of Christ, and both with a force of conviction all the more impressive for being so utterly straightforward. Our solidarity as men is confessed in the context of the active compassion of God. There is no flourish of trumpets, no chanting of slogans, no self-conscious anti-racialism or liberal condescension that so readily slip into postures of patronage. The Creed is beyond all these because it is not moving from any uneasy conscience nor searching for a face-saving compromise that will conserve the substance of privilege while conceding the spirit of equality. It is not remotely within this complex of inner reservation or potential hypocrisy. "Us men"—could there be a surer statement of human one-of-anotherness than this use of the plural, personal pronoun "us"—a pronoun in objective case because it describes an involvement made real and incontrovertible by a common status under God? Not "us whites", nor "us blacks": nor yet "us Jews" nor "us Gentiles": nor, again, "us blacks and whites", nor "us Jews and Gentiles"—simply, sublimely, "us men". For the Creed the wholeness of humanity is an incidental truth all the more secure and central for being so. In the reality of God in Christ it has a surer context than our frail assertion of it against the separatisms of our passion and our enmities. Is there anywhere a deeper, firmer 'humanism' than this clause in the Christology of Nicea, emerging as it does from the Biblical understanding of man in the world?

"In every field" then, as Teilhard de Chardin has it, "we will live constantly in the presence and with the thought of the whole"[1]—the whole extent of human dispersion as far as

[1] *Building the Earth*, London, 1965, p. 53.

the utmost isles, and the whole range of human endeavour. The intention of the Incarnation comprises every expression and evolution of men, everything human is counted fit for its relevance and is, therefore, the parish of its Gospel. "This is a faithful saying and worthy of all men to be received" says the First Epistle to Timothy. (1 : 15). Implicit in the nature of the Christian faith is this human inclusiveness making it 'native' in every context. There are no aliens in its reckoning, no monopolists or outsiders in its view of the world. It is chartered under God by this confession "us men", where the sense, and the acknowledgement, of a single humanity converge.

"For this God", wrote Fustel de Coulanges in a memorable passage, "there were no strangers". Christianity instinctively sought out the indifferent and deliberately undertook the recruitment of the world. If we may properly see in the Hebrew sense of election a supreme moral courage, undertaking responsibility in history towards a single, Divine authority, and in the Greek genius a profound intellectual courage in accepting the rational trust of experience and nature, we may recognize in the Christian Church in the New Testament a superbly loving courage in bringing together these two and accepting the single incorporation of humanity as a dogma and a task. With the Church the domestic, city-protecting, tribe-concerning deities of the pagan past were repudiated in an effective universalizing of the Divine and the human relationship. Christianity

> . . . was not the domestic religion of any city or of any race: belonged neither to a caste nor a corporation. From its first appearance it called to itself the whole human race.[1]

From this vocation flowed the opening out of Jewish particularism and the emancipation of conscience from the tyranny of statehood. Since it ceased to be necessary to exclude or despise the foreigner, law and patriotism could acquire a limited and so proper autonomy. Early

[1] Fustel de Coulanges, *The Ancient City*, trans. from the French 1877, p. 522.

century decisions. History is neither reversible nor anachronistic: historians may be. It has to be remembered that the universal is always in the trust of the particular—particular persons, conditions, occasions and places. The nineteenth-century is no exception. Our duty is not to dispute or disown the way it was, but to take the measure of the consequences, for a fully world-dwelling Church, of the suppositions and situations within which it was served, with energy and good faith, and without hindsight, in the nineteenth-century context.

The first and most evident of these lay in the fact of empire. The parallel histories of mission and colonialism are not yet free from the pride and prejudice which their contents provoke and which often quite fail to register the cross-currents and eddies in the stream of events. There has been nothing like the close juncture of "the flag and the Cross" that some writers allege. Instances of sharp, colonizing suspicion or obstruction of mission, and of vigorous missionary criticism of government are frequent enough to disprove any thesis of near identity between the two purposes. Their relation has been more complex and ambiguous than western assumption or non-western accusation has generally recognized. Yet that they were broadly parallel is not in doubt. European commercial expansion provided the occasions of Christian mobility and imperial authority, in its turn, utilized, or shielded, or answered, missionary imagination. "Their gain", Drake had said of the penetrated lands even in the sixteenth century, "shall be the knowledge of our faith, and ours such riches as their country hath". The priest and preacher could not long exclude the merchant, even when they had preceded him. It was in vain, for example, that King Affonso of the Congo wrote, in the same century as Drake, to King John III of Portugal:

> . . . we need from (your) Kingdom no other than priests and people to teach in the schools, and no other goods but wine and flour for the Holy Sacrament: that is why we beg Your Highness to help and assist us in this matter, commanding your factors that they should send here neither merchants nor

wares, because it is our will that in these Kingdoms (of the Congo) there should be neither trade nor market in slaves.[1]

Sadly, bread and wine have their sacramental dealings in the flesh and blood of the Lord only within the world that admits no less of desecration than of hallowing and where the acquisitive may explore the continents and exploit the flesh and blood of men for their perversity. In any event, it was with a plea to a king that Affonso hoped for satisfaction. Governments with their authority were necessary to curb rapacious traders, their own or others. Thus there was no escape from the political in the issues belonging to mission, either in the coming or the going. It were idle to ask for "a purely spiritual encounter".[2]

Examples of the fact are legion. Livingstone, supreme among nineteenth-century missionaries, was convinced of the desperate need for 'governing' above all else. Unless one could pacify it was mocking futility to evangelize. The tragic devilry of the Slave Trade could only be mastered when a peaceful commerce could be substituted, and this demanded an effective control by which to subdue the strife of tribes and cut off the occasions of human trafficking. Hence, in Livingstone's logic, the geographical enterprise of exploration as the prelude to the opening up of the continent to those pre-conditions of its benediction. Is it not fair to see in the magnificent loyalty of Susi and the other carriers in the explorer's service and their incredible devotion to his remains a mute African perception of the truth of his dominating purpose? It was as "a great chief" that they returned him to his own people to lie, his heart withal in Africa, among the mighty of his nation. Their gesture, springing from deep inner sources of African culture and courtesy, belonged reciprocally with the bigness that had come to them and reached out, in the token of his corpse, towards the other 'bigness' out of which he sprang. We can make no valid

[1] Quoted from Basil Davidson, *Black Mother*, London, 1961, p. 139.

[2] W. A. Visser't Hooft, in *No Other Name*, London, 1963, p. 119, calls for "a purely spiritual encounter" between the religions. The plea is valid as an insistence on deep, open, truth-loving relations; but if we want it absolutely then, as St. Paul says, "we must needs go out of the world".

comment on mission and government if we miss the dignity of this African relation with western authority in the trust of the dead Livingstone.

Charles Mackenzie's brief encounter with the tribes of the Zambesi in 1861–62 underscored the same lesson and logic of a military peace which, with attractive forthrightness, he took upon himself. The Universities' Mission to Central Africa, itself a fruit of Livingstone's visit to England in 1857, sent him, long before any flock existed, as Bishop of Central Africa. Mackenzie, with an honest insight, refused to preach. Prior to years of patient study, neither he nor any local informants could find any short-cut ways into the pagan mind with the vocabulary of Christ. But meanwhile compassion had immediate tasks. Mackenzie released a column of shackled slaves he met on the march and was at once involved in the whole complex of force and grace. Once freed, they needed defending against repossession and revenge by their late owners whose 'property rights' the Bishop had violated. This opened up in turn the prospect of full-scale engagement in quasi-military terms with a hydra-headed evil. Death intervened and Mackenzie's more discreet successor later withdrew down the Zambesi armed only with an umbrella. There can be little doubt with whom the truer realism belonged. Mission, in this revealing episode, lay in a stout personality, a few devoted comrades and their English guns and alliance with a local, friendly chieftain. It was an honest combination of crozier and musket, with the Bible, *The Imitation of Christ* and Keble's *Christian Year*.[1] Deplored as it was in the secure committee rooms of London, Mackenzie's venture, with its seal of tragedy, had within it the whole dilemma of the time. Its very pathos states the case for the missionary invocation of imperial, or at least forceful, pacification, alongside, but preferably not in the same hands as, the Christian mission.

The more eloquent these examples the more paradoxical the equation. The inevitability, to these Christian purposes, of power and control did not, and could not, obviate its

[1] See Owen Chadwick, *Mackenzie's Grave*, London, 1959, p. 70.

militancy, at the same time or in the long run, against many of the intentions of the missionary Church. In some places, the inability of missions to exclude or subdue the evil aspects of the openness by which the faith itself profited was painful in the extreme. In Tahiti, for example, and elsewhere in the Pacific, traders, planters, escapees, followed, as the 'saints' had done, in the wake of the explorers. Prior to the French take-over, the power-void only accentuated the distress of the Christian agencies.[1] While it is just to castigate them, as Herman Melville did so passionately in *Typee*, for their disruptive influence on local culture, it is idle not to see their consequences as part of a much wider complex. But the more one lays the final blame on the whole western irruption into the Pacific the more guilty, so to speak, becomes the 'innocence' one can thus reserve for the representatives of Christian faith. For their Gospel failed to proclaim heaven without the makings of hell or hold forth life in Christ without death from the West. Such were the ambiguities of empire and the lack of it, the benison or the bane of trade, as the context within which the Church moved, whether in sanguine expectancy or disquiet and misgiving.

In either event, it was a relationship of dominance which the over-all situation bestowed upon the western servants of Christ throughout the Asian and African worlds. As surely as Augustine, landing from Rome in sixth-century Kent, and far more overwhelmingly, they came as those who spoke from a superior society and enjoyed the authority of evident advantage in almost every realm of their relationship. For the most part, their penetration of alien or virgin territories seemed a confirmation of their right to impose their will, to colonize and appropriate. The dissemination of Christian faith fell all too readily into the same pattern. It was the spiritual dimension of the trust of the blest to the yet unblest, of the enlightened to the benighted. Evangelism was the occupational necessity of the few within the pride of civilization that was the occupational hazard of the many. The

---

[1] The story is vividly narrated in Alan Moorhead, *The Fatal Impact*, London, 1966.

laudable earnestness of the one was only dimly aware of the other and rarely cast it off. Missionary zeal, to be sure, criticized colonists and empire-seekers, but more often for particular hindrances to its own purpose, than for any fundamental suspicion about the whole shape of things.

To the 'imperial' aspects of Christian expression throughout the nineteenth century must be added, on every count, the 'white' factor. The race-complex, as 'western' peoples see it, must, of course, come in reverse into every reckoning. Missionary estimates have need to be vividly alive to those ruminations about 'whiteness' with which the author of *Moby Dick* prepares us for the mystery of the white whale. For they belong in grim measure with other men's retrospect of the white world.

> Though in the vision of St. John, white robes are given to the redeemed, and the four and twenty elders stand clothed in white before the great white throne, and the Holy One that sitteth there white like wool: yet for all these accumulated associations, with whatever is sweet, honorable, and sublime, there yet lurks an elusive something in the innermost idea of this hue, which strikes more of panic to the soul than that redness which affrights in blood.
>
> ... not yet have we solved the incantation of this whiteness, and learned why it appeals with such power to the soul: ... yet should be, as it is, the intensifying agent in things the most appalling to mankind.[1]

The recurrence of the phrase "the white man" in the contemporary literature of Africa and Asia, bears out how haunting this dimension was, and is, in the contact of Christianity with the larger world. Thus, for example, Achebe:

> Like many potent things from which people shrink in fear, leprosy is nearly always called by its more polite and appeasing name—white body.[2]

It is not a gratuitous remark—only a measure of the fascination of intimidating things. He goes on:

[1] Herman Melville, *Moby Dick*, Modern Library Edition, New York, 1950, pp. 188 and 194.
[2] Chinua Achebe, *Arrow of God*, London, 1965, p. 177.

We have a saying that a man may refuse to do what is asked of him, but may not refuse to be asked: but it seems that *the white man* does not have that kind of saying where he comes from.[1]

Apprehensiveness was at first sight instinctive.

Shaw spoke of his difficulties in overcoming the . . . repulsion which his white skin had aroused when he first visited the Dinka. Many of the people had never seen a European and so thought that a white skin was the disgusting pathological symptom of leprosy or some other disease. He was an object of terror from which children fled weeping into the bush.[2]

Such initial situations are no doubt part of pioneer history. But unhappily there is a parable in their very crudity which refuses to stay with children in the bush. A much more subtle and persistent unease pervades the reaction to white relationships, however sophisticated their character or their reception. It is, in perspective, one of the sorest liabilities of modern Christian mission that it has been so exclusively pursued by white humanity and served by white initiatives.

It was, perhaps, the assumptions of inferiority that the factor of colour somehow imported, the sense of dismay at a presence that could not be accommodated without submission.

> I feel, ridiculous among them, an accomplice . . .
> I feel ridiculous in their shoes, in their dress suits,
> In their starched shirts, in their hard collars,
> In their monocles and bowler hats . . .[3]

Or just a suspicion of irreducible alien-ness that refused truly human community:

They were kindness itself, these two beautiful Fotheringhays, these charming innocuous anachronisms; I reflected, driving home to Ovuzane, that although they had spent nearly all their lives in Africa, they had never begun to think of Africa.[4]

[1] *Ibid.*, p. 106.

[2] Quoted from H. C. Jackson, *Pastor on the Nile*, London, 1960, p. 118. Shaw was one of Bishop Llewellyn Gwynne's colleagues in the Southern Sudan.

[3] Leon Damas, *Pigments*, Paris, 1937, from a poem, "Wages". The poet is a French Guianan.

[4] William Plomer, *Turbott Wolfe*, London, 1965 edition, p. 114.

Laurens Van Der Post, in his powerful study, *The Dark Eye in Africa*, broods sadly on this aloofness in the white presence and the fundamental withholding of humanity. While interest among whites in new territories ran high where geological resources were concerned, with flora and fauna a poor second, being less lucrative themes, attention to things of mere human worth—dialects, customs, rituals, traditions—was almost nil.[1] The white invasion had, in the main, so keen a will to exploit that it had little mind to recognize the truest wealth.

Examples of this absence-in-presence, this partializing of the white amid the human, crowd all too thickly on the historian and the observer. Some readers will recall the dismaying picture of irreconcilability and chronic divergence with which E. M. Forster's *A Passage to India* concludes. Or this from Charles Hooper's *Brief Authority* on a church disused because its white congregation would not have it shared with Africans:

> Quite the hardest thing to bear was the melancholy state of St. John's. . . . The superlative action of the Eucharist would find its soaring words: 'In love and charity with your neighbours . . .' striking flat echoes from the walls, while Host and Chalice were elevated before the vacant judgement of unoccupied pews. This was the hardest to bear, because the refusal to worship with my neighbour is blasphemy: and the refusal to worship is rejection not of man but of God.[2]

Or, where white relationships have been in intention compassionate, they have often been patronizing in effect. Dr. Kenneth Kaunda writes:

> They gave many things but they did not give themselves. The relations tended to be one way, with the European dictating the degree of intimacy, deciding what he would give to, and what he would withhold from, the relationship.[3]

Or was it simply that human relationships complicated by race could not well survive the stress of political bedevilments?

[1] London, 1956, p. 42.   [2] London, 1960, p. 62.
[3] *A Humanist in Africa*, Letters to Colin Morris, London, 1966, p. 73.

There undoubtedly exists—at some point in its evolution—a certain adherence of the colonized to colonization. However, this adherence is the result of colonization and not its cause. . . . In order for the colonizer to be the complete master, it is not enough for him to be so in actual fact, but he must also believe in its legitimacy. In order for that legitimacy to be complete, it is not enough for the colonized to be a slave, he must also accept this role. . . . One is disfigured into an oppressor, a partial, unpatriotic and treacherous being, worrying only about his privileges and their defense: the other into an oppressed creature, whose development is broken and who compromises by his defeat.[1]

This fixing of 'images' has many angles and is reinforced by sheer contrast of culture. To the white, status and the 'value' of time create a habit of office which seems, in the African view, to make unavailability the badge of rank and inaccessibility the sign of power, in a total reversal of the familiar patterns. Habits of dominance, in any event, coarsen the finer textures of human exchange. And they provoke the 'native' to instinctive, perhaps militant, re-assertions of itself, or inspire divided counsels in a culture sensing its own demise. However impulsive the ill-judgement, there can be no mistaking its deep psychological validity. For a relationship of inherent, or exceptionless, inferiority is utterly insupportable to the human spirit.

These considerations of 'imperial' circumstance and 'white' aegis were reinforced by a third general factor implicit in the very nature of mission, for which one might well borrow the term 'managerial'. It was not only that sanctions of power, welcome or unwelcome, lay behind the Christian presence and that there were painful and inexorable antitheses of racial origin: it was, further, that western Christianity found itself for ever 'organizing' and 'officiating' in every context of its coming. This is in no way to ignore or discount the massive obstacles it encountered or the formidable energies it summoned to the conquest of disease, the

[1] Albert Memmi, *The Colonizer and the Colonized*, trans. from the French by H. Greenfeld, New York, 1965, pp. 88–89. Memmi, a Tunisian Jew, writes within the perspectives of North African independence struggles.

mastering of languages, the curbing of the ravages of man and nature. Yet for all this incredible resource of skill and character, pitted against extraordinary odds, it has in retrospect the semblance of enjoying a steady advantage with its technical, educational and cultural endowments. It brought with it the dispensary of all the benedictions a sick and hungry and ignorant world awaited. For the most part it found older faiths or cultures in strange atrophy of their finer ideals, or languishing, for a variety of reasons, in inertia or decay. Over against the social negligence of the religions, as their societies reflected them, it was all too easy for the Christian faith, like busy Martha in an uncaring world, to give its very seriousness and sacrifice a compromising tone of condescension. Surmount this, and there were still the implicit problems and pitfalls of necessary compassion.

If Christ is to be obeyed, ministries of mercy must be fulfilled. Doctrine, without action in its meaning, is a travesty. One cannot proclaim the love of God and forbear to meet the needs of man. Yet doing both, in missionary conjunction, is to open the situation to the charge of paternalism or worse. Medicine and tuition in Christ's name then incur the accusation of disguised bribery or may be said to reflect an inability to trust the faith to make any headway in the world without these aids. Hospitals, orphanages, schools, clinics, welfare programmes are seen, in such analysis, as so many masquerading inducements to allegiance, whatever their service to the beneficiaries. The possibility, as distinct from the distortion, of these charges only underlines the paradoxical snares of compassion, the exposures involved in mercy itself as a principle of relationship to men, the more so when the ministries of mercy are equipped with technical capacities beyond the reach, or at times even the comprehension, of the recipients.

All too readily something like the Prospero-Caliban relation lurked dangerously in the happy shadow of the hospital or school. The 'high priest' of medicine, with his white robe, his antiseptic 'ritual', his surgical wizardry and his scrupulous hygiene, wielded, so to speak, the magic wand that tamed and conquered the ills of Caliban, yet somehow fastened his uncouthness on him the more firmly thereby. Education, also, liberated aspirations which its incidence failed adequately to satisfy.

> You taught me language: and my profit on't
> Is, I know how to curse . . .

Or it tended to identify the progressive with the alien and the inferior with the traditional. It created an appetite for action which it was loath unstintedly to concede.

There was mastery, and there was tutelage, a long day. The form of relationship was oftentimes too much for human frailty either to transcend in full humility on the one hand, or in genuine independence on the other. Even the great Schweitzer is not immune from strong suspicions of 'benevolent despotism' and there have been lots of lesser souls who found in mission the satisfaction of an egoism which, in a field of more equal relationships, would have been healthily reduced. The whole imbalance between authority and subservience worked disadvantageously to both.

Conversion tended to generate in many quarters a posture of excessive compliance and deference, even on occasions an obsequious temper. The faith, after all, had been the precious gift of the missionary and he constituted the obvious court of appeal in all that related to it. Did he not expound the Scriptures, teach the music, order the worship, manage the budget, decide the questions, design the churches, enjoy the competence and settle the issues? There was, for him, all too little necessary dependence upon his local fellow Christians, except in strictly contributory capacities as builders, learners, trainees, listeners. Perils and martyrdoms, of course, befell the pioneers, and the progress of the faith exacted from heralds and hearers alike the toll of courage and self-expending devotion. But within the ranks of discipleship, the necessities of dependence were heavily in one direction only.

In respect of translation, truly, as Mackenzie's refusal of premature preaching emphasized, there was of necessity an urgent reliance on local partnerships of a prolonged kind. For the one thing, if no other, the missionary must needs 'receive' is the language in which to give. Yet even here, since the faith awaiting expression was his to elucidate, dominance, wittingly or unwittingly, could still remain with him and play a cramping role, as not a few early versions of the Scriptures, for all their painstaking, give proof. It is all too easy to foreclose the taxing transactions of vocabulary equivalence, or—more likely—the lack of it.

In the main, there was no one outside their own circle to correct the missionaries, and unquestioning discipleship, awed by gratitude or timidity and tempered by affection, was often uncritically tolerant of many forms of gaucherie in idiom, in music, in custom and in behaviour, or else settled down to a double kind of acceptance world, moving with only partial reconciliation between school and hut, church and village, faith and superstition, Scriptures and ancestors, trusting the while in a sort of double insurance, Jesus and the taboos, prayer and the beads, salvation and witchdoctors. This was neither deliberate duplicity, nor artful compromise; it was rather the co-existence of two worlds, the instincts of the one imperfectly permeated by the intentions of the other.[1] Many of the problems inherent here persist. For they are part of the perplexing mutualities of Christ and culture. Their point, in our immediate context, is simply their witness to the habits of authority and deference characterizing missionary relationships.

In the same realm, the analyst has to ponder the numerous factors complicating the reception of Christianity from external causes—the desire for English language as the sesame of education; the asset of dress, status or advantage; the need to have an eye in the white world's mysteries and masteries; the value of the influence of mission personnel in

[1] See John V. Taylor, *The Primal Vision*, London, 1963, pp. 15–25, "Classroom Religion". Cf. also Kenneth Kaunda, *op. cit.*, p. 30, "I suppose the standard retort would be that he has not yet been fully 'converted' to Christianity that vestiges of paganism still remain in his mind. It is not as simple as that. The African mind does not find it easy to think in terms of Either-Or. It is open to influences which make Both-And seem desirable."

quarrels with colonial authorities or their 'native' underlings behaving as lordlings with their own. There was economic gain, too, in Christian emancipation from the agricultural taboos, the bad earth superstitions and phobias of the pagan mind. 'Christian' freedom from the social vetoes or inhibitions of existing religions had its mundane as well as its spiritual attractions and thus entailed a confusion of motives, vexing to unravel and impossible to eliminate.[1]

Areas of mission, for all these reasons, tended to become "colonies of the spirit", with a docility of acceptance that made the emergence of a genuinely critical independence slow and tentative. It was easily assumed on all sides, that the western and the Christian were synonymous. The local wistfulness to imitate meant a too sweeping disparagement of the beliefs and mores that conversion displaced. Perspectives of patience were lacking, both in situations of ready accession or of embattled conflict. The very exactions of mission on the physical and emotional plane worked paradoxically to lighten its theological stresses, by foreshortening the ultimate problems of relationship to culture. This in turn contributed to missionary assurance. The Church, in its ready conviction as to the trust of the answers, did not always measure or heed the questions. And, like the empire, with its insistent full-dress parades, for example, under the hot Indian sun, the faith was liable to reproduce, in every place of its dispersion, the criteria and shape of its domestic character. Roman Christianity was transmitted in full Rome, Anglican in true Canterbury, Lutheran in pure Luther and Presbyterian in faithful Genevan.

The perils of generalization are notorious and there is temerity in thus attempting to summarize a vast complex extending over several generations and many lands. Yet, through the intricacies ignored, or even in detailed part violated here, the consensus of the nineteenth century

[1] Cf. Chinua Achebe, *op. cit.*, p. 55, "I want one of my sons to join these people and be my eye there . . ." And the same writer's *No Longer at Ease*, London, 1960, and D. Okafor Omali's *A Nigerian Villager in Two Worlds*, London, 1965, an autobiographical study of how white power worked to the opportunity of mission and the new faith disrupted tribal life.

legacy needs to be understood, if the contrasts of this third quarter of the twentieth century are to be properly measured and enforced. With that intent, a historian might well turn to a now memorable moment of truth in missionary counsels occurring with painful frankness at the Edinburgh Conference of 1910—the first of the milestones in ecumenical development in this century.

Vedanayagam Samuel Azariah, later Bishop of Dornakal, had only lately been made deacon at Madras. He was one of a very few Asian delegates in an overwhelmingly white assembly. When he had been asked by John R. Mott to speak, he had at first declined, but undertook to do so when assured that outspokenness would be welcomed. In an address of deep feeling that was to have long echoes in many quarters, east and west, he said:

> Through all the ages to come the Indian Church will rise up in gratitude to attest the heroism and self-denying labours of the missionary body. You have given your goods to feed the poor. You have given your bodies to be burned. We also ask for love. Give us friends.[1]

It was a plea for the fullness of personal exchange in the equal, reciprocal, quality of love and, in tribute to that vocation, a clear indictment of habits, instincts, or perhaps only impressions, of superiority, of patronage and of condescension in the posture of the Christian west to the Indian east. It is interesting to note the ambiguous handling of the speech by Temple Gairdner, himself a justly loved figure in Muslim Christian fields, in his official narrative of the Conference:

> an electric silence, broken now by a sort of subterraneous rumblings of dissent, or startled by thunderish claps of applause, is the least comfortable of all atmospheres . . . even if it were mistaken, the courage it evinced and the delicacy and humour with which the thing was done, entitle it to recognition. . . . As for the criticism, what does it matter even if criticism passed on us is false?

[1] W. H. T. Gairdner, *Edinburgh 1910: An Account and Interpretation of the World Missionary Conference*, London, 1910, p. 111.

He concluded that salutary rebukes "lose no particle of (their) point if the vision of . . . others is most unaccountably mistaken".[1] Plainly 1910 could not quite take it. Yet within that appeal for an equal humanity in Christ, in full personal expression, lay the crux of every other mutual liberty of cultures in their baptism into Him—men's right to think and to build, to sing and to pray, in the honour and freedom of their own idiom, subject only to the one Spirit of truth and holiness. Out of its own criteria, and by its own progeny, mission was being summoned to the inner obedience of its outward universality, to the self-oblation necessary in its self-fulfilment. The task is with us still.

The Edinburgh Conference is rightly taken as a climax in its time of that Christian worldwideness-from-the-west we have been reviewing. If Azariah's intervention is, likewise, truly seen as a fair register of the onus of the 'particular' ascendancy within that universality, then the incident in its dramatic quality constitutes a symbol to conclude our case. It remains in this chapter quickly to note the changed circumstances of the present generation and see developments since those halcyon pre-war days as urging, with their own insistent logic, the unreserved and equal prerogatives of all nations in the things of Christ.

The years since 1945 have seen the steady recession of empire and the eager emergence of independent, national states, asserting the political identity and self-expression of large numbers of formerly dominated peoples and races. By its apostolic criteria, the Christian Church greets with lively, and critical, sympathy this freedom for distinctive existence as the proper and equal right of all. But by legacy of its nineteenth-century history the Church finds itself wrong-footed, faulted so to speak, by its long near-identification with imperial order and by the habits of cultural partiality in which, despite its geographical dispersion, it has generally acquiesced and trusted.

Aspects of this disqualification of its near past by its far past are evident on all hands. There can be little doubt

[1] *Ibid.*, pp. 110–11.

which is the more congruent in temper with the new, external shape of things. The "in Christ neither Jew nor Greek" assurance, to be studied in the next chapter, for all the political quiescence of the Church within the Roman Empire, affirmed just that integral human-ness about all men which the new nationalisms of our time corporately assert against the imperial subordination of some to others. The opening up of the faith in Christ, on equal terms, to Gentile as well as Jew was the abandonment of a kind of imperialism of the Spirit by which Jewry, despite its magnificent potential universalism, interpreted election as a human privacy of its own and made accession to truth a sort of naturalization to itself. That, albeit beneficent, supremacy, the Christian Church in the New Testament disavowed, by the principle of a common open-ness in which birth and breeding had no decisive word. It is right to see in this spiritual non-imperialism of early Christianity an affinity with the impulses by which, in the name of humanity, all other imperialisms are disowned. Modern Christianity, however, has by contrast a long and inescapable association with the forms of political empire and a strong stake in its effects. It can only adjust in painful ways to the new post-imperial climate, even if, in doing so, it is learning anew some implications of its primitive intuitions. The end of the imperial era is for Christian faith a veritable disembarrassment, whatever the complexity and difficulty of the demands it entails.

It is well to remember in this connection that the faith itself has contributed in no small measure to the emergence of the forces by which empire and colonialism have been ousted. It may be over-exuberant to say with N. Sithole that "the Church may be regarded as the guardian angel of African nationalism".[1] What is true is that the teachings of the Christian Gospel and the ministries of healing and education have served to 'personalize' society in ways that

[1] Ndabaningi Sithole, *African Nationalism*, Cape Town, 1959, p. 59. He cites an occasion when a 'revolt' against a decision in a mission school, considered unjust by the boys, was referred in a petition to the head in a paraphrase of Lincoln's words that "government of the students, by the students, etc. should not perish from the mission's school".

Asian and African cultures did not experience or sustain before the Christian coming. The understanding of man and nature and history, in Christ, generated the will to self-fulfilment, the passion for independence, the resources of hope and energy, necessary to the expulsion of foreign authority and the transformation of the colonialized into the free. There have, of course, been many other factors. Repression slowly accumulates its own nemesis. Innate potentialities of race, creed and tradition, are aroused into conscious and then effective militancy through a variety of factors. It would be folly to over-state the strictly Christian factors or to underestimate, as some do, the primal human necessities of soul that empire violates.[1] Empire itself has engendered the forces making for its own eviction and has sometimes taught the very mechanics of revolt. Dr. Nkrumah learned to believe and assert his well-known mis-borrowing of the Sermon on the Mount. "Seek ye first the political kingdom and all other things will be added unto you",[2] because he saw, in imperial presence, precisely such a successful pursuit of political priorities, worthy to be imitated whenever the power balance could be turned. Yet all these

[1] Thus, for example, D. Westermann remarks, "Since they [Africans] have never had a national consciousness, they could not feel humiliated by foreign rule. This attitude of political indifference is changing only through the education the white man has brought with him." *Africa and Christianity*, London, 1937, p. 49. This is, of course, a purely European delusion, reflecting only a certain self-esteem and an insensitivity to local vitality. It is true that the articulate form of 'national' consciousness often emerges only in the 'education' of colonization. Many African writers themselves confirm this; e.g. Al Haji Ahmadu Bello in *My Life*, London, 1962, where he writes of British troops in Northern Nigeria in his youth: "I do not think there was any particular antipathy against them. It was the will of Allah that they should be there: they were not evil men and their administration was not harsh." p. 2. See also p. 158. Ahmad Amīn in *Ḥayātī*, Cairo, 1950, writes in very similar terms about his father's view of the British in Egypt. But if there was a time and an attitude for which foreign occupation was readily tolerable, the springs of that 'identity' to which freedom is due were always there and are in no way a gift of the alien or a creation from the West. To think otherwise is hopelessly opinionated.

[2] See his *Autobiography*, London, 1957, p. 164, a formulation of the policy of the Convention People's Party. It is in line with the unhappy statement on p. ix: "It is impossible to talk of equality of races in any other terms" (i.e. than the political). For unless there are deeper grounds than the political ones, the will to independence would have no legitimacy other than its chances of success.

34

powerful factors owe something of their fulfilment—not to say their opportunity in imperial 'conscience' and restraint—to Christian influences. Even the Bible itself has been a potent source of the dream of liberty and the will to 'exodus' from tyranny. "Go down, Moses" can apply to other bondages than Egypt and the promised Canaan fit the vision of one's native land.

In this sense, then, the Christian Church seeking trans-cultural fullness is making good its own handiwork and this fact needs to be seen as a stimulus to the large duties involved. But by the same token it is imperative to see also how strenuous are the difficulties created by the Christian connection with the old order. The new nationalisms all too readily dismiss the Church—and often with every apparent reason—in the vehemence of their own assertion. Its edifices, after all, may well be lined with tablets and bronzes commemorating western heroes and consuls and generals in wars against mutinies which contemporary history re-writes as sagas of independence. Its buildings are likely set in cantonments reminiscent of the military presence. Its architecture often reproduces the image of Victorian Gothic and its music stays with Thomas Tallis, S. S. Wesley and J. B. Dykes, worthies of the West but not gifted in the lyrics of India or the tones of Africa. Its administrative structure, likewise, presumes the controversies and traditions of the West and fits too readily into a caste society it ought to transcend or allows its ideal of the 'shepherd' to be deformed into that of the 'chief'.

These incongruities aside, self-awareness in the political realm requires its counterpart in every other, save technology, where it cannot be had. For ideology, religion, society, as well as government, there must be a general declaration of independence from what is alien. To say with urgency: "Thy people . . . not my people", is all too readily to mean also "thy God . . . not my God". If salvation is by statehood, then the state must be sustained with the religious traditions, the intangibles of identity, that its emotional assertion needs. Nationalism is a passion often too poor in nationhood to risk a large tolerance or to achieve as yet a secure indifference to spiritual diversity. It tends to sense offence in vestiges of the old order, such as the Church and Christianity often seem, however innocuous in practice. Its demands are liable to be solidarity rather than pluralism, identity rather than multiplicity.

The temper of nationalism, reaching back into its own history and inheritance, has brought a re-invigoration to the ancient faiths. Buddhism, Hinduism and Islam are, as it were, in mutual corroboration with their respective national-isms, giving cohesion and thrust to Burmese, Ceylonese, Thai, Indian, Pakistani, Indonesian, Arab, and other, expression and themselves drawing strength and chastening renewal from the urgencies of new national authority. The process may in due course tend to greater secular distraction or displacement—a theme to be studied in Chapter 7, and to easier plural co-existence of faiths, majority and minority. It is true, further, that in many instances it is not the devotional, constructive, 'spiritual,' dimensions of the faiths which benefit from current circumstances, but rather the elements amenable to political manipulation or emotional interests. But, in any event, Christianity, as the faith of minorities in many Asian and African situations, confronts an exacting complex of relationships, in the need to make good its own loyal part in national duty and its 'universal' bearings in and beyond the nation. Even where paganism, in contrast to the 'great' religions, seems doomed as a pattern of belief, much of it abides as a way of life in conscious retention, as in *négritude*,[1] of its role in African identity, and its preservation against western permeation.

These are some of the strong counter-actions the contemporary scene presents to the Christian obligation within every culture and to the ends of the earth. Nor should we be minded to invoke to its aid here the notion of 'gratitude'

[1] *Négritude* first used as a term by Aimé Césaire in *Cahier d'un Retour au pays natal*, 1947. A powerful element in West Indian and Caribbean negro literature it is also prominent in the thought of President L. S. Senghor of Senegal. See also Jean-Paul Sartre, Introduction to L. S. Senghor's *L'Orphée Noire*, Paris, 1948, and Janheinz Jahn, *Muntu*, Eng. trans. London, 1958.

on which some observers rely. Gratitude, in any case, is not usually a force of any political significance and, while it is easy for some Christians to imagine that what they see as generations of unstinted service to the nations ought to leave a residue of indebtedness that might facilitate the cause of Christianity, the actualities are much more untidy. Some observers, indeed, would see those generations of empire as obligated rather to penitence and apology. But even where gratitude might be expected to remain, is it not true that historical relationships cannot well be based on it, least of all in the setting of new nationalism? Let us here quote a western, in preference to an eastern, source:

> Even in those cases where we owe an idea uniquely to Christian insight . . . the full assimilation of it into our own view of the world calls for ingratitude. Our attitude to our Christian heritage, as to our Greek heritage or our Chinese heritage, is properly exploitative.[1]

In the perspectives of the Gospel this is not a conclusion about which Christianity can well complain. For the willingness for uncalculating self-expenditure is its proper vocation and the central meaning of its Cross. There are, for Christianity, no debts except those it is itself most bound to pay. "Brethren, *we* are debtors".

So then, antipathy itself may be exhilarating. The Church in the post-imperial world has a dimension of opportunity-in-adversity more thrilling than in any previous age. When all is rightly said, in line with our concern in this chapter, about western monopoly as an entailing disability for contemporary Christianity, the steady inter-penetration of cultures needs to be remembered as a circumstance of great import. There are today more and more common denominators of human existence. The will to independence and repudiation is conditioned, nevertheless, by the compulsion to inter depend. In many senses men in every religion are increasingly amphibians—if we may borrow Bacon's term for a different purpose. They live, as it were, in double

[1] D. G. Brown in W. Nicholls, *Conflicting Images of Man*, New York, 1966, pp. 95–96.

hemispheres and belong with a both/and mentality. The notion we have rightly stressed of cultural identity and so of distinction can easily be perverted into a kind of restrictive *apartheid*, if it is invoked with malice from without. *Négritude* is valid so long as it is self-generated and self-defined: it would be totally invalid as an imposition willed from outside upon those it fitted. "To call a march back to indigenous culture" as Ezekiel Mphahlele scornfully puts it, "and thereby help the government to reconstruct ethnic groups and help work the repressive machinery".[1] And so with every culture. The world is such that the will to be must be the will to become, and living at all living as one. Cultural identities turn, more than ever before in history, upon the inter-cultural whole.

> Whether he [the white man] liked it or not, our destinies are inseparable. . . . I have seen too much that is good in western culture, for example, its music, literature and theatre, to want to repudiate it. . . . The white man has detribalized me: he had better go the whole hog. He must know that I am the personification of the African paradox, detribalized, westernized, but still African.[2]

Pandit Nehru saw himself in something of the same sense as a western expatriate in his own India and an Indian expatriate in his adopted West. There are many factors that suggest we may anticipate an increasing incidence of this fusing of human existences into a contrasting commonness. In so far as that is true, it must surely moderate the picture we have properly drawn of the burdens for Christianity of its western custody.

Some there are who allege that the one-world quality of this time has in fact coincided with the irrelevance of faith and the outgrowing of worship. The measure of this view must be taken in a later discussion and its conclusion rejected. The Christian looks, rather, in this single and divided world for the means to the mediation of Christ, out from partial trusteeship more and more into the fascinating and contributory diversities of mankind. It was from just such a

[1] In *The African Image*, London, 1962, p. 36.   [2] *Ibid.*, p. 66.

sense of openness in the world and obligation with the Christ that the New Testament sprang and there precedent and example begin. There we learn to hold the universal as the constant corrective of all cultural privacy and the true context of all cultural fulfilment, in the embrace of Christ and the intention of God.

CHAPTER TWO

NEW TESTAMENT UNIVERSALITY: PRECEDENTS AND OPEN QUESTIONS

IN the poetic theology of the Early Church one of the tenderest images was that of the *ekpetasis*, the embrace of the extended arms of Jesus on the Cross and the open hands of welcome. The clenched fist is all defiance and retaliation: but one cannot be crucified that way. There was about crucifixion this parable of universality and inclusion in the very shape it gave to death.

Inscribed above, St. John's Gospel records,[1] was the *titulus*, or accusation, "in letters of Hebrew and Greek and Latin", the three official languages of the Judean province, that the text of the capital charge might be known readily to all. The words in fact needed little translation, for all but *Malek, Basileus* and *Rex* were proper names.[2] With deliberate ambiguity, this first recorded statement on the crucifixion embodied a double irony—Pilate's jest against the priestly hierarchy and Caiaphas' astute intimidating tactic with the governor. Our theme in this chapter is also a double one— to see the universality in the reach of the Cross within the particularity of its "superscription". What seeks all is initially told in a limited, trilingual situation and moves within the confines of Hebraic tradition, Greek thought and Roman rule, where along with this placard of indictment the whole New Testament exclusively belongs. The event and its telling, whether grim, terse and official, or deep, warm and apostolic, proceed through the languages and textures of Mediterranean history. Yet beyond the first instruments of its expression is a significance worthy to employ all the varied tongues of men.

[1] John 19: 20, and in some texts of Luke 23: 38.
[2] See, in chapter 5 below, a discussion of the operative word 'king'.

At every point the contrast with the nineteenth- and twentieth-century missionary situation is unmistakable. There is no context of privileged imperialism. The Church, on the contrary, is a community of catacombs and persecutions. It is facilitated, truly, by Roman peace and Roman mobility, and benefits intermittently from the indecisiveness or liberal apathy of Roman attitudes. But these give way more often to the virulent suspicions and ruthlessness of a political authority disdainfully implacable against any ideas or persons neutral or critical towards its demands of allegiance and conformity, as the Church most stubbornly proved to be. Thus the first three centuries belong to a victim Church, never secure against the imperial enmity and itself totally innocent of political power or pretension—a subject Church having no sanctions but the quality of its discipleship and the tenacity of its dangerous convictions. From those beginnings in precarious exposure and oppression it is a very far cry to the prestige context of Victorian Christian expansion, where, for all the private heroism and unstinted self-expenditure, there were the assets of imperial connection.

No less relevant is the absence from the early centuries of the 'white' associations of the modern Church. For all their sharpness, the Jew-Gentile, Greek-barbarian tensions at the time of Christian beginnings were not of that exclusifying character. Or putting the matter in geographical symbol, the Mediterranean is not an ocean. Mission in a basin is inherently easier than mission across a hemisphere or over an Atlantic, east or west. St. Paul, preaching in Athens or writing to an already existing Church in Rome, gives lively proof of a sense of defensiveness, even inferiority, before a culture which commands his respect. He does not speak so much of a shame at what he finds, as of being unashamed of what he takes. He moves in a temper of participation and even diffidence, not of estrangement or contempt. The world of his relationships is not opaque and foreign. For it belongs in most essentials with his own loyalties and education. He came always to his hearers from

41

within or, perhaps, as they surmised, from beneath, never from beyond or from above. His audience did not have to say of him, "The white man is like a hot soup and we must take him slowly, slowly, from the edges of the bowl".[1] More likely, as on the Areopagus, they called him "this rag-gatherer", and felt secure enough in their own superiority. This is not to say that there lacks in any culture an inherent sense of preferability to the new and the imported. But nowhere has this instinctive durability and pride of cultures been more disadvantaged than in the white and western invasion of other humanity under circumstances of political dominance, material power, economic strength and racial self-esteem.[2] It will be a long and arduous task in the better perspectives of the future to assess the Christian service and disservice of white peoples. But it is the kind of assessment, incriminating or at times vindicating, for which early Church history has happily no need. The first Palestinian, Greek and Roman custodians of the faith about the Christ had neither the temptations nor the privileges involved eighteen centuries later in being white in the same trust.

With their minority exposure and their cultural solidarity with their world, the first Christians had the further para-doxical advantage of economic poverty and social simplicity. "Not many mighty, not many noble . . ." was not a rhetorical flourish in St. Paul. Their mission moved in the stream of everyday participation. They blunted the evils of slavery by the quality of their brotherhood as between each Philemon and every Onesimus. They cared for travellers by the vigour of their hospitality and commendation, the 'provisioning' of which the Epistles speak. Their compassionateness among men did not proceed by the precious and elaborated patterns of modern mission, deploying resources of external origin and, for all its often selfless devotion, expressive of an alien

---

[1] Chinua Achebe, *op. cit.*, p. 105.

[2] One may cite at random on this score the attitude of Theodore Roosevelt in *The Winning of the West*, New York, 1926, Vol. II, p. 56, all the more apposite for the element of truth within its untruth, "The settlers and the pioneers have at bottom had justice on their side: this great continent could not have been kept as nothing but a game preserve for squalid savages".

and superior world. The problem here is no doubt part of the larger issue of desperate disparity between technology, medicine, skill and capacity in one part of the world and their atrophy or absence elsewhere. It would be as false to sentimentalize about early Christian *koinonia* and *agape* as to reproach the mission school and hospital of the nineteenth century for 'otherness' of character and quality in their ministry to illiteracy and disease, when this was inescapable. The fact, however, remains of a contrast of circumstance that saved the primitive Church from the temptations implicit in the very deliberateness and condescension, however costly and high-souled, of missionary action in recent generations.

On all these counts, the Church of the New Testament, as a source of eloquent precedents, provides a constant foil by which to identify the subtle contrasts of our own time and reckon with their implications. This is no doubt part of the benediction of the Scriptural documentation of apostolicity, to which, in duty bound, our self-criticism must continually return, lest we lose our bearings and obscure our temptations. The circumstances of general history, honestly faced and realistically accepted, make the context in which to work out the criteria of judgement, the emphases of decision, that derive from the definitive Scriptural history. The delineation of the Christian relation to the world is to be sought and found in the understanding of Messianic decision on the part of Jesus Himself. For in that Christly decision the Christian and the Church are constituted. In what did it consist? The answer takes us to the heart of the Gospels, to the ambiguous hope and final reality of Messiah.

"WHERE IN THE WORLD IS GOD?"

A fair question, indeed, and the sum of the Biblical concern. Beyond, and because of, His presence in the natural order lay the ultimate mystery of His action and His rule in history. Human experience, as lived and interpreted in the Old Testament, is simply and surely described if we say that it left a big place for a big answer. The yearning and wistfulness of Old Testament man came from his measure of the largeness and goodness of life. Sin mattered as the forfeiture of glory: wrong had to be taken seriously because life was assuredly blessed. Faith in God and hope in Messiah were thus one dimension: redemption was the self-consistency of the Creator. So clear-sighted is the Bible about man's high calling under God that it cannot but accuse the deep measure of his sin: yet so confident is it of God's sovereignty that it cannot believe the Divine initiative frustrated or withdrawn. "Deep calleth unto deep". History, as men in the nation Israel and under the Torah of Sinai, shape it in the Old Testament is a record of human defiance of God and of good, pursued within a setting of Divine goodness whose purpose is invincible. History, then, calls for a Divine answer to its human significance and Messiah is the crux of it.

But in what terms and by what means would Messiah accomplish Messiahship? Here the evident clues seemed to lie in the institutions of people and polity, of nation and law, which had been the central realities of the faith within which Messianic expectation lived and yearned. Could the law be the theme and guardian of righteousness and that law's exclusion of the ungodly *not* be the corollary of its Messianic establishment? Could Exile be the symbol of history gone wrong through sin and return for exiles into independence not be the sign and pledge of its correction? Could foreign subjugation, alien tyranny, imperial servitude, be the tokens of defeat, and statehood with liberation *not* be the theme of victory? Since "the people of God" were the heart of the problem, could Messiah's reign be other than their political, national, popular triumph?

So out of the very notions of Messiahship misconception sprang, and ideas of His Kingdom became part of what He had to save. The circumstances of Roman occupation in the days of Jesus made it natural for His hearers to assume that Messiah's task would be necessarily nationalist, external and Maccabean, magnanimous indeed, but nevertheless effectual and victorious. Despite the whispers of the Servant Songs and the dark perspectives of prophetic suffering, the books and views most widely loved of His disciples and contemporaries had no hint of humiliation or tragedy. No shadow of death, no Gethsemane, penetrated the Similitudes of Enoch, the Assumption of Moses or the Psalms of Solomon. Throughout it is the nation, for its own sake and in its own sovereignty, which dominates the picture. Even the New Testament hymnology, drawn from the older Messianic traditions, could be fitted to the same interpretation. "That we being delivered out of the hand of our enemies might serve Him without fear". Mary's own *Magnificat*, with its tender reversal of values, could readily be taken, or mistaken, for the traditional hope: "He hath put down the mighty from their seat . . ." Is it strange that people should have wished what Herod feared?

Jesus' disciples themselves moved in the midst of this Messianic ambiguity, cherishing hopes which tallied less and less with the increasing trends of His ministry towards suffering and patience, with His apparent disinterest in public acclaim and His readiness for growing defections. Why, they asked themselves, did Jesus care so little for corporate and manifest triumph or for the prerequisites of success? His works of compassion were deliberately neutralized by His policy of enjoining silence and of checking idle enthusiasm. Yet a popular Messiah needs all the enthusiasms he can muster, idle though they be.

Their mystification grew, too, from His habit of reluctance over an open Messianic confession, despite His apparent concern that they should know rightly His identity. We must not do them the deep injustice of supposing that their slowness to credit His predictions of tragedy sprang from any lack of devotion or of courage. It may be that they hoped to bring Him to a better frame of mind, or else they reasoned that He intended to convey that His mission entailed grievous risks and these they hoped to confine to themselves, while He went unscathed. For that was a proper logic: the underlings were expendable provided only that the central figure remained inviolate. Had not Peter said: "This shall never be *to Thee*"? That there was a prospect of suffering for the Messiah most of all lay beyond their comprehension

45

until the event had made it luminous. All in all, we conclude that Messiahship, as the answer to the human situation, was assumed to be in terms of national hopes and human desires and that Jesus, heroically and in loneliness, proceeded on a contrasted understanding of the mind of God.

If we ask why He saw it differently, the final reason lies in His openness to God and men, or, put in dogmatic form, because He was the Son of God. The Passion and the ministry are all of one piece as the expression of 'sonship' understood not first as a status, but as a quality of identity with the Divine nature, of attunement to the Divine will. He had already seen in the socially outlawed publicans and prostitutes the raw material of grace and had broken through the communal exclusiveness of the law. He sensed that popular Messiahship would be imprisoned in the moral exclusivism He had rejected and that, in national terms, it would leave the deepest evils untouched. Liberate Israel from Roman subjugation and you have still saved neither Jews nor Romans from the tyranny of themselves, nor achieved that universal redemption which the Old Testament chosenness of Israel foreshadows. Full and true Messiahship must break into the universal and the radical reaches of God's purpose or it is betrayed in the partial, the imperfect and the exclusive. "If the Son shall make you free, you shall be free indeed." Through Messiahship according to Jesus, in its suffering quality, the Jewish pride, the Roman injustice, the disciples' failure, the popular rejection, are identified, met and surmounted, in their whole range and in a quality of love which left no element, as all lesser salvations must, outside its reach of pardon and power.

Only when Jesus had been Messiah, in this redemptive encounter with evil, did the disciples know *who* Messiah was. For then they knew *how* He was. The two discoveries were obviously inseparable. Our Christianity, tested by its origin in Jesus as the Christ, means faith in *this* Messiah, as the clue to God and the answer for man. It is a faith about a Cross which leaves no room for pride because it pardons, no room for monopoly because it includes all, no room for anger because it is forgiving, no room for despair because it is in character and inclusion ultimate. The life and ministry of which it was the climax, it is true, had been spent in a single country remote from the centres of empire, and were closely tied to a sharp particularity to which Jesus Himself referred when He said, "I am not sent but unto the lost sheep of the house of Israel". Yet the mind of the Church, taught by the inner clues of His teaching and the reach of His Cross, has consistently seen that historical limitation to the Palestinian and the Jewish as a necessary confinement securing and preparing the universal relevance. So at least His followers understood the concentration in the transaction, turning them from disciples into apostles, by which it gave way to universal obligation. Implicit from the beginning, in a compassion that received the prodigal and saluted the faith of Romans and the mercy of Samaritans, was the impulse the Church knew in breaking out of Jewry into Gentile hospitality. The ethnic and cultural frontiers were already breached in Jesus' crossing of the moral confines of the law's regard. We have the secret of the universal Church in the conversation by the well of Sychar. What Jesus had prospectively seen and undertaken in the meaning of Messiahship, the Church retrospectively preached and exemplified.

" . . . IN CHRIST RECONCILING THE WORLD . . . "

The supreme, definitive precedent of the Church, then, consists in the nature and achievement of Messiahship in and according to Jesus, and Him crucified. This is why the core and theme of Christianity, in creed and allegiance, is in the simple confession "Christ Jesus, Lord" on which New Testament history turns. Messiah and community had always been understood as belonging together, the Son and the many sons. "Behold I and the children whom God hath given me." But instead of being racial, nationalist, or exclusive, this Messiahship means a community that is open, free and ecumenical. State-force or race-pride or patriot-cohesion—all these may have their partial authenticity. But Messiah may not be imprisoned within them, or He is no redeemer of the world. These partialities mean, in some measure, the exclusion of their opposites, the alienation of their foes, the exemption of strangers. They stand in birth-right or moral attainment or political identity and, as such, represent salvation with remainders, achievements which leave out of their range the enemies they outdo or secure a private immunity from evils still persisting.

Man is not restored by teaching alone: for he defies it. Not by law alone is he re-made, for law does not make actual the good for which it speaks. Not by statehood alone, in the service of law, or teaching, or election, for the element of force cannot reach the deepest evils nor include itself in the saving criticism. Teaching, law, education, legislation—all have their relative place. But there is no salvation for the human situation that is merely legal, or ethical, or political. So Messiah's action must be more ultimate than these. It is in the Cross alone that evil, enmity, prestige and sin find no answering and new-breeding return of their own image, and where, for that very reason, they find the liberating word. Sin is borne away only where it is borne. It is in this quality of grace that the supra-racial character of the Gospel lies and the steady realization of it is the great theme of the Acts and of St. Paul. Accidents of birth, race or culture do not now obtain in what is a personal discovery of a new sort of collective recruited by the common energies of grace and the common denominator of faith. "Thou hast opened the Kingdom of heaven to all believers" they sang in the *Te Deum* with an accent strange to the pride of Israel and folly to the ethics of the Greeks. What turns upon grace and personality cannot be racially received or culturally confined. It has to do with men as men, their sins and fears, and not with Jews as Jews, or Greeks as Greeks. Thus its unity majestically transcends the most stubborn divisions in humanity.

The New Testament narrative seems, by emphasis, to intend Saul's conversion as the representative exemplar of this discovered universality through Messiah-Jesus. It may be taken, in that sense, as the conversion to illuminate conversion, not of course in its dramatic circumstance (for this is more apparent than integral) but in its central logic. Contrary to some recurrent suspicions that Paul invented Christianity by imposing Paulinism on the Galilean Jesus, this view takes him as epitomizing what the recognition of Jesus means. It is by insight and obedience that he is representatively Christian, that the urge in his Gentile mission is one with the significance of Jesus as Galilee and Gethsemane knew Him.

The vision on the Damascus road, when we rightly understand it, is the crux and proof of this. Everything in St. Paul's theology and his travels is truly the sequel to that encounter and an active commentary on its meaning. It was there he found the calling into the world beyond Jewry for the single reason that there also he found the reality of Messiahship in Jesus.

We begin with bitter hostility to the Church, on the part of Saul, precisely for the reason that they claim in the crucified Nazarene the Christ of God. This antipathy of Saul is all of one piece with the enmity of the Pharisees to Jesus in His ministry. That He, before the crucifixion, had linked Messiahship and suffering and embraced them in His own claims and person was bad enough. That the disciples took up the same theme and, corroborated by the Resurrection, should insist that the actually crucified Jesus was in truth the risen Messiah, was worse than all. Little wonder that Saul, in the ardent priestly tradition, "breathed out threatenings and slaughter against the disciples".

This identity of the issues is confirmed by Jesus Himself, in the arresting words of the vision, "Why do you persecute *me*?" Saul's vehemence against the Church is all one with his veto on the Messiahship of Jesus. In harrying the one he is utterly repudiating the other. It is just this identity, on the positive side, between the exalted Christ and the victim Jesus, that the point of the vision affirms: "I am Jesus . . .". Not "I am Christ". Such a word from the heavens would have occasioned a well-taught Jew no surprise. Elation, perhaps, but not revolution. Was not Messiah expected to be riding on the clouds of power? But the voice identified

Dc

itself as belonging to the real Jesus and yet spoke from where Messiah alone could be. Here in one transforming focus was the whole mystery of "the Lord Christ Jesus": here in compelling power was the truth that in those very words— "Jesus Christ is Lord"—became the core of Christian creed and the theme of St. Paul's whole devotion and theology.[1]

"Obedience" to the heavenly vision begins in the capitulation of mind and will to this Lordship: "Lord, what wilt thou have me to do?" The whole trend and course of his ambition and his being are reversed. He found himself confessing the wonder which formerly he had found unthinkable. Yet the crisis had been slowly mounting in the patient logic of its own elemental mystery, in the authenticity of the way Jesus had achieved Messiah's ends, attested as that decision was in the steady demeanour of the Christians, the constancy of Stephen and the whispered misgivings Saul's own vehemence had struggled to forget. Hence the metaphor of the pricks. Once won by the crisis into acceptance and peace, he was ever dominated by the consequences of the Lordship he had come to own. Such a Christ must be the Christ of all: such a Cross takes in all peoples. The same voice that proclaims the identity of Jesus commands the mission of the new disciples: "hence afar unto the Gentiles". Or, as St. Paul later set it down in writing to the Corinthians:

> The love we saw in Jesus-Messiah is what carries us forward in its mighty flow. We have reached the firm conviction that in dying, as one for all, He laid all under the obligation of sacrifice. And this is the reason why, from now on, we no longer follow the world's way of looking at things and people. Why! the very way we used to think of the Messiah has been utterly and

[1] It may be useful to note, in the same sense, the force of a passage which, by exegesis little short of obtuse, has sometimes been utilized to suggest that Paul's Gospel was in fact disinterested in Jesus of Nazareth and centred round a Christ of faith of his own creation. The passage is 2 Cor. 5: 16, about "knowing Christ after the flesh . . ." The passage is in no sense debating whether the actual Jesus was known to Saul: it has to do with this-worldly ideas of the Messiah. We used to have our own nationalist, 'fleshly', racialist notions of how Messiah should be; but now having known the Christ we no longer think of Him, or indeed, of any people, that old way. It is surely worse than foolish to argue that St. Paul here, or anywhere, is disinterested in Jesus and Galilee: he is plainly acknowledging the Messianic revolution in Jesus Christ.

irrevocably changed. We no longer think of Him in those fleshly terms of prestige and Jewish honour. And so it is that everything is new, in Messiah, in *this* Messiah. The old way of looking at things is gone for good and all: everything takes on a new guise . . .[1]

This is the energy and the benediction which enable and enjoin an attitude of hopefulness towards all, since there is no reach of evil that can dismay this Gospel or take it unawares. All has been already faced in the transaction that gave it birth. So we are no longer bound to the old calculus of race or culture or heritage in weighing the possibilities for our fellow men.

Here, then, the universality of Christian faith belongs, rooted in the nature of its origins. Hence also the splendid extension of the community of this Messiah beyond its initial heirs in history, across the daunting gulf of Gentile distinctions and into the wholeness of mankind. St. Paul, within the New Testament history, is the main, but by no means the sole, protagonist of that inclusiveness which constitutes a ruling precedent for all subsequent time. If Jewry, with all its Old Testament tradition of covenant, had no writ to monopolize the Christ, no other cultural matrix of the faith can claim or will to do so.

The quality of that opening out of privilege is evident in the New Testament narrative, where it originates with nameless disciples from Cyprus and Cyrene, preaching in Antioch to Greeks, some time prior to the ministry of Paul. Despite tensions between localities and leaders in the Church, about which in their detailed complexities scholarship differs, there can be no doubt of the general unanimity of the New Testament in the basic decision for the open Church. Nor was it that the apostles, so to speak, de-Judaized their faith and worship in order to Gentilize it.[2] On the contrary: they held

[1] 2 Cor. 5: 14–17.
[2] Though, especially after the Fall of Jerusalem, strong factors developed to isolate the Jewish and maximize the Gentile elements. One unhappy element was the way in which Gentile influence fostered the use of 'Christ' as an alternative name rather than a definitive title, thus opening up the way for the sort of misunderstanding just noted of the sense of 2 Cor. 5: 16 and obscuring the full significance only the formula "Jesus *the* Christ" preserves. On the whole Jewish issue, see chapter 4.

tenaciously to their heritage of Scripture and psalmody, of prophecy and liturgy. They believed themselves heirs and servants of the universality latent in the very nature of election. They spoke of Abraham as being, centuries before Sinai, and the law and the covenant, the progenitor of *all* the faithful. Yet this steadfast hold upon their Jewishness admitted no compromise of their will to Gentile participation. They understood their obedience here, not as some gratuitous extension to others of what was inherently and possessively Jewish, but rather as the service of the essentially universal thing which had come about within a Jewish framework. "We (Jews) believe that we shall be saved even as they (Gentiles)" was the way they spoke, making the general the norm for the Jewish.

Their way was paved by the example of Jesus, interior to Jewry, in welcoming "publicans and sinners". For the problem within Israel of "the ungodly seed"—the souls who were physically "of the covenant" yet ethically its despisers—was in its essence the same problem inwardly as that of the godfearing Gentile externally, namely the problem of the law and "righteousness" not being coterminous. Inevitably this dilemma took its place among the Messianic themes. For clearly Messiah would have to address himself both to the unworthy sons and to the mystery of the wistful aliens. Were the ungodly inside the chosen people to be sifted out and perish? Were the nations to pay homage to Israel's God or be eliminated? How would Messiah relate to good hearts outside the pale? These were all aspects of the same burden. Jesus, as we have seen, proceeded by the same incorporation of grace in Galilee and Judea which the Church learned to translate into the wideness of the Gentile scene. So the Acts records the coining, by pagan spectators, of the name 'Christian', to denote the resulting community. For it could be described neither as 'Jewish' nor as 'Gentile' exclusively. The wits of Antioch chose with a rare perception, minting their gibe from the central clue of Messiah-Lord in a term that emerged from a new identity.

This "reconciling of the world" takes shape in the Acts and

the Epistles as a reciprocal movement of Jew-to-Gentile witness and Gentile-to-Jew solidarity. The one is a mediation of word and worship, the other a ministry of deed and care. There is the outward-reaching activity of travel and translation "from Jerusalem round about unto Illyricum" and beyond: there is the inward-returning sacrament of compassion in the Gentile offering. In the former, St. Paul expends his tireless energies of body and spirit: for the latter, he forfeits the very liberty to expend them. It is well to remember that of all the tribulations recorded in 2 Corinthians 11: 23–28 none seriously impeded his evangelism. What did so was his dedication to Christian unity in taking back to Jerusalem the symbol he called the "unspeakable gift". We set down the significance of this striking fact of New Testament priorities before taking in review the trusteeship of doctrine and fellowship by which Jerusalem and Antioch, as bases of expansion, had brought such responsible faith and compassion to birth.

The initiative, it would appear from 2 Cor. 8: 3, came from the Gentile Christians themselves. But the project seems to have grown steadily in St. Paul's mind to something of quite vital import. In 1 Cor. 16: 3 he writes of sending the offering to Jerusalem by any bearer of whom the churches approved, and adds: "If it be meet that I go also, they shall go with me". On further reflection, he evidently found it very meet, for this objective became an inflexible purpose, as timid friends discovered in trying to deter him. He determined to seal the whole enterprise with the special imprint of his own apostolic participation and set himself actively to promote its collection, using forwardness in one church to kindle liberality in another, and despatching Titus to Corinth to pursue an advocacy that had been effective in Philippi. He used only the methods of godly example and grounded the whole appeal on solidarity and mutual debt in Christ. These, he knew, would alone give substance to his brave boast about there being neither Jew nor Greek in the one Lord.

The successful partnership of instinctive humanity in the

churches and its personal nurture by apostolic enthusiasm resulted in a splendid precedent and a deep sacrament of unity, hallowed by St. Paul's deliberate jeopardizing of his freedom and his life, in a costly act of statesmanship. It would be worth anything, he reasoned, to show the hesitant "saints" at Jerusalem that Gentile grace in "the imitation of Christ" and so in the community of Messiah was real and effectual. This care for things Jewish and duties Jewish was no less real in the realm of his spiritual sharing the other way round. He was no wild betrayer of his people and his heritage, casting their pearls before those swine. He was, in both directions, the guardian and servant of a living authority of covenant, made good in a hospitable and transforming Gospel, and proving itself in the blessed creation of community. The relevance to Jewish scruples of Gentile conversion is thus to be seen as all of one piece, in Paul's mind, with his perpetual theological concern to justify Jewish realities to Gentile "debtors". He firmly rejected the view that Gentiles should be converted to Judaism before participating in Messiah. Yet for Jews as Jews the law still had validity. The new universalism required a right loyalty to the old particularism, in gratitude on the part of the newcomers, and in conformity on the part of the old heirs. Thus the apostle to the nations lived and died a Pharisee.[1] There was a genuine reciprocity in the unity he found in Christ, and an eastward as well as a westward crisis of decision in the biography of his ministry, which it is sober as well as poetic to call a circle of love. "God", he said, "was in Christ reconciling the world unto Himself and has committed to us the word of reconciliation".

"THE UNFOLDING OF HIS WORDS"

What then, sacramentalized in this compassion out of Europe, was the secret out of Judea and Syria by which it came to birth? the communication in deed derived from the communication in word: the work was the fruit of the faith

[1] On St. Paul's concern for his Jewishness see W. D. Davies, *Paul and Rabbinic Judaism*, London, 1948, chapter 4, pp. 58–85.

and the ministering a recognition of debt. Important New Testament precedents reside in those outward ventures of preaching among the Gentiles. A fascinating study opens out for the scholar of vocabulary transactions of a quite creative kind. There are, of course, differences of view about particular interpretations and a variety of controversial issues. But there can be no question that the Acts and the Epistles employ in the expression and commendation of the faith terms consciously drawn from, and directed to, the familiar world of speech and thought among Gentile hearers. It is equally clear that the new borrowings were in studied divergence from basic terms current in the Judean or Galilean context but either opaque or difficult for pagan, Gentile folk. A concordance suffices to trace a score or more recurrent ideas and terms in the Epistles that find little or no place in the Gospel narratives.[1] Even a partial list is impressive: γνωσίς, knowledge; παρρησία, boldness or frankness; εἰκων, image; ὑπομονή, patience; σοφία, wisdom; ἐκκλησία, assembly and church; βεβαιωσις, confirmation; ἐλευθερία, liberty; κοινωνία, fellowship; ἀναστρυφή, conversation or behaviour; ἁπλοτης, simplicity; οἰκονομία, dispensation or régime; καταλλαγή, reconciliation; πληρωμα, fullness; ἀρχαι, principalities; and κληρονομία, inheritance. Some, no doubt, arise from the simple change of milieu and the obvious necessities of Greek equivalents for the Hebraic originals of the Christian themes. Nor is it claimed that all this activity was of pioneer character within the Church. In the world of the Septuagint and a deeply Hellenized Judaism any such claim would be wild and extravagant. Yet when all due caution has been observed, there seems reason enough to posit a quite considerable effort of trans-language initiative within New Testament theology.

The *Logos* doctrine and the bold baptism into Christian usage of the term μυστηρίον are the most conspicuous examples of all. The contrast between the opening of St. Mark's Gospel and of St. John's illustrates the whole issue.

[1] Or when they do occur it is in a factual, not a conceptual, usage, as with εἰκων, image; and κληρονομια, inheritance.

55

The former has its deep theological affinity with the latter in its simple assertion, "The beginning of the Gospel of Jesus Christ the Son of God". But it plunges at once via a prophetic citation into the hard concreteness of John, and the crowds and Jesus coming out of Nazareth of Galilee. The Fourth Gospel presents the same figure of the Baptist with no less dramatic simplicity of fact, "There was a man sent from God whose name was John". But the statement takes its place in a profound and classic expression of ultimate theology, for which the Palestinian history recruits and shapes the central theme of Greek speculation. The essential unity of narrative events and philosophic thought, implicit in the whole character of the Fourth Gospel, is eloquent of Christian theological achievement in its integral task and its place within the New Testament Scripture canonizes that proceeding for all time. The Gospel is unmistakably rooted in texture of what happened from Galilee to Jerusalem but is equally the fruit and symbol of the engagement of those events with the whole world of Greek culture. It consummates in the Gospel form what is all the time proceeding in the encounters out of which the Epistles come.

The Scriptural status of these documents of engagement— the Epistles in their immediate relation to life around and the Gospels in their mediation of history—makes them ventures in interpretation that are unique and in that sense irrepeatable. The canon of Scripture has, *ex hypothesi*, the same ties of time and place as the Incarnation itself. The contemporary Church is not called to a theological involvement with other cultures of this definitive kind, since the principle of the canon argues that such Scriptural tasks of the Spirit are completed. But this very fact only makes more imperative what might be called the 'imitation' of the Scriptures. Our loyalty is in accomplishing the same creative trusteeship as they achieve and establish, in a temper that comes to them with an awareness of example as well as authority. If the 'Scriptural' (i.e. 'Scripturarizing') energies of the Holy Spirit in the Church, the activity, that is, by which Scriptures came to be, allowed phrases like "the kingdom of

Heaven" and "the Son of man" to lapse in certain territories by virtue of their disservice to their meaning, the lesson must not be lost on us today wherever there occurs a like opacity in "the Son of God" or "worthy is the Lamb", or "God the Father".

Such precedents of the New Testament Church must not be scouted by timidity. Few borrowings could have been more dubious than to speak of "the mystery of Christ", exposing the meaning of the Saviour to problematic associations attaching to mystery cults, with their esoteric doctrines and their exclusivist ideas. Here, indeed, was a strange, even embarrassing, piece of currency for the truth-interests of the Christian faith. Yet to have feared these dangers and refused the venture would have left the Gentile meaning of Christ alien, enigmatic and remote for many who would find in the new terminology the clues of discovery through discipleship, truth via trust, yearning in fulfilment, to which the new language pointed. These ventures, after all, were no more in their own sphere than the deliberate *argumenta ad homines* which Jesus pursued in the pattern of the parables. "Giving the new", wrote D. Westermann, mistakenly, in his *Africa and Christianity*, "means taking away the old".[1] On the contrary: it means harnessing its possibilities and setting up within it the revolution that will both fulfil and transform it. For if the old is taken away, to whom is the new given? Rather, in Christ, "the old passes" because "all things become new".

No adequate attempt can be made in this space to illustrate this New Testament adaptation to Gentile listeners, still less to justify all its detailed aspects in the face of scholarly discussion of particular points. In these matters theological prepossessions are often more at issue than the minutiae themselves. It is easy, for familiar reasons, to want the New Testament utterly innocent of the sort of vocabulary borrowing that might be perversely cited as syncretistic. But in that event it would not be the New Testament. The fear of syncretism, either as a charge then or a menace now, must not

[1] London, 1937, p. 2.

be allowed to obscure New Testament creativity of mind and usage or inhibit a present energy in the interpretation of Christ. We must be no less wary of the dread of syncretism than of the fact of it: in many situations the former is the greater danger. For paralysis with dogma is always worse than risk for it. There is no theological security more doubtful than the anxious search for it. Of this the New Testament is never guilty.

Take the earliest embryonic credal formula, "Jesus is the Lord", which borrows, as is the manner of the Epistles, the cult-title of the saviours of the Graeco-Roman world. The Greek rendering of Messiah, $\chi\rho\iota\sigma\tau\sigma$, was, as we have insisted, a vital key to the whole theology of the faith. Yet in a purely literal sense the Greek usage lacked the deep emotive power of its Hebrew original and had, therefore, to be paraphrased in day-to-day preaching and conversation —a situation which may well have contributed to the tendency by which it lapsed from an 'official' title into a personal name. 'Anointing' was not significant in Greek history or mores as a seal of kingship or priesthood, though common enough in domestic hygiene. Hence the greater need to designate the glory and authority of Jesus as the Christ by the 'Lordship' of Gentile speech, translating the *Mār* of the Aramaic congregations, echoed in 1 Cor. 16: 22. The usage, however, was fraught with peril. The table of the Lord Christ might be confused with the table of the Lord Serapis, as the same epistle recognizes in its sharp exclusion of any such equivalence (1 Cor. 10: 21, 22): "I do not want you to become partakers of the demons."

It is the necessity, perhaps more than the urgency, of this warning that becomes significant. The whole Church is moving, both in rite and word, within a setting of idolatry and all its cultic forms. The idols have, at one and the same time, to be dismissed as non-entities and denounced as menacing realities. They are innocent of power yet far from innocuous. The only positive Christian proceeding, within this 'negative' menace that attaches nevertheless to their actual unreality, is to affirm the one Lord, the living Christ, whose sovereignty fills the fullness where their folly masquerades and whose worship takes and refines the forms they falsified. Imaginations are not purged *in vacuo*: they are purified *in* their expressions. So the Christian Eucharist, most eloquent of all delineations of Christ-discipleship, readily and openly risks and vindicates itself in the spheres of pagan cults. Yet there is never a doubt that its 'mystery' abides in and with the theme of its institution and with its initiating history in the Upper Room.

All lesser movings of Christian existence within the terms and structures of the pagan world are implicit in this central Eucharist, where the inwardness of the self-commitment of men as Christians meets, in one transaction, the self-oblation of Jesus as the Christ, and does so in the almost universal context of eating and drinking in communion through the created order by consecration of the elemental symbols that nature yields for man and man employs from nature. The focus here of the redemptive in the natural, the economic in the regenerating, is surely, in sacramental terms, the plainest token of the involvement of the Gospel, however riskily, with the cultic reference of all men. The Christian faith fulfils itself, not by isolation from the elements of worship as men venture them, but by partaking, from within its own uniqueness of history, in their familiar patterns of celebration of harvest, of suffering, of remembrance or of gratitude.

Yet the Holy Communion was known intimately only from inside the faith. Not open to outsiders, it awaited the departure even of the catechumens. Thus the final onus for the illumination of ignorance, the dissipation of prejudice, the transmission of meaning, returns to the word. Though truly the Gospel might have said: "In the beginning was the Deed", it is "the Word" St. John's Prologue in fact prefers. "That which we have heard" takes precedence in the summary of things heard, seen and handled of "the *Word* of life" in the First Epistle of St. John. And so it is still. Deeper as "the image" or "the sacrament" may reach in their emotive power, it is the word, the idea, the "communication", that first tells and perpetually interprets and defends the truth, through all its other means. So we return to the initiatives of the Spirit in the art of the preacher. May we not find them exemplified in the encounter of Paul with his audience on Mars Hill?

All the dangers are there in the audience of idle sophistication and dilettante minds. There are some, too, who think that the apostle himself was not here at his happiest, with poetic quotations and philosophical excursions, said to be out of character. The passage, however (Acts 17: 16–34), is surely too significant to be discounted in that way. We must reject entirely the view that the speech was an ill-judged experiment which Paul later regretted and that self-censure over it is reflected in the determination of 1 Cor. 2: 2 "to know nothing . . . save Jesus Christ and Him crucified". There is no direct evidence in that Corinthian passage of any connection with Athenian events. Nor, outside theological prejudice, is there any ground for supposing that what the apostle said on the Areopagus was not a preaching of Christ and the Cross. Only by an assertive limitation of what such preaching should embrace could the sermon be excluded from it. Nor did his auditors hear him to the end. The narrative itself gives no hint at all of its being misguided: rather it is set down as clearly central to a whole movement of response within him to the context oppressively felt. It emerges from a deep stirring in his spirit, as the writer puts it, a strong emotion of mingled yearning and revulsion at the spectacle of Athenian idolatry. It would be sane and reverent to assume that what issues from such travail, unfinished address as it was, needs to be taken as an important, if not definitive, passage of New Testament precedent.

So St. Paul stands, a little awed perhaps but virile and articulate, on Mars Hill, a symbol of the encounter between his faith and the classical tradition. He takes his text from the wayside shrine and his clue alike from its aspiration and its ignorance, "To the God whom it may concern": to the deity we think significant but cannot identify. It may be no more than an altar of prudence, warding off the umbrage of some unwittingly neglected god. But whatever its meaning

for the makers, Paul proceeds to affirm an identity ("Whom
... him") between the God of its intention and the God of the
Gospel. He invites his hearers to a totally new assurance and
awareness, yet links it to the groping worship they already
offer. The Divine 'subject' is constant in either case, his and
theirs: it is their 'predicate'—"unknown"—which has to be
disowned. The Christian relation to that 'ignorance' is first
to reckon with its relevance and only thus to make it good by
truth. Such is clearly the apostle's ruling purpose. His answers
in Christ begin from the questions in men and, however
remote from their goal, they serve to preface the way there.

There is, doubtless, about this scene in Athens a certain
touch of 'atmosphere'; it has the quality of a contrived occasion. The historian says as much in noting the knack of
Athenians in turning philosophy into entertainment—an art
at whose hands theology could hope to fare no better. In this
they well reflected the capacity of the world to find the
earnest Church amusing. Yet the very honesty of this
feature in the narrative only serves to underline the resources,
—humour among them—which the faith must cultivate in
the Spirit, if it is to acquit itself worthily in such a world.

These paragraphs are far from a complete review of the
translation of the Word of Christ into the media of the
Graeco-Roman world from the Aramaic, Galilean, Judean
milieu out of which it came. We have left to silence the
evidence of the Epistle to the Hebrews with its "figures of the
true" and the several echoes of Stoic ethics in Philippians.
The precedent quality of the whole New Testament transaction in Jew-Greek inter-community is clearly incontrovertible. There is a genuine reciprocity within the new unity,
finding practical and sacramental form in compassion,
and there is a partnership of initiating truth with recruited
terminology. Does it not all fit into the vivid imagery of
Hosea 2: 23, which rabbinic writers cited when they
pondered the meaning of their own diaspora: "I will sow her
unto me in the earth"? The faith in the world is like seed in
the soil of the nations, yielding in their receiving ground the
increase of its own life. Whence the ringing assurance of the

prophet, "I will say to them who were not my people: You are my people: and they shall say: You are our God". Through all there runs, as integral to the sense of the universal, the new dimension of the person, the sense of men as men, not of Jews as Jews, or Greeks as Greeks. This effective discovery of personality, individual yet social, the self in its own right and yet properly in company, is the most remarkable achievement of New Testament religion.

"OPPORTUNE, IMPORTUNE"

Unequivocal in all their essentials, those magnificent precedents are nevertheless within the physical and temporal limitations of the Mediterranean and the Canon. The former, as we have seen, circumscribes the range of travel and translation and excludes, for example, the enigmas of the Ganges and the Yangtse. The latter, in some hands at least, tends to the temptation of inflexibility whenever the Scriptural authority is regarded only as decisive and not *also* exemplary and its creative language taken dormantly in an ever-changing world.

Plainly the sense in which the apostles were "in" the world was much narrower than the sense in which we are. Jerusalem and Illyricum are no longer a sort of completed orbit. Nor do we move in the Palestinian circuit of shepherds, fishing nets and temple sacrifice. Paul's travels, for all their heroism and endurance, knew nothing of the oceans and pursued no uncharted rivers to their unknown sources. The world of his assumptions offered a readier and a simpler amenability to dedication than modern life affords. The universal agelessness is there when Jesus welcomes Zaccheus or Mary Magdalen and the moral frontier of the law's esteem is breached. It is there when the covenant of the old dispensation is re-enacted in the new openness by which the movement of the Divine will is multiplied and the measure of covenant transformed.[1]

---

[1] A very useful discussion of 'covenant' and of the several themes in Jew, Greek and Christian relationships in this chapter will be found in F. W. Beare's "New Testament Christianity and the Hellenistic World" in *The Communication of the Gospel in New Testament Times*, London, 1961, pp. 57–73.

Yet, ageless as its promise is, the new comes to us in the necessary context of its particular history and is perpetuated in Scriptural definition according to the circumstances of its first apostolic—which is to say operative—understanding and obedience. Our duty is to renew that obedience in every changing setting of our world and more especially to make it good against the near monopolization of Christianity by western possessiveness which entails upon us, as argued in chapter 1, from the last two centuries. Our calling is to hear, as it were, within the precedents of our Lord and the early Church a great *a fortiori* for our own time. If these Jewish people of God, by sure instinct, surrendered their historical monopoly to a genuine *oikumene* of men, so much the more must all lesser and subsequent spheres of cultural dominance in the Gospel subdue themselves to its properly universal character.

The words of 2 Timothy 4: 2, then, are a fitting conclusion "Opportune, importune" as the Latin text runs. Be there alike when times serve and disserve: be alive and answerable in situations convenient and inconvenient: have a mind alert and expectant but aware also of the constantly deterring factors. The very sense of opportunity is a vocation to tenacity. Humanity provides the occasions for the faith—not to say for fidelity—in the very obstacles it erects against them. The Gospel makes good its welcome to the world by its patience with the world's obduracy. It is among the intractable things that grace comes to abound.

How are these qualities of New Testament mission and theology to be reproduced in our context? What do apostolic precedents of mind mean for a setting without precedent of circumstance like ours? Nowhere are these questions more urgent than in the encounter with men in their religions, and there, too, lies the most formidable aspect of the Christian commitment to universality.

CHAPTER THREE

A THEOLOGY OF RELIGIOUS PLURALISM

"IF you salute your brethren only", says the Sermon on the Mount, "you'll be failing to break out of the general human pattern". The Divine benedictions of sun and rain come, by contrast, with an openhandedness that does not first assess the virtues of recipients. The will to inclusive relationship, free from calculating discrimination, is the "perfectness" of ready hospitality in God which the disciple must somehow learn to emulate. But how it goes against the human grain! Writing of traditional Egypt, E. W. Lane so well describes the habits of first-century Judea which Jesus had in mind:

> Several of their most common usages are founded upon precepts of their religion, and distinguish them in society from all other people. Among these is their custom of greeting each other with the salutation of 'Peace be upon you'. . . . This salutation is never addressed . . . to a person . . . of another religion: nor *vice versa*. Should (one) thus salute, by mistake, a person not of the same faith, the latter should not return it; and the former, on discovering his mistake, generally revokes the salutation.[1]

Time and change have doubtless softened and outdated these communal insulations and compelled a converse of affairs across religious lines. Yet faiths themselves, in the citadels of their theology, are the most prone to introversion of all human things, the least ready for ventures of awareness beyond themselves. The concern in all that follows in this chapter is to attempt a Christian salutation in contemporary terms to those outside Christian community of mind and worship—a salutation that must include, as all greeting does, a worthy cognizance of the other and a ready giving of one-

---

[1] *The Modern Egyptians*, Everyman edition, London, 1908, pp. 203-4. This classic work originally appeared in 1836—"the most perfect picture of a people's life that has ever been written".

self in and with the world, without exoneration of will or exemption of spirit. We cannot proceed upon convictions of universality without incurring relationships with religions. Inter-cultural expression means inter-religious responsibility. For it is by their faiths that cultures have been historically determined and spiritually inspired. Christianity cannot address men and ignore their gods: it may not act in the present and disown the past or wisely hold forth salvation and withhold salutation. In seeking men for Christ's sake, it is committed to the significance of all they are in their birth and their tradition, both for good or ill. To obey a world-relevance is to incur a multi-religious world. Both require a theology of religious pluralism. How do we make brethren by one discipleship and yet greet more than these brethren only? How do we rightly evangelize and properly co-exist?

The first necessity is to face the plurality of religions as an irreducible fact of our human history. To refuse acknowledgement of the continuing there-ness of diverse faiths— whatever our understanding of the providence within it—is to be at odds with existence. "Then", as St. Paul said in another context, "ye must needs go out of this world". The degree of our Christian realism will be the measure of our sense of the faiths of other men. There can be no true claim to a Christian distinctiveness that ignores the actuality of divergent and alternative interpretations of human experience or lives by deliberate isolation from their significance.

We have, moreover, to reckon with those faiths, not only in their historical persistence but in a new, modern quality of aspiration that is much more than mere survival. This opinion, of course, runs counter to much recent, vocal expectation of the near demise of all religions. The secular impact, it is believed in some quarters, will soon rob creed and worship of all but antiquarian interest before the march of secularized technology. The main issue here is postponed to chapter 7, where the argument sturdily refuses this conclusion and bases itself on the staying power of the religious dimension in man, confirmed as it is by the urgent issues of science itself. Suffice it here to claim that many features of the present scene suggest an increasing relatedness, as far as Christianity is concerned, to the major faiths of the nations in what may more wisely be taken as a new lease of opportunity.

Or certainly, at any rate, of numbers. Human growth arithmetically is overwhelmingly greatest in Asia, where the populational centre of gravity of mankind is firmly fixed. Comparatively, the white and western segments of the world are in quantitative recession, despite phenomenal populational increases in the Americas. In so far as religions have their relative importance determined by numbers, Christianity is rapidly losing ground, dwindling from perhaps a third of humanity in the nineteen-fifties to less than a fifth three decades hence when the millennium turns. There are proportionately vastly more Hindus in India than when William Carey landed. In very few Asian and African societies does population increase allow the Christian communities anything but a sharply declining percentage. If the objective of the Christian presence in the world is to possess all nations in their masses, it is manifestly succeeding less and less.

There is, of course, much more than statistics in all this, and minorities have no historical justification for timidity or surrender or despair. But the sheer increase of numbers outside Christianity must remain to the sensitive spirit a deep aspect of the problem of religious pluralism, committed, as we are, to the central significance of persons in their societies. There can be no acquiescence true to Christ in a theology which is content to see the Church in complacent immunity from mankind, contentedly exclusivist, dismissing the big world as a proliferating irrelevance. That would be to greet the population surge of our time with an aloofness comparable to the worst arrogance of the gnostics in the early centuries, finding in statistical inferiority grounds for privacies they entrenched in intellectual sophistication. We cannot interpret a proper minority vocation as a self-conscious disinterest in our multiplying fellows. The need is to search for the positive meaning of this awesome human responsibility of faiths other than our own and of the providence that entrusts it in such critical plenitude of precious folk, of mouths and minds and millions.

The plural religious situation of our time is further solemnized by the new political engagement of other systems of dogma and worship, of code and cult. The present existence of the great faiths is by dint, in important senses, of a post-missionary resilience. We cannot treat or assess them as if the two or more centuries of modern Christian mission had not occurred. Undoubtedly, they have reacted, for their great advantage, to Christian presence and persuasion, absorbing into themselves, altogether apart from conversions —or do we say defections—into Christianity, vital and transforming elements of Christian faith and ethic. The Hinduism of Mahatma Gandhi and of Dr. Radhakrishnan is wondrously different from that which dismayed Henry Martyn so sorely in 1800.

Yet, when all is soberly said about the indirect impact of Christian faith upon the concepts and cultures it had primarily sought to convert, and about the unintended consequences for good of Christian thought and action, the fact remains that the faiths of the world effectively persist, their essential identities intact. There has been no capitulation; and ready assumptions of their disintegration, for example in the nineteen-twenties, have miscarried. They abide, chastened perhaps, but self-possessed, on this the nearer side of a long, and in certain senses highly favourable, period of Christian endeavour to persuade, facilitated as the Church was by the sort of factors appraised in a preceding chapter.

African paganism apart, mission has been held off by the religions; denied by Hinduism, Buddhism and Islam, its primary purpose of recruitment and baptism; and restricted in large measure to the indirect consequences those faiths, in the metamorphosis of their own traditions, were prepared to admit. Even African, and other, pagan systems, in the unequal contest of their primal views with Christian liberty and depth, have contrived a certain resilient perpetuation of their potencies, sometimes in the form of 'sectarian' hybridizing of the Gospel, or, more happily, in a unique spontaneity generating new measures of what Christian expressiveness might mean. Paganism is far from dead in its general defeat.

In the broad view, then, the pursuit of Christian mission, in circumscribed or strictly statistical criteria of what its achievements ought to be, must be seen in many quarters as a study in frustration. With some conspicuous exceptions, the incidence of baptism over many years compels a heart-searching in the ranks of Christian mission as to how its vocation should be defined and its ventures understood.

It is not surprising, therefore, if the intelligent and circumspect within the other faiths look with unabashed, if sometimes also respectful eye, upon the faith of the Church, after these two and more centuries of missions they have registered yet also survived. It is natural if the more ardent or belligerent among them should affirm and pursue a missionary relation in reverse, with emissaries, Buddhist and Muslim especially, prepared and preparing to guide a western civilization that Christianity has proved unable to discipline and save.

This assurance and aspiration provide an external exercise for energies that are also, of course, urgently engaged at home. The bias of population growth, already noted, is corroborated by the steady emergence into world responsibilities in the last half-century of the non-western nations and cultures. The recession of empire has meant a wider distribution of the capitals of power, a break-up, at least in form and constitution, of the imperial concentration of definitive decision-taking in the west. It is doubtless necessary to qualify this consideration by the harsh technological, military and nuclear facts of life which make a physical mockery of all notions of 'independence'. Nevertheless, the many new, politically self-responsible, states of the post-war world give voice and occasion in world affairs to the ideals and capacities of the religions they follow. In so far as the faiths determine the postures of nations, the world is less liable than in the heyday of Queen Victoria to be determined by a

Christian reference and more likely to register influences and determinants arising from the much wider spectrum of the religions. The Versailles Conference decided world alignments and affairs by its own lights and dealt cavalierly, for example, with the Islamic motivations of Indian Khilafatists and Arab nationalists. The plurally religious character of United Nations delegations and their counsels marks a striking contrast.

Emotionally, too, this will to articulate independence and to the exercise of their authority on the part of the nations, by renewing of their traditional resources, has been sharpened by the struggles of anti-imperialism. It is a commonplace that the political prisoners of the decades of resistance became the presidents and premiers of the new order. When the gears shifted from the negative eviction to the positive replacement of the foreigner, ideologies and their religious sanctions were necessarily attuned to the same mood of self-sufficiency. Inevitably the revival and assertion of Asian and African nationalisms involved a renewal and contemporary deployment of their Buddhist, Hindu, Muslim, or traditional, vigour, while Christianity, as broadly the faith of the empire-makers, suffered the liabilities of its external associations.

It is sometimes alleged in western circles that the religions are not genuinely revived, but only politically harnessed, in these events, and that the real making of nations calls for much more than the arousing of nationalisms. On this view the essence of the faiths is in fact prostituted by these political passions and involvments. Such a verdict, however, is suspect on two counts. It is probably premature, in the first place, to regard religious partnership with politics as no more than opportunism. Given all the complexities of the modern scene, the full implementation of self-responsibility must take longer time and be judged by a longer patience than these criticisms command. In the second place, they speak out of a western, if not secular, assessment of religion. When we complain that religion is simply 'used' by politicians and so perverted to 'irreligious' ends, we are largely assuming a particular view of religion as a-political, as a devotional and private exercise between the soul and God. The fact is that for most cultures political and social and religious elements are so intertwined that there can be no question of 'prostitution' in their intercourse. To look only for theology and devotion in Islam, for example, and not also for statehood, is to have missed its essential quality. For almost all religions, as for African *négritude*, the anti-, and now the post-, imperial scene means a lively immersion in total assertion of identity, which some western theorists of religion may find hard to understand and congenial to condemn.

By the same token, of course, the spiritual problems remain, provided we do not mentally isolate them from the entire emotions of nationhood in which they belong. There is no doubt that the religions in their role as sponsors, or, on the western view, abettors, of nationalism, become, in their deeper reaches, also its victims. Nor must we forget the whole Communist thesis, immensely reinforced by the Chinese colossus, that religion is a guilty redundancy in Asian destiny. But the immediate point in our present argument is that it is dangerous to discount, by merely western criteria, either the validity or the significance or the crisis of the religious element in the post-colonial situation and the new nationhoods. It must be seen that there is exhilaration, as well as peril, in the present juncture in the long history of the major faiths. That there is a new quality of dynamism both in their temper and their context is all we are concerned to say. But it is a claim about a large thing which so much in the mood of external observers is minded to question or ignore.

We have, then, both urgent, circumstantial, as well as ancient, essential reasons for taking our multi-religious situation seriously. There is a wise realism, as well as a deep loyalty to Christ, in striving patiently for a Christian theology about the religions in their continuity and their present responsibility.

Yet to reach one is a task which bristles with temptations and problems. There are the pitfalls of easy sentimentality and muddled thinking, of obtuse assertion of identities where distinction is urgent. There is the appeal to goodwill that disqualifies itself by bad faith: there is the superficial neutrality that evacuates issues of their real essence and, so doing, saps the integrity of the mind that moves within them. Or, contrariwise, there is the militancy that makes exaggerated claims, the aggressive fear that forecloses finer possibilities or invokes the menace of relativism and too readily levels charges of syncretistic disloyalty. The literature of the theme is diverse and exacting and there is hardly a question of authority, doctrine, temper and history that is not in some sense included in the range of our decisions within and around it. In the mystery and the burden of the plurality of religions there lies, surely, the supreme test of the meaning we intend when we say, "I believe in the Holy Spirit". That confession is at once followed, in the Apostles' Creed, by the clause, "the communion of holy things".[1] It is perhaps in that sequence of the Holy Spirit and hallowing relationships that we are wisest to move if we are rightly to confess the intervening clause about "the holy, catholic Church".

Understanding that our purpose is a *Christian* theology of plural religions—for only each faith of itself can define for itself a relation to the rest—the suggestion is to seek it by reflection on the inward and the outward aspects as they bear upon each other. What ought the diversity of men's beliefs to mean for the interior shape and temper of the Christian mind and for the exterior relations of the Christian faith among them? The two inquiries are intimately joined: yet they are usefully distinguishable for the sake of elucidation and decision. Hospitality, potential and actual, is perhaps the closest common factor to unite them: and hospitality, the capacity and the reality, is surely the closest of all analogies to the meaning of the Gospel, the transactions of worship, and the nature of God, as these are known and loved, in Christ. Thus conceived, Christianity might rightly be taken as "the open faith", and that sense of openness here

[1] Taking, as there is good warrant to do, the intention of the Greek text and the option of the Latin so as to understand "participation in holy things".

explored as both an inward disposition and an outward relation.

THE OPEN FAITH: CHRISTIANITY IN INWARD DISPOSITION

We begin, in a simple context, with two examples and follow their quality into deeper and sterner reaches to discover the problems that wait for the openness they exemplify. The first is a passage from *The Lost World of the Kalahari* and begins in narrative.

> From there we pushed on faster because the passage over the blackened plain was east. By eleven o'clock the highest of the hills rose above the blue of distance and between us and them lay a bush of shimmering peacock leaves. After so many weeks in flat land and level swamp the sudden lift of the remote hills produced an immediate emotion and one experienced forthwith that urge to devotion which once made hills and mountains sacred to man who then believed that wherever the earth soared upwards to meet the sky one was in the presence of an act of the spirit as much as a feature of geology. I thought of the psalmist's 'I will lift up mine eyes unto the hills from whence cometh my help', and marvelled that the same instinct had conducted Samutchoso to the hills to pray. . . . Jeremiah, who knew something of Samutchoso's story, stared hard at the hills. He had been for a short while to a mission school in Barotseland and now he said suddenly in a small voice: "Master, they look like the rocks Moses struck in the desert to let out water for the Israelites."[1]

The quiet perception of this account is echoed repeatedly in the author's journeys and writings in search and sympathy for the human cultures closest to external nature.

> With our twentieth-century selves we have forgotten the importance of being truly and openly primitive. We have forgotten the art of our legitimate beginnings. . . . of all the nostalgias that haunt the human heart the greatest of them all, for me, is an everlasting longing to bring what is youngest home to what is oldest in us all.[2]

[1] Laurens Van Der Post, *op. cit.*, London, 1958, Penguin ed. 1962, pp. 181–82.
[2] *Ibid.*, p. 151.

In that instinct, surely, the Christian spirit is bound to share, taught by its own compassionate Gospel an affinity with every human reverence. Or take, in a very different context, the following from Teilhard de Chardin's *Letters from a Traveller*:

> Three tall obos with their apparel of boughs and poles were a silent testimony to the sacredness of the spot. Standing there, I offered up the world of Mongolia to Christ, whose name no man has ever invoked in that place . . .[1]

Such emotions of kinship, it may be said, make few demands, beyond a poetic imagination, and shape no taxing controversy, conjectural and passive as their sources are. It is easy enough, if also magnificent, for Teilhard to remark, "I only came to China in the hope of being better able to speak about 'the great Christ' in Paris".[2] But Paris, not to speak of a now vastly altered China, may dismiss that better ability as a private dream. Mongolian obos are inarticulate about the Cross by which a Christian hallows them and Samutchoso's mountains have not cradled Hebrew psalms. Yet, for all that, the sensitivity vocal in these passages, and rare enough in the general Christian tradition, points the way to the open temper.

What we need is just this capacity to feel with the reactions and impulses of men in every texture of belief and unbelief and to possess, not merely as assessors, still less as aliens, but as companions of mortality, the world of their fears and sanctities. By and large, doubt and suspension of faith within our western societies, and varieties of religious allegiance among the rest of men, deserve more generous and lively relationships than they have usually received. The outsider to the Christian community has been all too often treated, in the interests of defensive theology, to a less creative, less imaginative, attitude from within it than Christian criteria demand. We owe a better deal to sceptics and to 'others'. In our eagerness to hear people say, "Lord, I believe", we have too often failed to overhear their whisper, "Help thou mine unbelief".

It is in this context that we need to suspect, and indeed

[1] London, 1962, pp. 118–19. 'Obos' are cairns of sacred stones laid by pilgrims.
[2] *Ibid.*, p. 88.

abandon, the frequent usage 'non-Christian'. It suffices as a kind of convenient shorthand, like 'non-recurrent' or 'nonsensical'. But it quite fails to denote the inner content of the cultures and faiths to which it is applied, even as 'non-Buddhist' would be rejected, or resented, as a descriptive of Christianity. Moreover, it obscures the significant senses in which whole areas of doctrinal 'intention'—as we shall argue below—or at least of spiritual content between religions inter-penetrate and co-exist. It is a blatant confusion, for example, to dub the deep transience-of-life perception in Buddhism, or the sublime creatorhood of God in Islam, as 'non-Christian'. But, worst of all, the mentality behind the usage is betrayed into a treachery. For it implies the negation of kinship, the exclusion of hope, and perhaps even of the acknowledgement of human neighbourhood. Necessary and sharp distinctions deserve to be reserved and pondered in much more hospitable and adventurous terms.

For it is often in a good cause that these habits of assertion and exclusion arise in the history of dogma and in the temper of the custodian-mind. "It seemed good to write and urge that you should be in anxious earnest about the defence of the faith", writes Jude (1 : 3), and we all appreciate his meaning. Yet, from another angle, an anxious apologist is a contradiction in terms, and the very assertiveness aroused by the concern to preserve tends all too readily to obstruct the purpose the preserving intends, making security of doctrine, as it were, an end in itself. Then theologians, it might with truth be said, are doing the wrong thing for the right reason—the reason being the unimpeded accessibility of Christ as Christians love and receive Him, the wrong thing the defensive preoccupation with the dogma that houses Him. There is a real sense in which we find truer loyalty by taking larger risks. Unrisking minds mean cautious trusts and so, in turn, diminished meanings. The claims of communication ought always to be paramount, since ensuring the truth is properly a function of having it received, and this is the guiding loyalty in having ourselves "received it".

There is here, no doubt, a paradoxical mystery and maybe

it is sharpest of all for the Christian spirit. Though dogmas are by nature possessive—even those about dogmalessness—and designed to ensure that nothing is unwisely given away or improperly forfeited, the religions they define have somewhere at their heart the obligation of yieldedness and of surrender. They exist for 'consecration' to the ultimate, rightly known to lie beyond their institutional or cultic selves. While sacrifice, therefore, can hardly be a virtue of creeds, it is essentially the theme of worship. Seen from the standpoint of beliefs, faiths appear, substantially, as ends in themselves: seen from the perspective of worship they are themselves for ends beyond them.

Self-possession and self-oblation belong in some sense even to the most tolerant and amorphous of systems where, as with Hinduism, tolerance is a fiercely intolerant rejection of every exclusive claim. But their conjuncture is nowhere more pressing than for Christianity where the self-preservation, to which creeds tend, is the very principle which Christ crucified refuses and abjures. So we have, for example, a long doctrinal contention for the status of the Incarnate Son; yet that very status in itself consists, not in prestige reserved, but glory self-expending. This is not to say that controversialists had a wrong concept to defend, but that their defence had, nevertheless, to do with a freely defenceless Christ.

It is urgent not to surrender either side of this paradox. There are times, for example, when Arnold Toynbee seems to be inviting Christian faith to forego exclusiveness in such a sense as to jeopardize the very presence, for religious reckonings, of those dimensions which the Christ of the Gospel embodies, and which doctrine 'holds' and receives, and so allows to be received, in expression and recognition.[1]

1 See Arnold Toynbee, *An Historian's Approach to Religions*, London, 1958, and *Christianity among the Religions of the World*, London, 1956. Toynbee sees Christianity needing to apply to its own institutional, and perhaps doctrinal, identity the principle of its own Gospel, namely "dying in order to live". His own clear insistence on the need to break out of the circularity of the argument, which rests uniqueness on the assertion of it, lends force to his concern and there is no mistaking his own profound recognition of Christianity. There is still, nevertheless, the dilemma of doctrine as the guardian of the very meanings by which it learns that guardianship requires self-oblation.

There are other voices too, in a different context, that appear to be so interpreting the Incarnation, as a kind of abnegation of the Divine by the Divine and as a principle of historical relativism, in such wise as to dissipate every meaning of the transcendent which, according to its true majesty, the Incarnation is understood as disclosing.[1] Where this happens, the whole situation with which theology is dealing loses the very tension by which it is constituted. If, so to speak, we de-exclusify doctrine, in these terms, in the name of the humility of God or of the hospitality of Christians, we finish by evacuating that humility itself of the significance it can only possess on the ground of the glory the doctrine uniquely affirms, and thus we end, also, in having no home of faith in which to practise hospitality. It is not by surrender of the Name of God, theologically told, that we shall truly come with others to the God in whose Name, sacredly loved, we surrender ourselves. What the Spirit of love in Christ calls us never to exclusify possessively, so as to repel or discredit "him that is not with us", the Spirit of truth in Christ requires us to affirm with fidelity, so that he might be "with us". The two lessons cannot be detached. It is only within that sanctuary of incorporation that we learn it has no walls.

So it is not by evaporation of its uniqueness that the Gospel embraces the faiths. But the more clear and controlling this conviction is, the more necessary to seek and pursue the openness it enables. Our very assurance is disloyal unless it learns the utter non-assurance it addresses. The criteria unbelief demands have often more relevance than we suppose. The faiths of men are, in part, the stuff of their dreams and of their poems, and our faith, in meeting them, has not simply to contend with their pre-possession, but to do business with their incredulity and befriend their wistfulness. It has no commendation except by relation with the hearer's world and by virtue of a listener's part. Attentiveness is only generated by its like. Communication is nothing if not the focus of communion. Only by the latter can the former happen. Both are an exercise in openness offered and rewarded.

[1] As, for example, in T. J. J. Altizer. See chapter 7 below.

This willingness to be accountable to other men's thoughts is hard for the doctrinal habit, all too readily a stranger to its own strangeness and accustomed to the practice of authority. It can only come by exposure to the questioning and the indifferent, learning to frame their perplexities as they do and not contract out of their indifference. We may recall Robert Graves' poem about the apologist and the sceptic:

He is quick, thinking in clear images;
I am slow, thinking in broken images.
He becomes dull, trusting his clear images;
I become sharp, mistrusting my broken images.
Trusting his images, he assumes their relevance;
Mistrusting my images, I question their relevance . . .
He continues quick and dull in his clear images;
I continue slow and sharp in my broken images.
He in a new confusion of his understanding;
I in a new understanding of my confusion.[1]

The disposition to openness here in mind is not understood if it is seen as a sort of tactic or approach, a conscious policy of 'contact' to help the case. Some Christian thinkers in this field have conceded, readily or reluctantly, the necessity of 'points of contact' in order to facilitate their witness. But these, if so conceived, represent no genuine openness and confess no truly mutual possessions in the spirit. Once their tactical purpose is served, they tend to be quickly overtaken: the truth in them is merely serviceable to ends that may ignore it once they have a foothold. Relationships are then reduced to strategies and, in this temper, the heirs of 'revelation' easily lapse into postures of condescension or accents of distance.

For all his vast erudition and formidable authority, Hendrik Kraemer may not unfairly be cited in this sense. In his *Why Christianity of All Religions?* he insists that the problem of religious plurality must be posed "correctly". This means, for him, the non-derivative, primary, original "given" of Christianity, that is, "the Person of Jesus Christ". "Through God's revelation in Jesus Christ, and through

[1] *Poems, 1926-1930*, London, 1931, p. 40, "In Broken Images".

77

nothing else", "what true and divinely willed religion is" is known. All else is "error", including much in historical Christianity—though why *that* faith, with its historical source in the person of Christ, should be so on grounds like other religions, is nowhere faced and met. Biblical truth rules out the possibility of relevant truth elsewhere, though somehow, even at the heart of their error, we can sense amid other religions, that "God has passed this way". God, however, only *makes known* in Christ. We leave aside here the inner problem of rightly identifying the whole meaning of 'Christ' in this context, and of doing so without accretion, yet not—inevitably not—without association of Scripture, tradition, witness, church and much else besides. That hurdle apart, and taking Kraemer's position, what are we to say of a theology that characterizes all other religions, indeed all religions, as essentially misguided and abortive? By this Divine absolutism in Jesus Christ Kraemer reduces the content of all other faiths to incidental traces, not essential elements, of what God has decisively chosen to vouchsafe outside them. If being thus exclusive is a reproach, the Christian Gospel just has to accept it, for it is God's doing, though, in some eyes, it be not marvellous. In his doughty way, Kraemer even goes further and scouts some debates on plural religions as "a stick to beat the Christians".[1]

It follows that he is reluctant to see affinity between Christian faith and other religions even where to others it might seem evident enough. He speaks, for example, of 'mystery' as lying "quite outside the sphere of Christianity", and sets that term and concept over against 'revelation'.[2] Yet 'mystery', as we have seen in chapter 2, was one of the basic translation terms of the New Testament, where the kinship between 'mystery' and 'revelation' would seem to forbid the harsh disparity with which Kraemer sunders them. There may be some room for debate here: it is the doctrinaire stance which stirs disquiet.

[1] London, 1962, pp. 76, 79–93, 103–4.
[2] *Ibid.*, p. 45, though see also p. 78, where Kraemer modifies the point a little.

More serious is the rigorous confinement of the revealing initiative of God to the Christian Gospel and the curtailment of other religious significance and experience to an opaque sort of antecedent contact for that evangelism. Is it not truer to that revelation itself to see its commendation as moving, by travail, in significant community with men? Kraemer, it would seem, would have us be "God's spies" in a very uncomplicated sense. The openness of Christianity surely means much more a taking upon ourselves "the mystery of things"[1] that absolutist views of 'revelation' scarcely measure.

Yet when we do deepen that sense of the vastness and burden of the world in which we witness, there are seen to be no easy solutions for our theology. Other Christian views of inter-religious relationship soften considerably the rigorism of Kraemer, see positive and kindred meanings in all faiths and approve a Christian confession of indebtedness and fellowship. Yet, these more genuinely relational attitudes still involve suppositions that tend to qualify the temper of openness for which we are concerned to plead and pre-determine their conclusions. We are all too readily attracted by positions which contrive to have the best of both worlds, showing hospitality and, withal, conditioning the guests. We like to think of all faiths as being a *praeparatio evangelica*, a preparation for the Gospel—and, indeed, there is much to commend the belief when properly subdued to all its duties. We fasten on the conviction that, whereas in Christ God moves authentically to men, in other religions men move, more or less authentically, towards God. In the Gospel we have the Divine initiative, elsewhere the human; the one indubitable and inclusive, the other dubious and partial. We allow the relative value of natural reason, natural law, religious aspiration, the instinct of worship, and whatever else it be, so long as it is clear that these are broken lights, or streams feeling their way towards the tidal estuary where the waters of revelation flow powerfully in to make the river of

---

[1] Recalling, of course, *King Lear*, Act V, Scene 3, ll. 16–17:
   And take upon's the mystery of things,
   As if we were God's spies.

truth. The faiths find such validity as they possess in their conformability to Christ or their preparability for the Gospel.

An outsider might feel that there was something less than honest here, a readiness to allow a case once we know we take it, a conditional sort of recognition, the opening of a debate when its conclusion is foreseen and sure. This is not to argue insincerity in this approach. The fault, if fault there be, is much more likely to arise from over-simplified sincerity and the wish that the world were tidier than it is and the Divine Spirit more orderly. As an interior hypothesis of the Christian mind, it is a formulation consistent with a will to actual encounter which may, in turn, admit of fuller engagement than its 'theory' defines. As such, it may enable, and in that sense justify, more than it concedes. In issues so tangled as those between faiths, a degree of practical mobility of mind, even within a theological position of partial reservation, is a useful thing. No doubt other religions also come to meeting with similar qualifying attitudes officially maintained, while allowing themselves relational freedoms better than their formal judgements. Inside Christianity itself, in what has to do with ecumenical developments, the heart that wills has often been readier than the head that reasons. It would be sanguine to hope that the whole of orthodox faith would easily muster the prerequisites of complete spiritual encounter. It will be well, therefore, to foster such ventures as may be feasible. If we can elude, or preclude, the vetoes, we need not passively await the unqualified authorizations.

Aside from this consideration, there is truth enough, from within Christian premises, in seeing a 'preparation' for Christian faith in the meaning of other religions, provided we see that they have the right not to view it that way, and provided we explore and serve this understanding of ours with a properly sensitive humility. This we shall aim to do below. But we must also see that we do not exhaust external significance in these terms, and beware of a less than reciprocal approach in proceeding on it. It is, for example, a crudely inadequate form of this expectancy to exclude Divine action from the realms outside the Gospel, just as it is to exclude human searching from the Christian 'scheme'. On that latter assumption, revelation itself could not occur, since it is always an enabling of men's receiving and not merely a communication of Divine 'informing'. Revelation is always relational, answering to human anticipation, however revolutionizing the answer it brings. The Gospel must apply to itself the principle by which it evaluates all else, namely that it is into receptivity that Christ comes. This is only one instance of the self criticism we need, the sense of alertness to all we imply, if we would avoid the pitfalls of the 'preparation' view, and keep integrity with the expectation. For, in the end, the force of that conviction will turn on the qualities which can deserve to have it so.

This conclusion is only reinforced by a glance—there is no time for more—at the careful and complex thought of Dr. Karl Rahner, one of the most notable and forceful Roman Catholic theologians in this field. For all its admirable initiative in striving to reconcile the uniqueness of Christ and of the ecclesial community, of the Gospel and the universal Church, with the spiritual reality of the world's religions, the reader who does not start out from that uniqueness is probably impressed more with a resourceful, theological will, than a successful theology. Rahner accepts the actuality of religions and, from a belief in a Divine mercy through 'nature', as men in their social and cultural settings belong with it—settings that are necessarily informed by religions— is able and ready to validate those religions as spheres of Divine grace and truth. These last are not rightly thought of as 'added' to man's natural being, seen as a closed system when the Gospel comes. They are there already, though grace in Christ is their perfect work. By this intrinsic view of nature and grace, Rahner is able to hold on to the perpetual necessity of mission and the Church, and yet believe in a sort of "anonymous Christianity" among men in their religions.

His view involves four general propositions. Christianity is the absolute religion and, because of the Incarnation, holds the one fundamental relationship between God and man and the continual presence of Christ in His Church. But this

central fact, as it were, legitimizes what, either in time antecedently or in place concurrently, is outside the conscious
possession of it. Its absoluteness, therefore, does not impera-
tively apply before it is known or where it is unknown.
Moreover, mercy, integrity, even penitence, as benisons of
the Divine grace, must not be excluded from situations
external to the known Gospel or the accepted Church. Thus
Christian preaching and ministry awaken and make explicit
what is already there in the depths of men. By evangelism, so
to speak, men come out of their anonymity and recognize
what is not, thus far, altogether unknown. Meanwhile,
religious acts, whatever their error of doctrine or frailty of
form, may be acceptable, by a moral integrity, as the worship
of God. The Church, finally, should consider herself the
tangible form in which, historically and socially, salvation is
to be found, but not as the exclusive society of the saved.[1]

The work of this pioneering theologian has strongly
affected recent thinking within his Church, though, of
course, it is not 'official' doctrine. As a means to Christian
openness, it promises much. It gives a significant Roman
Catholic shape to the *praeparatio evangelica* theme and must
be welcomed for its practical consequences in banishing
hardness of heart and pride of absolutist belief, and in
mediating, on the personal level, between custodians of
faiths. All this is enormously to the good: if it is the necessary,
perhaps even the proper, form of Christian preparedness for
fruitful colloquy, so be it, gratefully. At least, that means a
certain reciprocity from the Christians' side to their *praeparatio* view of the other 'sides' in the issues of pluralism. Yet
a certain disquiet must remain. Is there something forced
about the whole picture? or contrived? Plainly there are
sharp problems. Could the notion be reversible, and we
Christians be anonymous Buddhists, Muslims or Hindus?
What if the 'anonymity' declines its perfecting? Is Christian
silence a safer tack than Christian preaching? Are the
Christian premises of 'salvation' and 'Incarnation' too
partial as clues by which to regulate the whole plural scene?

[1] See, *inter alia*, Karl Rahner, *Nature and Grace*, London, 1964.

Is this, as a way of making absolute claims spiritually tolerable, a still inarticulate awareness that they ought to be abandoned for a co-existence that does not attempt a coherent explanation? If so, are these ideas a stage in further adjustment of the dogmatic to the empirical, a half-way house where orthodoxy and sympathy are still in incomplete negotiation within the Christian mind? Or could they perhaps make a true and abiding Christian ground for mutuality, where openness can both contain and orientate orthodoxy itself?

It is too early to say. Certainly it is a theology which faces the right way. The suspicion, however, persists, whether for Christians or for observers, that it achieves too tidy and systematized a conclusion. Ought we to be ready for a less secured position, to be freer from the moorings that reassure and more ready for the open deep? Perhaps in the end our situation calls for a capacity to hold together the finality of loyalty to Christ and the will to 'concede' the other faiths, without asking for an answer how. Need the courage of the Christian necessarily enjoy a system devised to make things neat and guaranteed? Is it not more a matter of the "negative capability" that Keats described, "the state of mind when a man is capable of being in uncertainties, mysteries, doubts, without any irritable reaching after fact and reason"? Would it be better to live imaginatively with unanswered questions, rather than gather them into a commendable framework of answer that may still do violence to the ways of the Spirit? Can we at once confess the dimensions of our problem, as being too big for our theology, but not for our faith? Believe that they fit into the ultimacy of Christ without our particularizing the terms?

This posture may seem too risky, too exposed, too approximate for some: yet, for others, those very adjectives may represent the only options open to us. Is there not a sense in which our commitment to Christ in commitment to the world can, and must, be big enough to live with loose ends of explanation, with unresolved tensions of logic, with incompatibilities of stated creeds, and, despite that circumstance, or even because of it, be vindicated as a right loyalty? We may seem to be concluding that the right theology of pluralism is the lack of one. Hardly so. What we are saying is that we shall only find it in proceeding—the very word theology uses of the Holy Spirit. Further, that the proceeding is in Christ, and with Him, and that no other securities can finally avail.

There is one postscript to these reflections about the inward disposition of the open faith. Some readers, not least those of Barthian tutorship, will probably have been asking all along: Has not the exposition forgotten that religions are the expression of the very perversity of men? This notion of openness is culpably naïve in its apparent acceptance of religious man at his face value. In the Christian perspective, it is clear that men are never further from God than when they purport to worship Him. Are not religions in fact a device to escape from God in the very acts that supposedly do Him honour? Is not history proof of the inherent depravity of religious forms where men elude reality itself in myths and cults?

There is here an important truth. But the charge of religious perversity is no proper disqualification of the whole dimension, still less a plea by which to discriminate against particular faiths. The moral theme is in no sense a cause for repudiating the transactions of openness. On the contrary. These features are only indicted as distortions of what ought to be. If, essentially, there is nothing but deceitful illusion, there is nothing authentic to reproach. What is valid in these strictures only makes more integral the concerns of relationship, the more so since the deep compromises afflict in some measure all institutional religion and beset every form of cult or creed. They cannot rightly be invoked to sustain doctrinal uniqueness, for they have to do with moral failure and there are no systems here that can be merely external critics.

So we return to our starting point, not dismayed into a clamour for religionlessness, but ready to live with permanently unanswered questions, to refuse the over-simplifications of a crude evangelism or an easy sentiment, and to undertake the double task of openness to all in compassionate realism and openness to Christ as the one necessary loyalty. "There are times", observed Herbert Butterfield, at the end of his lectures on *Christianity and History,* when "we can never meet the future with sufficient elasticity of mind".[1] The present among the religions is one of them.

THE OPEN FAITH: CHRISTIANITY IN OUTWARD RELATION

What does the foregoing mean when translated into external activity? It means the grace to be in ultimacy without being absolutist; to hold positive premises without negative inferences; to reproduce the forthright witnessing of the New Testament while sharing a like principle of expectancy. There we find Zaccheus whom law, absolutized, must condemn, chosen by Jesus for His host. Cornelius whom Jewishness, absolutized, must avoid, is none the less a Roman first-fruit unto Christ. Mary of Magdala whom purity, absolutized, must disown, is first to learn the Resurrection. Is there a temptation, likewise, to absolutize the Gospel in such a way as to forfeit expectations the Spirit allows? Or try, too conservatively, to ensure the Gospel's meaning and impact? Is it not well also to remember how autobiographical is so much allegiance? Birth is likely to have a closer relation to belief than any other factor, at any rate in the non-western world.

The open faith, then, with a mind for all these considerations, knows there is a wind "blowing where it lists", and studies to set sails for it. Its central concern is to relate itself to the 'intention' of other religions, in so far as this can be identified and understood. It aims to take faiths in their own seriousness, to serve them in their own societies and recognize them in their own wistfulness and worth. It sees a Christian relationship as inviting them to state fully and positively their own apprehension of reality, with a radical and critical self-awareness.

[1] London, 1949, p. 146.

This objective has the merit of eliminating purely contentious debate about peripheral things. It precludes, at least in large measure, the kind of barren and inconclusive situations in which attacks are made, and resented, dealing with issues not of the essence, which have engrossed controversial exchanges in the past. These frequently terminate in *tu quoque* accusation or disavowal. The critic is often forced to be the devil's advocate, almost seeming to want other religions to remain at their worst, so that the unfavourable contrast may be maximized. In that atmosphere, answers are often self-exonerating and self-insulating, and concern aspects which wiser questionings would have excluded, or banished from the centre of attention.

This search for the inner 'intention' of faiths at their heart should not be deterred or diverted by the sort of external concern to convert, which inevitably provokes a closing of ranks—and minds. The revolutionary impact of Christ can be trusted to take care of itself: our duty lies with the Gospel. Its capacity to shape crisis and demand action is more rightly implicit in its content than explicit in our speech.

It may be urged by some that the 'intention' of faiths is too indefinite a concept, or too imprecise. Are Hinduism, Buddhism, Islam, and the rest, not vast, inclusive, diverse, even heterogeneous, accumulations of beliefs, behaviour, cults and superstition? Can we be sure of discharging a Christian responsibility by seeking an elusive, perhaps, or a debatable, 'core' of value, which many devotees themselves would fail to recognize as theirs? Or shall we be tempted, in this proceeding, by an image of ourselves, our hopes and wishes? And what shall we say of the fact that the Buddhist, or other, 'intention' belongs, if at all, in a welter of accretion and actual distortion? Does not realism, as in Communism, require a much more ruthless programme?

Yet is ruthlessness at this, or any, juncture properly the Christian temper? We have seen elsewhere our western liabilities, the traditions of antipathy, the frustrations of aggressiveness. But these practical matters apart, may it not be claimed that there is better teaching in learning, surer speaking in hearing, wiser telling in inquiring? It is possible that in the respect to which faiths are invited to declare themselves, they may also discover themselves with more detachment from their prejudice, more sense of their seriousness, less instinct for assertiveness. There are notions of grace in Hinduism, of compassion and self-transcendence in Buddhism, of inter-dependence and human solidarity in *négritude*, of saving indignation in Communism, of God-wardness in Islam, of a people's consecration in Judaism. There are, in the traditional hostility or scepticism of all these about Christ crucified, elements of meaning that are in positive alliance with what the Gospel truly itself 'intends' and achieves. The misunderstandings need to be dispersed, if only that the essential crises of relation may be known and faced. But misunderstandings are not dissipated in one direction as long as they are harboured in the other.

It is the purpose of the three chapters that follow to make this Christian attempt to reckon with the 'intention' of Judaism, Islam and African religion. These three in no way complete a world perspective. But the hope is that the venture in these areas may illustrate what it might mean, in other hands, in respect of the rest of faiths.

This difficult objective may be prefaced, and these reflections on its theological framework concluded, by final reference to a striking statement of intention by St. Paul. In Romans 15: 16 he writes:

> I have written somewhat boldly . . . in virtue of the gift I have from God. His grace has made me a minister of Christ Jesus to the Gentiles; my priestly service is the preaching of the gospel of God, so that the worship which the Gentiles offer may be an acceptable sacrifice, consecrated by the Holy Spirit.[1]

It is a highly significant passage, referring of course within the orbit of Jerusalem and Illyricum of which he speaks, not of Benares, Meshed or Mecca. He uses a vocabulary that

---

[1] Using the footnoted alternative of the New English Bible translation. The version in the text, like most other renderings, takes what St. Paul "offers" to be the Gentiles themselves.

belongs with cult and 'liturgy' and oblation and it seems right to suppose that he has primarily in mind the hallowing, through the advent of the Gospel, of the worships the Gentiles bring. He makes his evangelism an act of priesthood. The two realms of ministry, so often at tension in Church history, he holds in one. He is priest-preacher and he is preacher-priest. By proclamation of Christ he claims to be achieving the central role of priesthood, namely presentation to God. So regarded, the sacramental and the evangelical are one, the Gospel has become, as it were, itself a missal.

Who, or what, does he 'offer' by his preaching? It is difficult, though popular, to answer: the Gentiles. Difficult for the crucial reason that, in Christ, the only oblation is a self-offering. "Present yourselves" is the call. No apostle, no herald, may, from outside the sacredness of personality, make a presentation of his hearers to God. That is a prerogative of the person alone and the whole quality and shape of the Gospel sets it in profound respect. It is unlikely that St. Paul holds a theory of the priestly effect of his evangelism in terms that override it. If we want to take the persons of the Gentiles, it is not St. Paul who offers them. Yet his language plainly speaks of a hallowing which he accomplishes.

We must look for the answer, then, in the effect of his preaching, received and implemented by his hearers. As, by word and travel, he brings God to the world in Christ, by the same token he brings the world in Christ to God. The outreach ingathers: the good news is itself a "sacrifice", not, here, in the sense that it costs to take it, but that its acceptance brings about the true Godwardness of men responding to it. Answering faith takes its place in the very setting of the self-offering of Christ. The table of the Lord is furnished with guests, guests who find that in coming to take they stay to surrender. Sought, they are found, and found, they are claimed. The Gospel of the Divine sacrifice conforms, as well as invites, us to itself, and does so universally. From the Old Testament patterns of priestly worship, the Gentiles were excluded. The priest consecrated only the labours, the persons, the harvests and the wealth, of the chosen. There

was, as we shall see in chapter 4, an education in sancti-
fication but only by its limitation. Now in the preaching of
Christ, with St. Paul as its exemplar, the stake of God in all
and of all in God is made known and made good.

So the preacher is priest and the priest is preacher. By his
pastoral ministry, St. Paul strives to make the presentation
perfect (Col. 1: 28), the fullness of a discipleship in which
his people have first given themselves. Worship is the return-
ing home to God, through hallowed men, of that initiative
of God which in the Gospel goes out towards men. Preaching
is the centrifugal, and priestliness the centripetal, movement
of the same love.

In this context, the words of Romans 15: 16 may be
rightly seen as a clue to the hopeful Christian view of every
form of worship. The Gospel is here taken as the crux of all
that men have for their hallowing—the gratitude of the
pagan, the awe of the primitive, the pilgrimage of the devout,
the honesty of the sceptic, the prayer of the faithful. Men
hearing the Gospel cannot be distinguished from men fre-
quenting or pondering their own shrines and temples and
mysteries. By their relation to Christ, potential or conscious,
those intentions, inseparable from their humanness, are
taken up, refined, realized, in the recognition of their
redemption in the sacrifice of Christ. The Cross presents
itself as the place the world's worship always meant.

CHAPTER FOUR

CHRISTIAN CHURCH AND
JEWISH DESTINY

Would it really be the triumph of God if the scrolls of the Torah would no more be taken out of the Ark and the Torah no more read in the Synagogue, our ancient Hebrew prayers in which Jesus himself worshipped no more recited, the Passover Seder no more celebrated in our lives, the law of Moses no more observed in our homes? Would it really be *ad majorem Dei gloriam* to have a world without Jews?[1]

THE faith out of whose loyalties these questions spring is clearly the first and most urgent direction of the Christian essay in relationship which the previous chapter aimed to define—a relationship that wrestles deeply from within Christian discipleship with the continuity of other faiths. The very genesis of Christianity was a profound crisis within Jewry, a crisis of universality and election, of law and righteousness, of fulfilment and expectancy. If we are to enter into what St. Paul described as his "priestly service in the Gospel of Christ", there is need to dwell searchingly, both for our hearts and theirs, in the issues about which the Jewish withholding and the Christian embracing diverge so radically at the common point of Messianic meaning.

For "priestly service" means a fundamental reverence, a desire to possess religiously rather than dispute rationally the intentions of other men's allegiance, a will to the consecration thankfully in Christ of all that will rightly admit of such consecration. Just as a Christian 'orthodoxy' may confess the truth of Christ in such wise as to evade and neutralize the reality of His grace,[2] so an external non-

[1] Rabbi Abraham Heschel, "No Religion is an Island", in *Union Theological Seminary Quarterly Review*, Vol. 21, No. 2, Pt. 1, January, 1966, p. 129.
[2] Cf. Karl Barth in *Church Dogmatics*, Vol. IV, 3, i, p. 259 discussing "the resisting element in man" which can participate in the confession of Jesus in such a way as to immunize the Word of grace.

confession may yet participate, by its very deliberateness, in dimensions to which that grace belongs and points. It is these which a "priestly service" will strive to recognize, to hallow and to gather into the worship of faith. This pattern of relationship is nowhere more appropriate or more strenuous than in the mutual situation betwixt synagogue and church.

The Christian Gospel, as set forth in the New Testament, claimed quite simply that Jewry should both lose and find itself, transcend and fulfil its chosen uniqueness, in "the body of Christ", as a realized achievement of the Christ-meaning and so of Old Testament destiny. With no less insistence, after an early period of genuinely open option, Jewry saw compelling reason for abiding in unimpaired and untransformed Jewishness. That decision, and the Christian conviction which it refused, have continued, through many devious chapters of history, unchanged to this day.

> The Jew is to the Christian the incomprehensibly obdurate man who will not see what has happened: and the Christian is to the Jew the reckless man who, in an unredeemed world, affirms that its redemption is accomplished. This is a gulf which no human power can bridge.[1]

Sharp as that issue stands, it is important to keep in view how genuinely open the original option was. Despite the fact that it was Jewish humanity within which the themes of Messianic definition contended in such tragic terms, it was to universally human emotions of fear, pride and passion that they belonged. In the New Testament initiation of the Gospel there is no hint of any essential 'dejudaizing' of this faith in Jesus Christ.[2] The ultimate decision must be seen as a Jewish self-exclusion, as a decision for a perpetuated privacy of destiny for God and with Him. The choice was made in the context of the most powerful pursuit of the will to universality that ever arose in the soul of Jewish history, a will uniquely

[1] Martin Buber, *Mamre; Essays in Religion*, trans. by Greta Hort, Melbourne, 1946, p. 31.
[2] By 'dejudaizing' here is meant, not its being accessible to non-Jews, but its becoming, on that account, something other than authentically Jewish. The later near-equation between 'Christian' and 'Gentile' was neither necessary nor valid and derived primarily from decisions within Jewry.

energizing the precedents from which it learned in the splendid impulses of Hebrew prophecy and of Hellenized Judaism. Was it the very zeal and inclusiveness of that Christian welcome to the wider world in the trust of Jewish heritage and faith that, in the event, provoked the emphatic nature of that counter-decision? Through all the centuries of parallel existence it has persisted—Jewish consciousness of destiny withheld, within and without, from part and lot in its great, and different, counterpart—the Christian community. That community, in turn, with equally devoted logic, sees itself as the abiding might-have-been of Jewry, the abiding ought-to-be about Jewry. So it is that Jewish continuity, in any terms consequent upon the nature of the Gospel and upon that nature Jewishly disallowed, has seemed a perpetual disclaimer, from the most vital source, of the Christian conviction about Christ, and about the nations. It is a claim for exemption all the more significant in that it comes from within, and on behalf of, the very people who provided the founder-members of the Church.

The New Testament does not tell the story of that counter-decision. It happens outside the narrative range of its history. But the issues it concerns are there in biographical theology in the career of St. Paul, whom it identifies as the main, but by no means the sole, architect of Jewish-Gentile inclusion in Christ. That theme was carefully explored in chapter 2. The point here is the integral nature of Jewish participation in New Testament Christianity as a pattern which might have been perpetual—a participation all the more real and vital for the parallel fact of Jewish involvement in the very crisis of enmity, out of which the teaching and Cross of Jesus came into their universal fulfilment. The circumstances may rapidly be reviewed.

When, in Antioch, the local citizens first invented the name 'Christian' (Acts 11: 26), it was in jesting necessity to describe a new phenomenon—a group which was neither Jewish, nor Gentile, but both. The term, significantly, was minted, not in Jerusalem where the Church began, but in Antioch, the great Syrian metropolis from which its 'Asian' mission originated. "The people of this way" had hitherto been called 'believers', or 'disciples', or just 'brethren', and with these fully Jewish denominators the Church might well have remained content. For they were capable of universal range without differentia, including all without discriminating between any. It was the surrounding populace in Antioch who produced the nickname to denote a new thing—a fellowship in close intimacy composed of both elements, yet different from the familiar pattern of proselytes to Judaism, folk, that is, who were accepting a religious naturalization in becoming Jews. These people, by contrast, were common initiates in a new loyalty, still feeling its way, in which there was "neither Jew nor Greek", but a single entity. For this the Antiochenes coined well. They minted a word from Christhood, with a coarse humour thrown in, that uncannily focused on the fact that the shape of the choices of Jesus as Messiah had veritably begotten a new human family, fulfilling and yet abrogating election.

This common bond, dissolving old distinctions, is one from which Jewry as a whole steadily turned away. The very term 'Christian' came increasingly to be taken as virtually synonymous with 'Gentile'. This process, never necessary in the spirit, grew more marked in the last quarter of the first century and beyond. It is probably to be closely linked with the Fall of Jerusalem in A.D. 70. Strangely, at the very time when 'Christian' universality reached maturity of conviction, Jewish consciousness, with no less deliberation, withdrew into self-sufficiency and seclusion. It was a marked reversion. For Judaism, between the time of the Septuagint and the rise of Christianity, had been at its most hospitable towards the Gentile world. The synagogue itself, as the Book of Acts shows, was a most formative factor in the growth of the Christian Church. It afforded a nucleus for evangelism, if also for controversy, and it symbolized the concern for the nations of which the Church was the heir. It was, one might almost say, in its diaspora energies, on the way to becoming in measure, a 'church', a body of more than ethnic quality in one bond of faith and worship. But when the faith about Jesus

93

as the Christ emerged to crown and institutionalize that very promise, Judaism drew back decisively into exemption and assertively separate identity. And thus it has remained.

It was, however, a decision which makes undeniable the option it refused, namely of sustained inclusion in Christianity. Many factors contributed tragically to the obscuring and, soon, the annulling of that option. Dr. Heschel, with ample justice, writes that

> A Christian ought to ponder seriously the tremendous implications of a process begun in early Christian history. I mean the conscious or unconscious dejudaization of Christianity, affecting the Church's way of thinking, its inner life as well as its relationship to the past and present reality of Israel—the father and mother of the very being of Christianity. The children did not arise to call the mother blessed; instead, they called the mother blind.[1]

Yet the first of those implications is that the essential dejudaizing occurred within Jewry itself in the form of a cumulative, inner, verdict for non-inclusion, taken *vis-à-vis* a community of which their own genius, leadership and history were constitutive and where their presence, in definition and in deed, was by the nature of the case implicit. Initially, dejudaizing was by withdrawal of persons, not antipathy of content. The mother called the children wayward, for their new companions: but they still sang her psalms, read her lections and delighted in her Scriptures. The utter necessity and permanence of the Old Testament writings within the New Testament thinking were staunchly asserted and maintained by the Church in the face of powerful contention for their elimination or dilution. So faithful has the Church been to its ancestry, in liturgy, tradition and temper, that Christian auspices have constituted in history an immense Gentilizing or terrestrializing of the God of Abraham and the worship at Jerusalem, giving these a diaspora and a penetration of human cultures they neither sought nor found of themselves. Yet—from the Christian reckoning, tragically, and from the Jewish, sublimely—the personal, the ethnic,

[1] *Op. cit.*, p. 124.

94

the 'Torah' continuity of Jewry lay resolutely outside the Christian institutions.

It is common, but none the less false, to see that fact as of necessity arising from the role of local Jewry in the actual Gospel situation. The ministry of Jesus certainly proceeds through themes of controversy in which Jewish attitudes and instincts are a steady foil, in repeated antithesis to His words. There is here a deep and vexing problem. But it must be seen, in the last analysis, as essentially a crisis *for*, rather than *against*, Jewry, a controversy within, rather than around, it. Both the teaching situation of Jesus and the theological issues of St. Paul, and, most of all, the Cross itself as the bond between the two, are alike elements in a deep and searching dilemma of Jewry. For that very reason, the Christian relation to Jewry, in that role and crisis, and the Christian reckoning with the meaning of the events and Jewish part in them, are correspondingly crucial. Here the New Testament is clear and unequivocal: the only enmity the Gospels and Epistles have to do with is an enmity the Gospel takes away. In the very texture of their history is the reconciliation they proclaim.

There is, it is true, a certain 'animus' in the New Testament narratives, especially St. John's Gospel and the Acts, against "the Jews". It derives from the pain and pressures of controversy inseparable from the momentum of Christian conviction towards an open people of God and from the counter-thesis of Jewish uniqueness and proper, elected, persistence of identity. The very fluidity of this issue, vital as it was to both sides, during the years when it was in stress of decision, tended to sharpen the urgency of each, with legacies that hardened when the die was finally cast. These factors no doubt influenced the actual shape of the New Testament narratives. There are fascinating related questions comprising much detailed scholarship. But all this should never be allowed to obscure the salient fact that the circumstances of Jewish recalcitrance in the course and climax of Jesus' ministry and in the travels of His disciples and apostles never prompted their exclusion from the welcome of the new faith. Jewish involvement in antagonism, in word or deed, to Jesus was always seen, not as something 'Jewish', but something inherently human, the climax of which could most surely be described as "the sin of the world".

These are remarkable and interlocking facts. The New Testament firmly inculpates Jewry and just as firmly exculpates them. ". . . That same Jesus whom ye have crucified . . . the promise is unto you . . ." (Acts 2: 36–39): ". . . Ye . . . killed the prince of life . . . God . . . sent Him to bless you . . ." (Acts 3: 15 and 26). There is an incorporation of those whose action is seen as, representatively not uniquely, culpable. If these apostolic perspectives had been allowed to control all future attitudes we would never have known the enormity of an anti-Semitism generated from the event of the Cross. "Father, forgive them . . ." in no way rightly develops into "Father, hold it against them . . ." nor "they know not what they do" into "with perversity they knew and meant it all". This understanding of Jewry and the Cross is not exoneration since it is never condemnation. What, in this situation, is historical is also abidingly the symbol. There is no unilateral reproach about the Cross: it is the human quality within its making, not the national or local context of the enmity, which is the ultimately significant dimension. To realize that the trust of the sequel, including the apostolic preaching and the Gospel documents, lies squarely within the Jewish community is only to reinforce this conclusion. Even remembering St. Luke, it is fair to insist that the whole New Testament Scriptures are a Semitic entity, utterly removed from the temper of medieval Christendom where Jewry, in Sartre's words, suffered as "men condemned to live in a society that adored the God they . . . killed". There, as in Kafka's *The Trial*, a perpetual attrition, an "interminable trial visibly wastes them away".[1] The themes of the New Testament, in total contrast to this appalling tragedy, have to do wholly and only with an interminable forgiveness even wider by far than the "letters of Greek and Latin and Hebrew" that told the accusation.

[1] In *Anti-Semite and Jew*, New York, 1948, pp. 67 and 88.

Yet, in view of centuries of vindictive 'discipleship' that have thus betrayed the Son of man with a kiss, it remains the more necessary to keep the controversies of Jesus' ministry properly within the criteria of the Passion which was their climax. For otherwise those issues habituate us to the treacherous notion that the reprehensible is invariably the 'Jewish'. We are all too readily tempted to suppose that we have measured the familiar parable about prayer in the Temple, if we learn to "thank God we are not as this Pharisee". The danger to take the ever human for the merely Jewish is so pervasive that the vigilance must be continual. The 'legal' righteousness of the Scribes is always in the context where we learn to reckon with the message of Jesus and the Kingdom. We begin to understand the publican in the Temple in his ardent penitence, by dint of the contrast with the rigorously self-evaluating Pharisee. We enter into the compassion of the Samaritan but not without the priest and the levite playing their indifferent roles. The parable of the vineyard and the husbandmen presents its incisive commentary on both the Old Testament and the ministry of Jesus, as a study in official obduracy and gathering contumely. We too "perceive that He spake of them". The eating with publicans and sinners makes its benediction for us in the setting of the opposing spiritual aloofness of the priests. We hardly esteem the self-expending Messiahship understood in Jesus unless we measure and reject the self-preserving, self-expanding, militant Messiahships of Zealot conspiracy or pious eschatology. When all these themes of otherness culminate in the rejection and the Cross we find it hard to forbear the perpetuation into the absolute and the chronic of every element in the antithesis.

So it comes about that somehow the very appreciation of Jesus our Lord is involved in the depreciation of His contemporary people Israel. Right as it is to say, "We are the Pharisees", the historical confrontation of the teaching with *those* Pharisees has an emotional persistence in our Christian documentation of ourselves which all too readily obscures their essential reproduction within ourselves. The stress is

Ga 97

continually joined between the objective history of the one and the subjective necessity of the other. Even when, as we have argued, we are truly implicating ourselves in "the sin— and the antecedent sins—of the world" we are doing so in terms of historical analogues of that identification that leave the Jews in the central role. They are the prototypes of our evil natures, in a far more crucial sense than the Canaanites, for example, were figuratively so for Old Testament moralism.

This complex within the Gospels is extended and sharpened in the significance of St. Paul, who is, at once, the archtraitor and the central protagonist. Universalism has its crisis in his own person. The travail of his theology was an inner decision both for and against his people. It is the doctrinal formulation of his experience in Tarsus, Jerusalem, Damascus, Troas and the rest. As with Jesus' parables, so also, and even more sharply, with St. Paul, there is controversy with Jewry in the very gist and genesis of Christianity. Christian liberty stands in contrast with Jewish 'legalism'; the openness of Christ with the ethnicism of the covenant; the acceptance of the Gentile with the "hardening of Israel". All the great Pauline themes become a debate with or a disavowal of the ancient temper of "the seed of Abraham", stirred to anger by the defiance they encounter or the jeopardy they sense in the convictions and intensity of Paul. These tensions emerge very plainly in the narrative of the Acts and dominate the argument of the Epistles. On all counts, Christianity, in its origins, its Scriptural documents, its nerve centres of doctrine and emotion, constitutes an interior crisis of controversy in the soul of Jewry. It is a crisis which passes, by Jewish decision, as well as by Christian, into uneasy and abiding duality, a state of being separated by a single heritage and divided by a common language.

It is then the more urgent that neither the Old-continuing, nor the New-deriving, should allow themselves to be under this history as a tyranny. Under it, by spiritual charter, they most certainly are. But it needs to be subdued to the necessities of an inner obedience. What deserves their final loyalty belongs only with their positive divergence—God with this people and God in this Christ, the Torah in Israel and the Cross in the world. It does not lie with every clinging resentment, alienation or satisfaction stemming from events and circumstances attending those contrasted decisions.

This, no doubt, is asking a hard thing, the more so as injustices and intimidations from the Christian side have been so tragically multiplied through the centuries. We must concede that it is an ambition for which among the generality the necessary attitudes will justifiably be wanting. Yet without dismay and without reserve it must be ventured. For only in the utmost openness to Jewry can Christians rightly substantiate the open faith of Christ crucified. And only in the utmost openness to Christianity can Jewry vindicate the set of its soul, in whatever terms, towards a still 'messianic' future and a still 'messianic' relation to the world on God's behalf. 'Messiah', one might say, is for Christianity the vision of a fact and for Judaism the fact of a vision. The one, by definition, belongs with God in Christ reconciling the world; the other with the ever-present Torah and the ever-elected people; and both with the ever-living Lord.

What, from within Christianity, should this openness mean? what is its duty towards Judaism in steady continuity of non-recognition of those central Christian claims about the redemptive accomplishment of Jesus as the Christ in which Christian faith finds the clue to its understanding of God, the pledge and energy of its ministry and its view of the world? By what is this withholding of community in *this* Christ essentially inspired and how should the Christian mind and heart respond to the sources and consequences of that self-exemption from the Christian Christ?

The answer would seem to involve three crucial areas of common, yet divergent, truth. They comprehend, and should discipline, numerous other issues and obligations of history and dialogue too varied for present analysis, except in the strict context of the chosen fields. These are: the destiny to universal benediction, the vocation to Torah-achievement and the patience of loyalty in a world unredeemed. None can be broached on the Christian side save

99

with humility in the trust of relationship, pain for its many travesties and gratitude over its deep privilege.

THE DESTINY TO UNIVERSAL BENEDICTION

The heart of Jewry lies in the conviction of election. "I will be their God and they shall be my people"; "You are a chosen generation unto Me"; "You only have I known of all the nations of the earth". Election, it might be said, means Divine experiment: it supposes a sort of test case of humanity: it involves a focus of Divine purpose. For otherwise, as the Old Testament so deeply senses, a choosing God would be a tribal God, establishing a partisan relationship with a single people. It is monotheism which saves the full concept of election from this danger and enables the universal to be safely particularized and the particular to be rightly universal.

Biblical election is purposive for all: it has the benediction of all as its end and its justification. These are its conditions and its perpetual criterion. Acceptance, still more enjoyment, of election are intolerable arrogance, or empty fantasy, unless set towards the human whole. "In thy seed shall all the nations of the earth bless themselves" was the Abrahamic word. The only final credibility of chosenness is the readiness to make good its universal relevance. Let no one complain that such a condition says some moral "Nay!" to a Divine arbitrary sovereignty and deprives God of options that are not accountable. The Old Testament itself is the surest discipline of the elect in denying their status any security other than within the Divine ends. We do not go outside Jewry's own judgements for the insistence that election, covenant, chosenness, are spiritually disqualified when possessed in forgetfulness or repudiation of the Divine intention.

Universalizing of the covenant and the benediction of all the nations are, therefore, the supreme 'good faith' of the self-awareness of Israel. The 'Christian' question, then, to Jewry is: Where and when is the 'end' of election achieved? The faith of the Gospel offers itself as the point and form of the answer, in that a Divine grace is at work effectuating an incorporation of humanity without distinction of covenant, or birth-standing, into one redemption. Judaism disallows that belief—for the most part, totally, or by allowing it a validity that obtains only for Gentiles. Thinkers like Franz Rosenzweig, pondering the Jewish significance of the Christian Church, have been ready to see it as an authentic 'Gentilizing' of the covenant. Conceding the broad *de facto* dispersion of Jewish inheritance—psalms, liturgy, wisdom, prophecy—to the ends of the earth through the agency of Christian churches, and delighting in the Old Testament's currency in the wide world by dint of its presence with the New Testament in the Christians' Bible, thinkers of this school have gladly accepted that New Testament as the Gentiles' share in 'Israel' whereby the debt is paid.

Gratefully as this position may be acknowledged by Christians—and it is at once bold and generous in the light of long Christian enmity towards the Jewish world—it quite fails to meet the deep issue. For it lives by self-reservation. It is a readiness for the New Testament that violates the first principle of its nature, namely that "in Christ there is neither Jew nor Greek". It involves the paradox of an election fulfilled only by exclusion from its range of the people whence the fulfilment springs. Can we have the host saying, "I pray thee, have me excused?" or can one be absent from one's own hospitality? Christianity has continued steadily to incorporate the Old Testament in its Scriptures, its heritage and its solidarity of faith: yet Judaism sees this only as a token of Gentile wisdom. The Gentile world may share, thus, in what is Jewry's but without Jewry sharing.

There are, of course, compelling historical reasons for this position, many of them criminally owing to Christendom— Gentile rejection of Jews, persecution, the perils of assimilation, the long, dark shadow of Anti-Semitism. It is perhaps futile to make purely theological assessments. Yet Rosenzweig's position, as a feasible Jewish reckoning with the obligation of the elect, requires thus to be weighed. The sequence of thought, however, must move on to further aspects and deeper reaches of this self-exemption of Jewry from the Christian account of their election's goal.

Two discernible answers face us from within Jewish thinking about an irreducible chosenness and the disallowance of a universal in which Jewry has only equal part. The one insists that election is not liable to a goal and an end: the other that it is never feasible of an end, since it is a calling in which there is no discharge. For the first, it is simply not accountable to universality. Privilege is self-justifying and covenant self-sufficient. For the second the goal is historically unattainable: the vocation abides because to believe it accomplished would be to have it betrayed. For both these views, the diaspora has been the common circumstance, though provoking contrasted interpretations of Jewry in and for the world. On the one count, the scattering among the nations has seemed a privation and a tragedy, to be outlived by steadfast rejection of assimilation even at the price of seclusion and the ghetto. At its most paradoxical this was a sort of security, as it were, by persecution. On the other count, Jewry, by its presence in diffusion through the world, was the leaven, the Godward life, of all societies. This vocation implied some degree of assimilation as the means to the salvation of all culture and the revelation of the indwelling glory of God. For this second view, vocation was fulfilled even in rejection. It meant a metaphysical community in experience of the Shekinah. In these terms, Jewish thinking reaches towards some of the concepts of 'church', of community through which, collectively, the Divine Name is recognizable and the Divine will done, a homage of all men to God brought vicariously by a representative people of holiness.

Yet this version of how universal relevance might be realized has been qualified by two interior factors—the fear of absorption through permeation of other cultures and a reluctance to have it accompanied by vigorous recruitment of discipleship. It was as if the presence by which God was known had to hallow the nations but not baptize them, to exemplify the Godward meanings without offering equal and unstinted community to responsiveness. All this raises the question whether 'presence' without conversion or 'witness' without spontaneous incorporation are finally viable. Could Jewry fulfil its universal role in these terms without turning into 'church', without, that is, an uninhibited welcome to mankind, completing the will to represent God by the will to be one representativeness with all answering humanity?

Out of these aspects of the Jewish soul, duty-bound to all yet duty-bound to itself, given to humanity yet with equal insistence preserved from them, arises the constant trend of mind, and more recently of will, towards concrete nationhood. Politically conceived, this is the passion of Zionism. In its most assertive form that claim for statehood amounts to a tacit, or avowed, repudiation of the universal obligation. It is the assumption of 'privacy' in the sharp and forceful posture of nationalism. In more temperate hands, it may proceed under an interpretation which sees the national, political element as the necessary, if compromising, form of effective and defensible 'mission' in the world. Thus E. Berkowits argues that "national existence" is a prerequisite of universal obligations. "The community of obedience" has to be a nation: only in a political expression of Jewish dominance can Judaism be securely actualized. The same author, it is true, warns against a possible "collective assimilation", repeating the atrophy, as he sees it, of diaspora assimilation, by a statehood merely imitative of ordinary nationalisms. He relies, paradoxically, on continuing dispersion of Jewry outside the Jewish state, to save it from this danger. But without a majority dominance politically assured somewhere Jews will be on sufferance as Jews everywhere, even if they have tolerance enough as men. Their claim to common humanity must include, and be granted, the nationhood that humanity in general demands and enjoys. To serve Judaism truly, however, this political organism must be a real instrument of Torah and not just another nation-state.[1] For Berkowits, as for Martin Buber, the state is not an end in

[1] E. Berkowits, *Towards Historic Judaism*, London, 1943, pp. 69, 138 and 41.

itself: yet it is the sole means whereby the end in itself can be achieved.

Even very conservative thinkers in orthodox Jewry, who deplore the Zionist state as a false deification, a violation of the Second Commandment, nevertheless allow it a certain pragmatic justification. Even if mistakenly motivated, it may be providentially over-ruled. It is, however, by its ardent advocates that we must test its compatibility with any real retention of the vocation to the world. In the ultimate reckoning, both by fact and theory, Jewish statehood would seem to tend decisively towards the view that Jewry is not finally accountable to anything outside itself, and that its covenant is an inviolable possession, conferring a uniqueness, even a mastery, which need no validation otherwise than in Jewish self-awareness. This Ahad Ha Am (Asher Ginzberg) sees in terms "as old as the hills", having to do long before Nietzsche with a superior humanity.

> Judaism . . . has never subordinated its own type of superman to the mass of mankind . . . There was no thought of the advantage or disadvantage of the rest of mankind: the sole object was the existence of the superior type. The Jews have retained this sense of election throughout their history . . . The Jews as a people have always interpreted their mission simply as the fulfilment of their own duties and . . . have regarded their election as an end to which everything else was subordinate.[1]

Any bearing this genius may have on the rest of mankind is not a matter of debt. Gentiles may come to seek it if they wish. Jews have not sought conversions, says Ahad Ha Am, with only occasional exceptions—a situation attributable, not to any narrowness, or extraordinary tolerance, but simply to a consciousness of superiority.

There is no doubt a certain impetuousness in this viewpoint, explicable as part of the galvanizing process he deemed necessary to energize Jewish nationalism and set it free from the mission in the world philosophy of some assimilationists. The same writer, elsewhere, sees this masterful quality as

[1] See *Philosophia Judaica*, trans. from Hebrew by Leon Simon, Oxford, 1946, pp. 80, 81, in an essay on "The Transvaluation of Values".

benefiting mankind. Yet, even with these features, his inner mood remains symptomatic of an attitude to covenant status quite in contrast to what is understood by 'church' as a supra-national community with compelling concern for mankind as a whole and, that, without benefit, or pride, of state power. It would seem fair to conclude that nineteenth- and twentieth-century developments within Jewry have emphasized anew the self-preoccupations of the covenant. Those who find in the age-long sense of election no more than the religious dimension of a self-consciousness that owes no external obligations have received powerful reinforcement in recent decades.

If that is fairly said, we return to the question of universality and to the fear that, with its disregard, the particular forfeits the truly religious, as distinct from other, validity which its own history foresees and enjoins. Election is self-centred and to that extent disloyal unless it moves towards its own enlargement, unless, in a word, it accepts a church vocation and makes openness the theme of its fidelity. The Christian Church, it is true, has frequently succumbed to a comparable self-sufficiency and to a near identity with other criteria of its collective nature than an existence for mankind. Yet by apostolic constitution, it has always been meant for accessibility, and evangelism, and a refusal of monopolistic cultural expression. Is it not clear that any finally authentic notion of election must be bound over to the world?

Here, at all events, the issue is drawn. It is not for observers outside Jewry to venture the inward answer. A Christian duty consists in working out a relationship to the continuing convictions that only Jewish thought can vindicate. One possible approach to the mystery of an election self-retained is to see it as an education of all humanity in the sense of a nationhood contributory to the human whole. Jewry might then be seen as a sort of pioneer and prototype of how all nationalisms might find courage and humility in a total, or cosmic, reference.

Every nation is in some sense a peculiar people. Berdyaev[1]

[1] N. Berdyaev, *The Russian Idea*, trans. by R. M. French, London, 1947.

may be cited as a Russian exponent of this conviction, while William Blake and Herman Melville, among others, have given it eager currency in respect of America. Every people, by this count, is called to be its own 'Israel' under God, making the same commitment of their strength to Divine sovereignty and heavenly ends. The Old Testament could thus be seen as the progenitor of many 'covenants' of nations with their times and with the whole. It is a view which need not preclude the Biblical development from Jewry to the Church, from the Old to the New in its inclusive and redemptive character: such a sense of metaphysical nationhood rather accords perfectly with the supra-nationality of the Church, extensive through every state and nation.

This 'sharing' of election as an analogy relevant for all ethnic self-awareness need in no way disserve the unique quality of its first exemplar. It would, moreover, go far to meet and disarm that reaction of emotional 'retaliation' which has for centuries either simmered or exploded in mankind at the sheer, insistent distinctiveness of Israel. The enmity between Joseph and his brethren could hardly have been dissolved, in their context, by all becoming Josephs. But had they all been dreamers his solitariness could not have provoked them.

The whole theme merges into the issues of law and Messiahship to follow. There remains here one final consideration. May it not be said that covenant and election continue validly as long as the conviction of them abides? To think this does not compromise the external necessity of the Christian abrogation into universality already studied. As an exclusive persistence of uniqueness before God, the New Testament regards Jewry at an end. "Ye are all one, in Christ Jesus"—of unequal debts but of no unequal status. This achievement of the Christian universal is the proper destiny of the history that inaugurated it. Yet, within that assurance, there is room for the belief that a covenant meaning in Jewry's unbroken history continues authentic. The urge to this belief is not in some concession to tenacity, still less as a palliative for grim centuries of Gentile animosity and persecution. Jewry, anyway, would sharply repudiate it on any such count. It derives from the sense in which conviction as to covenant *is* covenant. To believe is to have. From the beginning, Biblical election has to be understood as a pattern of self-awareness, a profound interpretation of history, a way of taking the past and facing the future. Its objective reality is mirrored in the inward assurance and obedience that accept it. Where these abide is it unilaterally annulled from Heaven?

As such, covenant has its final end in its true end: its climax lies in consent to its enlargement. But there can be, in the dimensions of grace, no compulsion to such a consent. Neither Jew nor Gentile have their antecedent worlds denuded of the Divine patience in order to enforce their consent to Christ. On the contrary: the ways of grace are long and sure enough to contain all obduracy until it can be rightly drawn into surrender. In something of this sense the New Testament affirms that "God has not cast off His people" (Romans 11: 2). By this it means no arbitrary perpetuity or Divine favouritism. It means, surely, that there is a continuity of hope and mercy abiding with the generations whose history was in sum the generation of Messiah, and who are for all time the children of these fathers in whom they are beloved (Romans 11: 28). The New Testament, it is true, sternly dispossesses the guilty husbandmen and supersedes the old custodians of the vineyard. For the equalities of grace are uncompromising and there is no mistaking the meaning of the dark shadow that falls across its readers— the shadow of the destruction of Jerusalem. The genesis of the Church is no mild and painless incident, but crisis and tragedy and visitation and supersession. But the abiding phenomenon of Jewish integrity, with its manifest experience of covenant conviction as an interior secret through long subsequent centuries, is not thereby discounted. On the contrary: in its Gospel of the Christ of universal grace, Christianity has no reason to doubt that God still moves into Jewish lives along the pathway of their faith, while it waits, within its own loyalties, for their recognition of Him.

THE VOCATION TO TORAH ACHIEVEMENT

With its category of faith as the condition of inclusion in Christ, rendering birth and merit and every other antecedent relative, Christianity has encountered from its earliest days the issue of "faith and works". What did a saving faith involve? Judaism has incurred a parallel problem of "birth and works". St. Paul states it with his usual forthrightness: "He is not a Jew who is one outwardly", "they are not all Israel who are of Israel" (Romans 2: 28 and 9: 6), and when he reinterprets the meaning of "the seed of Abraham" in Galatians and Romans. As long as that "Seed" remains in any sense ethnic there is necessarily the question of "the ungodly Jew", the law-breaking son. "Whoever is born an Israelite", writes Hans Joachim Schoeps, "is a member of the covenant by virtue of his birth". Yet "it is he who lives by the Torah" and fulfils his duty who is heir to the promise.[1] As we saw in chapter 2, it was precisely here that the beginnings of the openness of faith took shape in the ministry of Jesus by His welcome to the prodigal and the publican whom the law had to condemn and His recognition of faith and goodness in unlikely Gentile places. It is true that thinking in Judaism speaks of a "return" to the bosom of Abraham for the members of a "biological election",[2] without the "detour" of the new birth, by dint of repentance and righteousness. The law in that sense transcends all actual insubordination. Yet the tension persists, as long as, by the ethnically ordered covenant, 'foreign' righteousness is excluded and 'participant' recalcitrance made to differ somehow from external evil doing.

This issue, however, only serves to focus the inner theme of law fulfilment, where, it would seem, lies a deep possibility of Jewish-Christian mediation. But first it is necessary to clear away two impeding misconceptions—the one that

---

[1] Hans Joachim Schoeps, *The Jewish Christian Argument*, English trans. by D. E. Green, New York, 1963, pp. 163 and 168. Cf. M. Buber's paradoxical phrase "the hereditary actuality of faith". See *Two Types of Faith*, English trans. by N. P. Goldhawk, London, 1951, p. 98.

[2] *Op. cit.*, p. 166.

Christian faith has mistaken legalism for law and castigated Judaism superficially for a compromise it has itself repudiated; the other that the Christian doctrine of grace and regeneration is involved in a romantic neglect of the real task of righteousness.

Many Jewish thinkers have reproached the New Testament, and notably St. Paul, for an alleged disregard of the nature of Torah. Hence the title here: Torah Achievement. Christians need to recognize unstintedly that Judaism, rightly understood, is quite other than a system of rigorous legalism, of scrupulous bondage to the letter of law. The inner concept of Torah is a Divine invitation to human co-operation, a walking with God. The very reverence with which the law was surrounded, as the sole vehicle of Divine authority, with the end of prophecy, naturally tended to the development of meticulous minutiae and codal tyranny. But these are the excesses and accidents of a vocation to be responsive to the Divine mind, vouchsafed in the grandeur of the law and hallowed in the exchanges of the covenant. To reproach this conviction and its translation into conduct with legalism is either, by its own criteria, to identify a perversion or, otherwise, perversely to mistake its real character. Centuries of history have been involved in this theme.

It has, however, to be equally clear that St. Paul's conversion and theology were not some mere rejection of legalism, as Jewish critics have usually supposed, so that he could be dismissed as extravagantly breaking with his heritage over a misconception. His quarrel with his people goes very much deeper than the menace of legalism into a realm that is integral to the ultimate concern of Judaism itself, namely the law's fulfillability, or the ethic of the heart. His quest was for that very rightness with God of which the Torah was definitive and of which several contemporary thinkers in Judaism have written insistently. Dr. Schoeps is, again, a spirited example.

The Hebraic covenant, he declares, is above all the vicissitudes of the law's reception. St. Paul's ideas of the "hardening" and rejection of Isreal are on that account invalid. Within the power of God who reveals the law is its indefeasible fulfilment and within this fulfilment, in turn, covenant will preserve the covenant's people. As a co-relation of God and man, Torah cannot be abrogated nor its people discovenanted. St. Paul would have agreed. It was "the fulfilling of the law" for which he yearned. Only he saw in that fulfilment at once the enlargement and the de-ethnicizing of its "people"—and both for the very reason of its indefectible ends in the purpose and authority of God.

"The law", writes Dr. Schoeps, "is not ruined by the disillusioning actuality of sin"[1]—a profoundly Christian assurance also. The question for St. Paul lay in *how* that actuality of sin was countered and the law achieved. His whole biography in sonship to the law issued into the conviction that "by the works of the law no one could be justified". For, when it was obeyed, the law generated a sense of merit, and so of meritoriousness, which first compromised and then disqualified the actions that fulfilled it. And when it was transgressed it had, necessarily, to reproach and condemn and by this necessity tended either to hardness or hopelessness of heart. Imperceptibly it ministered to its own defeat in that it nurtured a false pride of attainment or else a defiant or wistful state of non-attainment. Both aspects of this issue of the law worked to condemnation by the very standards of God-oriented goodness which the law enjoined and to which its origin in God bore witness. So "by the law was the knowledge of sin": yet in that knowledge of sin was the inner testimony to the law's authenticity. Man could not escape the dilemma either by repudiating the law —for that way lay darkness, or by 'attaining' it—for that way lay either corrupting pride and self-esteem, with censure of the lawless, or culpability, perverse or wretched.

This human situation, distilled in New Testament experience, is one of which thinkers and souls in Judaism are deeply aware, even if they rarely have patience with its passionate exposition in St. Paul. Some, it is true, tend to decry it as an unfortunate, even vulgar, over-emphasis by

---

[1] Hans Joachim Schoeps, *Paul*, Eng. trans. by Harold Knight, 1961, London, p. 282.

Paul on 'justification', an excessive and individualist demand for rightness. But there is no justice in such dismissal for that demand is, in fact, the law's own. To desire rightness is simply to take the law seriously. Moreover, if in the end we will not have justification in the way of grace, we shall either have it in the false shape of self-justification, or else repudiate the law's claim. In its fullest interpretation, Torah is the call for a "metaphysical rightness", a quality of relation with God that is beyond merit and beyond defeat, a fulfilment of Divine intention.

With some writers that fulfilment must needs be eschatological. For others it hinges on a capacity in the law's people to distinguish between the covenant obedience and ethical self-justification—a distinction men must never impatiently ignore or dismiss. For then they believe themselves the people of God too readily and too conveniently.[1] Or, in other words, sin has a greater ingenuity, a subtler deceptiveness, than legalism, or even honest law-abidingness, have understood. "The foreground course of the world"—to use Buber's phrase about evil—has a radical and pervasive nature such as no loyalty to Torah can rightly or safely minimize.

Here, surely, Judaism and Christianity, albeit beset by misconceptions, are very close together and both are taught by the profound psychology of the Hebrew prophets. Here, in the diagnosis of self-justification as a foreclosing of the law's purpose (Judaism) and as a necessitating of grace as alone the adequate answer (Christianity), they stand on common ground. The issue between them is not some superficial argument about law engendering legalism and thus deserving to be abrogated or requiring to be more fully understood. Christianity, not least in Paul, does understand it "more fully", and abrogates, not its intention but its self-justification. Judaism, in sum, is in no sense a bare legalism and may be assured that its deepest Torah-vocation is at the heart of New Testament religion. The difference belongs, not here, but in the shaping of "the people of God" in a co-relation with Him that is beyond self-justification. In the

[1] Schoeps' words are "quickly and rectilineally", *op. cit.*, p. 282.

end, Judaism is set to find, or to await, that climax in "its hereditary actuality": the Christian Gospel seeks it in "the righteousness which is by faith in Christ" and takes such faith to be the end of merit-works, the power to love-works, and open by spiritual birthright to all humanity. The distinction, both would say, is Messianic throughout.

THE UNREDEEMEDNESS OF THE WORLD

"Standing bound and shackled in the pillory of humanity, we demonstrate with the bloody body of our people the unredeemedness of the world".[1] How then can Christians say that the world is redeemed, that the Saviour has come? How can they hold that evil is conquered? What sense can be made of Messianic actuality in the light of the world as we see and suffer it?

At this point belong the sharpest and most tragic of Christian-Jewish misunderstandings. This theme of the Messiah brings all other issues to their climax. The Christian claim about Jesus as the Christ gives rise to bitter Jewish protests of romanticism, individualism and escapism. Here, it is alleged, is a Gospel which proffers a salvation-experience that travesties human realities, both social and personal. "Such gifts of grace", writes Leo Baeck, "are alien to Judaism: it does not pretend to be able to bring heaven to earth".[2] It is, on the contrary, a religion of tension that has no final solutions. The allegation, on this view, is that the Christian's 'finality' makes his faith merely a romantic "self-congratulation in the state of grace", and that, further, his pride in universality is really a fraud. For how can that community be 'universal' that abnegates whole stretches of human experience and 'solves' human problems only by first over-simplifying their nature and partializing their range? It meant, in fact, an acute 'privatizing' of its own which adds only irony to its reproach of Jewry. Corresponding to the finished man of romanticism there

[1] Quoted in Ernst Simon, "Martin Buber: his Way between Thought and Deed", *Jewish Frontier*, Vol. 15, Feb., 1948, p. 26.

[2] In *Essence of Judaism*, Eng. trans. by W. Kaufmann, Philadelphia, 1948, p. 13.

was the finished mankind the Church.[1] Both are unreal.

Martin Buber echoes these same strictures, in *Two Types of Faith* and other writings, adding the note of Christian impotence over against the evils of human history. "*De facto*, the redeemed Christian soul stands over against an unredeemed world of men in lofty impotence . . . The picture of the abyss is spanned by the halo of the Saviour".[2] Jews, Buber seems to be saying, refuse in the Christian way any private salvation by faith or, rather, they are able to refuse it because they are already 'safe'. Since privacy with God is by covenant their hallmark, they can dismiss the 'private' salvation of personal faith.

From this, Buber is led into an insistence that the whole character of 'faith' is different within Jewry, where distinction is not between belief and unbelief, but between fidelity and infidelity, realization or non-realization, within the abiding covenant. Faith is a position in which one stands, not an act that one effects. By its very supra-nationality, the Church, unlike the 'nation' Israel, is unrealistically abstracted from history. Without the corporateness of flesh and blood, "it is born outside the historic experience of the nations" and is, so to say, "in retirement from history in the souls of individuals to whom the challenge came to believe that a man crucified in Jerusalem was their Saviour".[3] This 'Christian' unreality is proven, in Buber's view, by the instinct of Christian theology to consign the world and history to demonic forces and, so he alleges, to lay greater stress on the Fall than on Creation, as the crucial doctrine. So the whole salvation scheme is a propositional, cerebral, individualized thing, far removed from the warm, incorporate, trustful self-awareness of Jewry.

Reaching as they do into aspects of controversy which cannot detain us here, these themes of contention hinge on the issue of man's "redeemedness" in Christ. Like those of law and self-justification, they are in fact very close together, if we see them freed of misconception. What does Christianity

[1] See Leo Baeck, *Judaism and Christianity*, Eng. trans. by W. Kaufmann, Philadelphia, 1958, p. 291. [2] *Op. cit.*, p. 113. [3] *Ibid.*, p. 172.

mean by "accomplished Messiahship"? Not, certainly, a
Messiahship which leaves no tasks remaining or supposes,
by some logical, perhaps, but abstract reckoning, that souls
are merely to be saved out of a society consigned to evil. On
the contrary: it is a Messiahship which enjoins its essential
principle of a love that bears and overcomes evil, as the
central law and secret of a community of ongoing redemptive
action and compassion. "It is enough for the servant that
he be as his Lord." At the heart of the interpretation of the
Cross is the Holy Communion—a perpetual invitation to
identity with the redemptive principle.

When Briboeuf, one of a devoted group of Jesuit priests
carrying Christian faith to the 'Red Indians' of Canada,
described to his colleagues a vision of the Cross which he had
seen beckoning them deeper into the wilderness and towards
fiercer tribes than before, his partners questioned him about
the size of the Cross he had seen. "It was large enough",
he answered promptly, "to crucify us all". Was it not in
these terms that St. Paul wrote: "I complete what is lacking
in Christ's afflictions . . ." (Col. 1:24), when those sufferings
were in fact entire, final and lacking nothing? In their
redemptive power, they were perfect and perfected: yet
to recognize them so is to know an invitation to their
perpetual imitation. They are at once the place of our
finished, and the pattern of our ever unfinished, redemption.

The "redeemedness" of the world in Christ is not, therefore, an idle assertion, capable of being sustained only in
detachment from the real world, or of being operative only
in a pietistic, personal salvation. All that Jewry asks of
realism about the evil world as yet being God's created realm
of law and love is there in Christianity and there, not in
impairment, but rather in enabling emphasis, by the conviction that there has occurred, once for all and concretely,
in our human history, the one perfect and inclusive sacrament of that power by which, in the end and in the whole,
all evil is redeemed. The Cross does not exonerate in its
redemption: rather it energizes men to its own reproduction,

and all the more surely for their sense of its redeeming authority already within their souls.

In this Christian meaning of the redemption in Christ crucified as at once achieved and prospective, actual and imperative, there is room for the Jewish concern to transcend a purely individual salvation. The Christian shares the Jewish instinct to find in Messiah that which is ever to come and that by which every achievement of history must be judged. Yet, for that reason, he will not require that Messiah must never be historically identified, or that Messiah disclosed is Messiahship betrayed. Would it not be fair to ask whether a Messiahship that could never 'come' could, by the same token, ever be 'thought'? The ability to believe, in a Jewish sense, in the prerequisites of Messiahship even as an always 'hidden' secret, is not inconsistently invited, by Christian belief, to open recognition of how those criteria might be translated in the concrete. To be able to think Messiah is surely to be in the way of identifying Him, provided, of course, that commitment to His actuality is loyal to all the unfinished aspects of the Messianic task.

Is this not precisely where the Holy Communion belongs in the Christian whole? The Lord's Supper is only a celebration of redeemedness because it is an invitation to live redeemingly. "In remembrance of me" does not concern a possessive or private state of grace but the energy of a realized salvation set towards humanity. When controversial insensitivities and prejudice are laid aside, the Jewish sense of the Messianic hope and the Christian persuasion of the Messianic faith may yet attain a common Messianic service, the one anticipating, the other recognizing, its cost and mystery. At all events, Christian Messiahship, in accomplishment, is no outwardly successful thing: it is one that requires and awaits discipleship and re-enactment after its own mind and has, therefore, girded itself once and for all to exemplify and energize that response by its own decisive encounter with the issues of redemption and has thus become, for all who will, the sign and sacrament of the redeeming among the unredeemed.

Buber once defined Christian faith as a "facing about"

in contrast to Jewish "persisting in", conversion rather than covenant, credence and rescue rather than faithfulness and 'immediacy'. And he added: "To the man needing salvation in the despondent hour salvation is offered, if only he will believe that it has happened and has happened in this way."[1] "If only . . . has happened in this way." The relation of the Christian to the Cross is well stated in these phrases, yet wholly misconceived. "If only" is not some arbitrary or formal requirement. Nor is that Cross an artificially imposed scheme or way. The necessary faith means a standing in the sort of transaction the Cross constitutes. It means becoming party to the very elements of evil and of love in their correlation as the Cross makes it plain. It means identifying in that whole transaction the nature of the sin in which I am by my humanity and the love in which I am by His embrace. Thus I find myself at the focal point of pardon and discipleship only in that I also find myself at the focal point of history and of thought, whence in turn my heart's affections kindle and begin to seek the world.

Here the argument must stay. Jewish stress on "unredeemedness" evokes one final reflection, bearing on the themes of chapter 7 and providing a point of contrasted departure into the confident theism of chapter 5. It is that this intractability of the world to the canons and concerns of faith, this insubordination of men, have a peculiar modern sharpness in our present generation, with the growing abeyance of belief and the seeming sway of an unbelief disinterested in its own 'conversion'. Judaism and Christianity alike tend to find themselves in a post-Judaic, post-Christian, time. In this situation, Dr. Schoeps argues, "the Church is beginning to share the external impotence of Israel" and learning the bitterness of being powerless and despised,[2] undergoing, so to speak, an exile from its traditional securities of privilege and acceptance. If this brings the Church closer to the experiences which for centuries have tempered the souls of Jewry, it may perhaps also release into new recognition the authentic dimensions of the Cross.

[1] *Ibid.*, p. 10.　　　[2] *The Jewish Christian Argument*, p. 171.

CHAPTER FIVE

CHRISTIAN CREED
AND ISLAMIC WORSHIP

High up on the back of a long mountain range, between its eastern flank which is the last bulwark against the Arabian desert and its western which is the side of the vaster basin of the Mediterranean, lies Jerusalem, facing the desert . . . yet so close to the edge of the basin as to feel the full sweep of its rains and humid winds . . . She hangs on the watershed between East and West, between the Desert and the Sea. (But) the whole exposure of the City is to the east . . . It is as if Providence had bound over the City to eastern interests and eastern sympathies. Hidden from the west and north, Jerusalem through all her centuries has sat facing the austere scenery of the Orient and the horizon of those vast deserts, out of which her people came to her . . . In certain states of the atmosphere, and especially when the evening sun shortens the perspective by intensifying the colour and the size of the Moab mountains, the latter appear to heave up towards the City and to present to her the threshold of the Arabian desert immediately above the hills of her own wilderness . . . the Mohammedan, as he looks down her one long vista towards Mecca, feels himself securely planted on her site.[1]

"THAT eastern bent and disposition of the City" is in striking contrast to the "westward ho" character of Christian expansion within the New Testament, studied in chapter 2, where the whole direction of expression, of travel and translation, was towards the Graeco-Roman world. Illyricum and Spain, not Hadramaut and Ceylon, were the limits of that story, the Pillars of Hercules not the Straits of Malacca. In the seventh century, however, the eastward tilt of Jerusalem had a dramatic counterpart in the possession of the city by the faith of Islam, riding in power from beyond the threshold of Moab. It was a bare four

[1] George Adam Smith, *Jerusalem, The Topography, Economics and History from the Earliest Times to A.D. 70*, Vol. I, London, 1907, pp. 3, 4, 10, 11 and 12.

years after the death of Muhammad and less than three decades from the first revelations of the Qur'ān. The purpose of this chapter is to ponder that "long vista towards Mecca" from within the Christian meanings of Jerusalem.

Hence the deliberate title about 'creed' and 'worship', in contrast to the emphasis on 'church' and 'destiny' in the discussion of Judaism and on 'mind' and 'symbol' in respect of Africa. Symbol and sacrament are, of course, deeply active in the scheme of Islam and a powerful sense of destiny belongs with the Muslim experience of God and revelation. But just as 'election' and its correlatives set the immediate sphere of duty to Judaism, so very properly worship and the doctrines that sustain and inform it take primary place in relation to Islam. It is in the mutual misunderstandings and exclusions of these realms that the urgent questions and the potential reconciliations are to be found. If, as we have said, our aim throughout is to take other faiths in the core of their seriousness, then, however much we may yearn to elude the trials and pains of dogma and move away into the territory of the practical or the mystical, we shall find the doctrinal waiting for us as the unfulfilled business in our relationship, and without it all else will be evasive.

Reasons of history in the very genesis of Islam lie behind this situation. Islam is the only major post-Christian religion. From all other faiths Christianity has a remoter quality of criticism, in that the critic, be he Buddhist, Hindu or Confucian, deals, as it were, with a newcomer, with a late arrival from a different world, whose doctrines have had no part in the origin of his own faith and for their assessment require of him an exploration of beliefs and attitudes already ancient. Only with Islam is Christianity antecedently formative of doctrines which disallow it and of judgements that contest its convictions. Only in the Qur'ān is there a definitive Scripture which has a consciously 'Christian' pre-occupation in its themes and emphases.[1] This fact makes the

---

[1] Christianity, of course, is responsible for the Old Testament being so named but does not affect its content or its ethos. Judaism, one might say, is defensively preoccupied with Christianity, not definitively so, as is the case with Islam.

Christian relation to Islam doctrinal in content and collateral in nature. Here lies its difficulty but also its great promise. Arabia reaches to Jerusalem in a territory that is religiously as well as physically akin. The city turns a special wistfulness towards its desert prospect.

That initial coming of Islam within its walls had all the marks that have characterized the people of Muhammad—vigour, assurance, authority and power. The Caliph 'Umar made a special journey from Medina personally to receive the cession of the city at the hands of the Patriarch Sophronius, after Amru, his general, had ensured the withdrawal to Egypt of its Byzantine commander. Islam never had more magnanimous expression than in the incorporation of Jerusalem into its dominion. The city of the Muslims' first and temporary *Qiblah* began to pray in the direction of Mecca and its historic associations with Abraham, David, Jesus and Muhammad were gathered into the physical custody of the Medinan state.

The characteristic circumstances of Islam are a far cry from that experience of exile and apparent impotence in a disregarding world with which the previous chapter closed. Not, surely, for Islam the sense of a post-Islamic world, of a setting in which the authority of belief has to live with neglect and disregard, with implications of irrelevance and the disinterest of an inattentive and unresponsive world. Not, surely, for this eminently confident and uncomplicated creed the question about the Lord's song in a strange land or the right hand forgetting her cunning in an elemental perplexity. Deus Semper Major: Allah akbar: God ever great and greater: this is a confession by nature perpetually assured and essentially irrefutable. Here is a faith that lives by the unity of God, the efficacy of His Prophet, the sovereignty of His law, the certainty of His will and the finality of His power. Here is the authority of Sinai, re-uttered in Arabic for all mankind: here the ultimate expression of religion.

Yet the paradox is that Islam had birth as a vocation to serve the reassertion of Divine reality in a negligent and

God-depriving humanity, to rehabilitate a true worship in a world where God was left out of the reckoning. Mission on behalf of God and for His due recognition is the central meaning of Islam both as a concept and a community. The *raison d'être* of Islam has to do with "letting God be God"— a theme nowhere more finely expressed than by Martin Luther commenting on Galatians:

> The chiefest thing that God requireth of man is that he giveth Him His glory and divinity: that is to say, that he taketh Him not for an idol, but for God . . . This being done, God hath His full and perfect divinity, that is He hath whatsoever a faithful heart can attribute unto Him. To be able, therefore, to give that glory to God, it is the wisdom of wisdoms, the righteousness of righteousness, the religion of religions and sacrifice of sacrifices.[1]

THE GREATNESS OF GOD IN THE LIFE OF MEN

Truly "taking God for God" was the heart and nerve of Muhammad's sense of vocation, as the Qur'ān embodies and fulfils it. The story of its genesis and climax has often been told and need not occupy the present argument. There were doubtless powerful other factors—social, political, personal—underlying the whole emergence of Islam as a religious achievement, some of them defying clear or precise analysis in the perspective of history. But, in and through them all, was this overriding concern for the Divine due, educated in part but unsatisfied by the Jewish-Christian precedents for monotheism, and set to permeate and subdue, as they had failed to do, the immediate Arabian environment of polytheistic division and disaffection. Historical analysis may be over-simplified but religious meaning is validly told, if we say that the gist of original Islam was to bring about a rightly worshipping world.

That objective in the human situation is a task of endless complexity and vigilance. Its most obvious and urgent necessity there in the seventh century was the speedy liquidation of pagan idolatry. Hence the sturdy iconoclasm

[1] *A Commentary on St. Paul's Epistle to the Galatians*, edited by Erasmus Middleton, London, 1810, pp. 250–51 (on Gal. 3: 6).

of Islam from the moment of its external power and the steady rejection of idolatrous practices in the early years of its minority status and struggle. Hence, too, the bitter animosity of Meccan vested interests, apprehensive of their pilgrimage prosperity in a world devoid of idol shrines. Hence, again, the whole Islamic philosophy of power as necessary to the reduction of these entrenched partisans of the idols and the disqualification of their commercial and political empire. In this sense everything in Muhammad's career can be understood within the logic of a thoroughgoing elimination of idolatry. Iconoclasm is, in this way, the single thread that links together preaching, propagation and political sanctions in original Islam. It is the common theme in the relation of Mecca to Medina and of the Hijrah which linked their dual role in the fruition of Muhammad's purpose, a purpose instinct with the assurance which Milton in another context put into the mouth of old Manoah, father to Samson:

> . . . for God,
> Nothing more certain, will not long defer
> To vindicate the glory of his name
> Against all competition, nor will long
> Endure it, doubtful whether God be Lord,
> Or Dagon.

—"against all competition", and against all compromise, against all complication, against all concession and against all compulsion to the contrary.

Through all the stages of the Qur'ān there runs this same insistent theme—the folly of idol worship, the ingratitude of the Divine neglect, the impoverishment of the world by the non-recognition of the signs of God, and the frustrations of the *mushrikin*, the people who commit *shirk*, or the alienation from God of all that is due to Him. One of its recurrent phrases in relation to these is *min duna*, "to the exclusion of . . ." with God (either the noun or pronoun), occurring some seventy times. The idolater excludes God from his reckoning, "lacks Him", is, we might almost say, "minus God in all his affairs", because he serves or loves alternatives that displace the true worship. Barred or banned

121

by the act of unbelieving, God is not allowed to be God: the pagan entrusts himself to patrons, lords, protectors, intercessors, "other than He". The task of all the patriarchs and prophets is to condemn and reverse this tragedy, to expose its vanity and give warning of its menace. Thus Abraham, in Surah 19, tells his people: "I will separate myself from you and from that on which you call, to the exclusion of God". Surah 29 is named "The Spider"—for the simple reason that the trust of the idol-worshipper is as frail as that creature's web (v. 41). The 'adoption' (the word is frequently used) of such deities means the deification of non-entities, the elevation to worship of forces, powers or factors in experience, natural, tribal, mythical, which have status, if at all, only as servants and instruments of a single and inalienable sovereignty.

Islam bent all the resources of religion to affirm and enforce this undivided worship. They may be studied in five general, inter-acting spheres. The first was the Scriptural authority, the documentary Qur'ān, whose genesis as a Scripture was a "recital in the name of God". It was a guidance and a reminder, a warning and a criterion. It declared, in its great positives, "the straight path" and identified, in sharp contrast, the way of those who have the Divine favour and the path of the wandering and unblest. This distinction of the opening Surah, *Al-Fātiḥah*, is perpetuated throughout the entire Book. All its exhortation, example, injunction, remonstrance, undergird this one consuming will to unity and worship.

The second means to the right Godwardness was liturgical practice and the benediction of habituation. From early days, Muslims had a unifying direction of worship—first Jerusalem and then Mecca—both powerful symbols of a single focus, the one making primitive repudiation of the shrines central to Mecca under Quraishi authority as long as Islam was cradled there; the other evoking the Abrahamic associations of that same capital once purged of the compromises that had necessitated Islamic revolt. On the *Qiblah* the familiar sequences of Muslim ritual prayer unified the faithful in the habituation of praise and the rhythm of prostration. Five daily prayers, frequent *Zakāt* or alms, annual fasting in the month of Ramadān and the annual obligation of pilgrimage for the community once Mecca was retrieved from idolatry—these were the recurrent devotions of the believing people, all the more effective for the solidarity and sacrament by which they were characterized, with the postures of prayer, the geographical centre, the congregational setting and the social sanctions. Public and private duty were welded together in a single cultic expression. Personal piety had a corporate stimulus and the community had the strength of individual commitment. The whole practice of Islam, with its ordered recitation of the Qur'ān and its demands on both the body and the imagination, conduced to an effective emotional dethronement of the idols, which otherwise might have persisted in inner affection beyond their dogmatic overthrow.

The third factor in the demise of the idols was undoubtedly political. Islam had no sense of impropriety in the invocation of physical sanctions against the evils it reproved. The vocation of Muhammad as a prophet came to incorporate a vocation to rule and to subdue. Not for him the word only or, as some would say, not merely the word spoken or preached. For this by Islamic criteria would have been an inoperative word, a word contradicted by its own omissions. Instead, the faith Meccan idolatry had ousted itself ousted idolatry from Mecca. The authority of the political arm corroborated the work of the messenger. Islam was realist: men in error and perversity were not to be corrected merely by verbal castigation of their evils. The *Hijrah* purposefully repudiated both their sins and their hegemony in order to prepare the termination of both in one proper triumph. The limitations inherent in this pattern of victory were, as we shall see, only occasionally sensed and noted in the Qur'ān. Muhammad and Islam seem to have been emphatically at rest in the conviction that state and statehood were necessary and valid instruments of their effectiveness. And so it has remained. The twentieth century is unanimous with the seventh that power is the proper destiny of Islamic expression and the due partner in its cause.

A fourth but different element was the historical sense Islam generated of a continuity in the recognition of God most great, its effective assertion of a kinship as old as Abraham. The assurance that their faith was no innovation, but the essence of all true religion before God, gave Muslims a confidence over against the older systems and precluded the inferiority that lateness might otherwise have occasioned. There were, it is true, other factors underlying the vitality of Islamic beginnings. But the sense of community with history and the doctrine of prophetic culmination in Muhammad were deep sources of psychological strength and so to speak turned the tables on the earlier Scriptuaries in synagogue and church. They claimed Moses and Jesus in Islamic terms and rejected as distortions of their teaching many of the characteristic convictions within Judaism and Christianity.

In this way the new faith was able to assert a participation with them and at the same time a correction and displacement of them. The final criterion of monotheism, it was claimed, had passed to Islam, turning the handicap of Arabian remoteness into a veritable asset, without which Islam's concern for the elimination of paganism might otherwise have tended to the enlargement of Christian or Jewish theism. The yearning for an Arabic revelation was, of course, deeply involved in this independence of the earlier prototypes, as the Qur'ān indicates by its reiterated reference to the "Arabic Qur'ān". This, however, was only the counterpart of the general dominance of the Graeco-Roman Byzantine culture in Christianity and the virtual identity of Judaism with Jews. In the self-consciousness of Islam there came about a powerful amalgam of this independence of will and an insistent belief in solidarity with all right worshipping in every age. The new departure was, as it were, continuous with all the past: yet the perpetuity of theism from antiquity now had its ultimate sponsorship, fresh, uncorrupted and authentic.

This double theme of history, the sense of a worship

unchangingly old yet properly renewed in Islam, is constant in the Qur'ān. The narratives of the patriarchs have to do with the same crusade for the recognition of God and are throughout associated with the parallel of Muhammad's mission. Their example engenders tenacity and their vindication is a reassuring education. By its mediation of prophetic precedent the Qur'ān evokes for its readers a sense of solidarity with the ages like that which the rhythm of prayer establishes for each contemporary generation.

Through the Scriptural, the 'liturgical', the political and the historical, as Islamic sources of the right worship, there runs, of course, the 'theological', the actual sense which Islam conveyed to believers and adherents of the Divine Name and nature as the ground and end of their allegiance. There is no more ultimate answer to idolatry than the realization of God, no surer wellspring of worship than the Divine worth. Theology lies at the root of all wise iconoclasm and of all authentic prayer. Since it must judge and condition all else, it is more properly taken as the climax in any study of the Islamic care for a rightly worshipping world. Theology, in any event, is for the most part only known in widespread experience religiously through the Scriptures and the rites, the rule and the community, in which it is embodied.

Assessed by criteria internal to Islam, the theological realm has features of strong and compelling simplicity. There is vigour and assurance in its emphatic creed and directness in its sense of the Divine majesty and mercy. Man knows where he is in this universe of authority, of revelation, subordination and decree. The transcendent Lord is nevertheless near, real and merciful. By His Names He is addressable, while the reservations of 'negative theology' preserve His impenetrable greatness and supremacy. The Divine unity, we might say, uncomplicates the human situation. External nature, to use a contemporary phrase, is "disenchanted", and this ensures a dominion to men in which the works of husbandry and culture and, at length, technology, can take their proper empire, freed from the endless spirits and spells of the pagan cults animating every well, or mountain, or wind, or tribe, with scattered and disorderly items of mystery. Yet this liberation of the hand and soul of man from the tyranny of polydaemonism did not connive, as so often do modern secularizers in their context, with the evaporation of wonder, surprise and gratefulness. These "virtues of delight" were ensured and kindled in the Quranic doctrine of "the signs of God", by which men were called to recognize in the external world the tokens of a single authority and mercy, binding together man's dominion and God's worship as blessedly correlative.

In all these ways, and many others familiar enough from numerous expositions, the theology of Islam has effectively educated and nourished the human activity of worship and imbued it with a scale of dimensions, sharp in intensity, strong in character and strict in discipline. Its postures of prayer, erect and prostrate, again erect and prostrate, symbolize the ultimate meaning of its doctrine—man in submission and dignity, God in sovereignty and compassion.

The misgivings that arise by Christian criteria belong in acknowledgement of that strength and simplicity and in a common concern for the right redemption of man's idolatry and the due realization of God. If Christianity is serious about a world perspective and "a priestly service", then here is a will to let God be God worthy of the deepest, positive concern. Within the terms outlined in chapter 3, that response must relate to the core of the theology, beyond resentments and beyond merely controversial tradition or competition. It will have to do essentially with the Islamic intention itself, tested by its own cares, as these are experienced and illuminated by the kindred cares of Christian theology. It will then be found that there are Christian considerations which bear profoundly on its purposes of right worship. "Wherever I go in my mind", wrote S. T. Coleridge, "I meet Plato on his way back". Wherever I go in theology, the Christian would say, I find Christ taking me further—an experience that is movingly so about Islam.

"THIS BEING DONE, GOD HATH HIS FULL AND PERFECT DIVINITY"

Three areas of significance in particular, for Islam, await this enterprise in relationship from within the Christian mind. They have to do with what might be called the zeal for God, the persistent power of false worships and the understanding of the criteria about God both for worship and doctrine. If these are briefly reviewed the ground will be ready for a simple relating of the main themes of distinctively Christian creed to the Islamic will for a right adoration.

There is in Surah 8: 39 of the Qur'ān a passage which sets the course for Muslim action against idolatry and unbelief. "Fight them until rebellion is no more and religion is entirely Godward"; or, more loosely, "Do battle against them until idolatrous resistance is ended and the religious obligations are entirely God's". Here is the uncompromising and forceful campaign of the Islamic community against all pagan opposition. The command contains the inclusive and evolving word *fitnah*.[1] It means, in early days, the persecution of the Muslim minority and in the time of power the sedition and disaffection that still resisted "the cause of God". Epitomizing in this way the inner transition of Muhammad's people from underlings to masters and so from victims of oppression to objects of conspiracy, the term itself symbolizes the danger inherent in the reach for power as the instrument of Godwardness. The transition to statehood is clear. For only states suffer sedition: one cannot intelligently talk of persecuted power. Yet there is a deep religious contrast between fidelity under persecution and action against rebellion.

This is not to say that religions are only right and pure while they remain minorities, or that there is any virtue in a deliberate taking of suffering instead of responsibility. Clearly the relations of religion to power are inescapable. What matters is their final form, and the reservations in those relations. Where there is an implicit tendency to

---

[1] A useful study of this term and an imaginative application in another context may be found in Kamel Hussein, *City of Wrong*, Eng. trans., London 1959.

identity between the claims of religious belief and the exercise of political power there occurs a situation perilous to the former and indulgent to the latter. What is proper for states is not *ipso facto* proper for religions: what is necessary to political authority is often inimical to religious integrity. There are always demands of ultimacy to which faith must bear witness, if need be, *against* the civil or political arm. If faith equates itself with the interests and sanctions of that power it necessarily forfeits the ability to curb its distortions or defy its compulsiveness. It reserves no critical independence. Without this, the Divine priority that is the core of worship is steadily jeopardized by the vested interests, political and even religious, of the institution in itself.

A story in *The Arabian Nights* has the issue in a quaintly searching passage. "The Tale of the King who kenned the quintessence of things".

> There came to a king of the kings, in his old age, a son who grew up comely, quick-witted, clever: and when he reached years of discretion and became a young man, his father said to him: "Take this realm and rule it in lieu of me, for I desire to flee from the sin of sovranty to Allah most high and don the woollen dress and devote all my time to devotion." Quoth the Prince: "And I am another who desireth to take refuge with the Almighty." So the King said: "Arise, let us flee forth and make for the mountains and there worship in shame before God the most great."[1]

"Worship in shame"—there must always be this element in our acknowledgement of God, not only in a *post facto* withdrawal from power but in the immediate exercise of it. Its pitfalls cannot mean its abnegation, except of course to other hands. For its feasible service to righteousness cannot be abjured, least of all in Islam. The problem is to keep vivid "the sin of sovranty" within its actual pursuit. Only so is there a proper judgement over the state and a true sense of its compromise and partiality, lest its necessary instrumentality to faith become a perversion of faith's duty to God. The perpetual need for a religious criticism of the political

[1] *The Thousand and One Nights*, Richard Burton's trans. Vol. ix, p. 137.

realm, as indispensable to a right worship, demands a dissociation of faith-loyalty from state-interest.

This is the more urgent where the zeal of iconoclasm is involved. "Be ye angry and sin not" says the New Testament. Precisely when we are on crusade, temptations wait for us. "Thou that abhorest idols", asks St. Paul in Romans, in an apt if puzzling question, "dost thou commit sacrilege?" May there be in the very action that uproots the idols a paradoxical self-idolatry, the more pervasive for its enthusiasm and assurance?

Some more strictly theological aspects of emancipation from idolatry belong with a later paragraph—the need for reassurance as to the relevance to God most high of finite man so that the lesser but more comforting 'deities' may be abandoned and the idolatry of prudent insurance and 'double protection' brought to an end; the proper, because disciplined, understanding of natural forces, within the Divine order; and the sense of release, in God, from the intimidations of mortality, of ancestors or of human ill-will. No doubt these aspects of 'salvation' from the love or the fear of idols may be served in part by robust action in idol-breaking under the wing, and by the will, of politically based authority. Yet in the farthest reaches of their dominion, idols are not accessible to axes and hammers, nor their devotees to forcible persuasion. And even when they seem to be, the quality of their conversion may well be diminished by these means.

Islam has been traditionally the most possessive of all religions over its community, the most ready and confident in state-reliance, the most forthright against 'apostacy', the most prone to believe itself in God's hands in a reciprocal purpose. May it not be that this characteristic has oversimplified the cause, the goal, of a right worship, has underrated the complexity involved in "religion being wholly God's"? The urge to go forward in the custody of revelation with the patterns of authority familiar to this world may easily miss the measure of the human problem, the lengths of men's self-idolatry, the chronic pride and defiance of the Divine, the insistent autonomy of mankind. If we tend to marry the correction of these with the acceptance and the authority of an external order, of a Caliphate or a government, shall we have taken them in their full reality or redeemed their whole damnation? Shall we have any sure vantage ground from which to judge and save that authority itself, as no more than an instrument, and accountable to God Himself? Is it not possible for us to deny "His full and perfect Divinity" precisely in constituting ourselves its champions? We can thus be idolatrously pursuing the negation of idolatry, substituting the self-centred service of God for God Himself.

As the Qur'ān itself recognizes, "the rule of God", and religion, must be uncompulsive (Surah 2: 256). For there is no worthy religious relationship that is unfree. Unbelief and idolatry, therefore, can never be retrieved except conformably to the omnipotence of God Himself, which is always willing to wait, or even to fail, until it can rightly succeed. There is no remaking of men against their will and no true shaping of their wills to their remaking, where factors of prudence, time-serving, necessity, or sanction, direct or indirect, are present. Vigorous external action in the direction of right worship and for the serving of true religion may properly be taken by sinews of earthly power. But these are at best only contributory to the larger, sterner, tasks of the spirit. It is here that the Islamic intention and the Christian criteria meet.

Their meeting is the more vital because of the sharper tests of our present situation. Arnold Toynbee has given eloquent currency to man's new temptations in the deification of technological power and sheer human achievement. Contemporary secularity as the testing ground of Christian theology and the common denominator of religions today will be studied in chapter 7. Clearly, practical atheism is a readier option for man, emotionally and perhaps intellectually, than at any earlier time. While there is nothing new in the posture that finds the Divine negligible, superfluous, or simply absent and meaningless, there is a new plausibility or cogency about it, in the light of man's extending empire over things. By the same token, the aim of a right worship, neither slavish nor immature—a worship of God fully rendered from within the technological competence of man—calls the more for an alert theology, whereby the sense of the option to get along without God may serve to a new perception of His presence. The question, for both Muslim and Christian, is how adequate and responsive their theologies, and their souls within them, are to these demands.

Certainly the cause of right worship encounters heavy contrary pressures in our time. Scientific civilization reprieves or at least cushions human society from many of the ills and fears which formerly gave powerful impulse to the sense of ultimate dimensions. Or, putting the matter conversely, men now tend to find refuge from the burdens and enigmas of existence in different 'ultimates'—in Caesar, or technocracy or other 'Leviathans', or else in an individual indifferentism that shelves and suppresses them in a convenient scepticism, while pursuing such diversionary happiness as temperament may allow and technology can furnish. In this context, the growing complexity of human organization, its massive proportions in megalopolis and the intensifying redundancy or irrelevance of the human element through cybernation, have together threatened a sort of 'evacuation' of meaning, or at least of traditional significance, within man himself. When he seeks for a self he cannot find, it is little wonder if he ceases to find a God he cannot seek. For he is in inner atrophy, or nearly so, in respect of those very emotions of wonder, seriousness or surprise, out of which all true religion comes. The literature of our time mirrors this vacuity in man more pathetically than familiar theologies in Islam, or in the Church, have compassionately known.

In some circles, the vacuity is met by a sort of turning of necessity itself into a virtue, crudely associating the Divine only with attitudes of human frailty or haplessness that are now scientifically outgrown. This view imposes, in a quite unwarrantable way, on the ageless status of humanity the birth-growth-maturity cycle of individual life, and tidily identifies our present dilemmas with a God-dispensing adulthood. By this proceeding it quite misses the existential equality of all generations, and evades the exhilarating duty to define and attain a contemporary worship and take the technological competence in consistency with that unchanging human-ness, hallowing both in a living awareness of God.

This calling to be truly human and rightly alive to God, as the double form of one vocation, is vital in the whole field of contemporary Muslim life for the reason that, as elsewhere in Asia and Africa, the changes and stresses of technology and the dissolution of the static order have come with such speed and intensity. Europe's two centuries of apprenticeship to scientific and nuclear civilization were leisurely indeed in comparison with the telescoped pressures on the societies of the eastern hemisphere. The consequent bewilderments or intoxications of mood are correspondingly more severe. There are certain handicaps, arising from local situations and traditional assumptions, to impede the full Islamic response—the external origin of the disturbing factors, the rigidity of some conservative attitudes, the satisfaction in some quarters with merely doctrinaire reactions, the relative immunity of official theological guardianship from frank experience of the modern temper in all its range of anxiety or scepticism, and the preoccupations of leadership with political or economic priorities.

These, however, are potentially outweighed by the solid assets of Islam—assets deriving from its Semitic and Greek ancestry in faith and philosophy, as well as from its native genius and vigour. There is the sense of a 'sacramental universe' in the signs of God, of nature as a realm of human dominion, of creaturehood in man as two-directional—imperially over things and dependently under God. These are the groundwork of a living worship that hallows the technological precisely in that it is neither feared nor enthroned. The Islamic will to deny idols, fully interpreted, is itself a most powerful veto on the tyranny of the absolutisms which men so readily establish, falsely, in their societies. Its doctrine of the Divine lordship, if related coterminously to the whole of contemporary life, can discipline and secure the human empire in a proper reverence, fortified by its sense of law and prophecy as an ideological structure of values.[1]

This is not meant at all to suggest, even in the most summary way, a balance sheet of Islam and modernity, but only as a preface to the deepest consideration for Christian relationship. Agreed that a right worship is still the authentic condition of human fulfilment—not the less but the more so, both as to its sources and its ends, by virtue of the contemporary history of man—then the question has to do with the reach by which man finds it. What is its depth within the mystery of his own being and its business with his inner waywardness—a waywardness that takes persistent shape in the falsifying of worship? Or, in other terms, how comes man's true *islām*?

The characteristic emphases of Christianity at this point are radical to a degree uncongenial to Islam. Muslim thought readily reproaches the Christian doctrine of sin for excessive seriousness. It echoes Judaism here, reproving what it considers, though mistakenly, to be a consigning of mankind to demonic authority and an exalting of the Fall over creation, in doctrinal priority. Yet that Christian sense of the seriousness of evil is not only the measure of the glory of the intention in creation, but of the fallenness which idolatrous worships enshrine. It could not be the one without the other. Thus, in the ultimate reckoning, any zeal of iconoclasm must take us into the issue of sin. Its final expression, therefore, in the dethroning of idols means the redemption of every inward evil whence those varied rejections of God arise. The Islamic passion for a rightly worshipping human world involves, in its fullest obligation, the Christian diagnosis of what thwarts or misdirects that rightness. The very sincerity of the will to "a full and perfect" acknowledgement of God involves us in the full measure of the wrongness to be retrieved and repaired. Our hope must

[1] See, for example, Isma'il Ragi al Faruki, *On Arabism: Urubah and Religion*, Amsterdam, 1962, in which the author, though with a certain stridency of tone, expounds "the total commitment of the whole person to the total realm of value" (p. 225).

be that the realism and frankness befitting our current situation may enable Muslims and Christians to perceive and possess the mutual relevance that belongs with the whole iconoclasm in the one faith and the whole salvation in the other.

Such hope is bound up with the related theme of their respective concepts of the Divine, of God known and acknowledged, of theology formulated and fulfilled in belief and devotion. Ideas of God are necessarily at the heart of worship. The 'Names' by which He is addressed are those by which He is described. A false worship will be implicit in an imperfect theology, except in so far as intention may redeem its distortion or mercy make good its ignorance. Wrongly to think of God is by that very token wrongly to esteem Him and thus, by Quranic principles, an improper theology, even if only intellectually so, is a form of *Shirk*, since it alienates from God what is due and 'associates' what is false. The image in the imagination is more vital than the image we manufacture. Idols are relatively innocent compared with the concepts they embody and far less subtle than the unworthy notions of God that have no embodiment but only adjectival, credal or conceptual existence. The ambition for a right worship turns on the will to a true theology, and both depend on criteria of the Divine that are, so to speak, divinely derived. Authentic worship Godward on man's part can only obtain responsively to authentic disclosure manward on God's part. It is here, as well as in what relates to idolatry and evil, that Christian awareness of God, in self-giving to the world, has so vital a bearing on the central worship-conviction of Islam.

"The Beautiful Names of God" in the Qur'ān and Islamic theology[1] are the formal satisfaction of this need. In them, God is rightly described and addressed, denoted and adored. Yet the insistent Muslim tradition about them, as it seems by Christian assessments, is so instinctively 'negative' as to diminish both their theological significance and their religious adequacy. If they have to be interpreted always

---

[1] Reference may be made here, for brevity's sake, to the writer's reflections on this topic in *The Dome and the Rock*, London, 1964, chapter 8, pp. 83–93.

with a careful exclusion of their human relatedness, and are true only so long as their truth is a matter for silence, then a certain anonymity attaches to the Divine nature. This reluctance in Islam to think of the Divine as in any explicit sense denoted by human language matches its reluctance to involve the Divine with the human in other realms. On both counts, the Christian faith offers a relationship of bold reassurance towards these reservations of Islam, a confidence about Divine readiness for human relatedness, and sees such a ministry as a powerful, if not indispensable, element in the informing and sustaining of that most Islamic of goals, namely, a right worship.

Doubtless, the human relations of the Divine are there in Islam. They are inseparable from creation, revelation, prophecy, mercy and judgement. The Names which have to do with these, and other, avenues of Divine initiative towards men and of human response and access towards God are firmly rooted in the life of Muslim devotion. The reservations, however, persist. The Divinely 'inappropriate' is to be excluded by the knowledge of the Names but itself includes their full or confident interpretation. It is as if an anticipatory anathema on the Incarnation, on "the Word made flesh", demands a firm preservation of theology from the analogical and from humanly grounded significance.

This situation of a partial anonymity in God for Islam, checked as it is by the robust emphases of Islamic religion and law, makes, by Christian thinking, for a certain disconcerting elusiveness in Muslim theology. In some quarters this may be regarded as a source of strength, coinciding as it does with the Islamic deprecation of what are seen as the complexities and dogmatics of Christian belief. We need, however, to beware of this kind of assessment. While there is no virtue in complexity for its own sake, there is certainly no legitimacy in the mere criterion of simplicity. Islam and Christianity could well cease to be divided by that sort of consideration about allegedly elaborate, and aggressively plain, creeds. The issue lies, not there, but in the adequacy of theology for the achievement of worship. It has to do with an awareness worthy of the greatness of God, with an enterprise, in the very relation of God to men, giving itself unstintedly to the expression of all that worship is to greet and love and answer.

Strange as the suggestion may seem, initially, on the Islamic side, it is perhaps through the thought of Divine 'vulnerability' that we can most truly bring together Muslim and Christian relationships to God. With this reflection we can cross over into our concluding review of the bearing on all the foregoing of the Christian creed about "God in Christ".

Islam lives in the conviction that human life is constituted, totally and essentially, by Godward accountability. God's will and worship are the terms of reference of human existence. For the guiding and enabling of that destiny in man comes the manward movement of the Divine purpose and power, and thence, in turn, the reciprocity of creation to submission, of law to obedience, of prophecy to allegiance, of revelation to witness and of compassion to frailty and dependence. Islam, in its deepest consciousness has powerfully known, and made known, these areas of Divine human mutuality—a fact that stands beyond all the controversies kindled by lesser perspectives.

Yet, for all its belief in omnipotence, it has apprehensively held back from the full implications of this Divine reciprocity with man. In holding so profoundly to the conviction about God as Creator, Lawgiver and Revealer, it is necessarily involved, however reluctantly, in a sense of God as 'vulnerable'. Its instincts to repudiate this only imperil its definitive beliefs. For there cannot be a Divine demand turning, as *islām* does, upon human response, without a sense in which Divine interests are staked, to the point of jeopardy, on the human answer. There can be no real enjoining of men to "let God be God", or to "take God for God", if His being not so taken is impossible or a matter of indifference to men or to Himself. The whole feasibility of idolatry, the evident option of atheism, make plain that God's due worship is not inviolate. And His worship being not inviolate, He is not invulnerable. There is no escape from this logic except into unreality and pointlessness. Even the merest urge to find a contradiction for it takes us out of Islam. Despite all the attendant, and proper, insistence on sovereignty and immunity in God, there abides this inherent 'vulnerability'—this standing of the power of God in the power of men—their power to repudiate, to gainsay, to diversify, or to ignore. Only by the reality of this 'exposure' to man does the validity of Islam exist as a faith and as an imperative.

Christian relationships exist to invite this lively recognition of Divine demand and its corollary in Divine 'expectation' into their deepest implications. Seen beyond contentious prejudice and misconception, Christian faith begins in this same dimension where Islam belongs. But it understands that Divine vulnerability to man as more intimately open, more unreserved in the will to seek and to care and thus more tenderly set to restore the human waywardness.

It comes, then, not as a qualification of the Divine greatness but as that greatness after another measure: not less great, only differently greater. That "being done" whereby "God hath His full and perfect Divinity" is understood to consist not alone in man's ability for surrender in acknowledgement of law and power and mercy in his Lord, but more in the Divine capacity for grace and long-suffering and the costly hallowing of man.

Here all that belongs with the Islamic struggle for a due worship of God comes into its own—and yet a different 'own', in the gentler shape of a birth and a death, of a Father seeking and a Shepherd finding, of the Word dwelling among men, and of a Cross on a hill. All these are other than Islam, and yet they are akin: they belong with a single goal that "religion may be wholly God's" and that "God may be all in all."

TE DEUM LAUDAMUS:
"THEE, AS GOD, WE PRAISE"

There is a striking similarity between the emphatic pronouns of the *Fātiḥah*, or Opening Surah of the Qur'ān:

"Thee it is we worship; Thee it is we seek for succour . . ." and of the opening verse of the Christian *Te Deum*: "Thee, being God, we praise . . ." The kinship continues at least through six verses of the latter, and even beyond to "apostles, prophets and martyrs" (though in variant sense). But with verse 10, and "the holy Church" acknowledging "the Father . . .", and the "only Son", the divergence seems complete. We are in the midst of traditional antipathies concerning the Divine unity and 'Sonship', the Incarnation and "the precious blood". Beyond these, however, we come out into themes again congenial to Islam: "govern", "magnify", "keep", "let Thy mercy lighten . . ." and "let me never be confounded". Our task now is to set these central verses about "the King of glory" and "the sharpness of death" alongside the Muslim sense of the confession "We acknowledge Thee to be the Lord", and with the help of Islamic awareness of what such 'acknowledgement' requires, explore its Christian force.

To this enterprise there is a negative and a positive side, having to do with terminology, holding, for the Christian, a Scriptural and credal sanctity and, for the Muslim, persistent misapprehension. The situation may be well served by a parallel. There occurs, in St. John's narrative of Jesus before Pilate, a brief but crucial exchange hinging on the word "King". Pilate takes it up with the opening question: "King of the Jews, I understand?" Is Jesus to respond to this with a Yes!? He cannot do so; for if He does He will play into the hands of Pilate's notion of kingship, which as a Roman's was wholly and unalterably political. To answer the governor in the affirmative will convey the idea that He, Jesus, is a political pretender. If, to exclude this error, He answers: "No! I am not" He denies or confuses the sense in which He is. He can, therefore, answer neither Yes nor No until the point of the word is clear. Hence the initial response, which is in no way evasive: "Pilate, are you using this word 'King' as you would as a Roman or are you quoting it from some reported context?" Pilate, in military brusqueness, is impatient with this seeming subtlety and retorts: "Am I a

Jew? it is your own people who have you under charge: what is your offence?" Still intent on the original issue, Jesus replies: "My kingdom is not of a this worldly kind: for if it were I would not be here without a fight. My subjects would have seen to that. But my kingdom is not of that character." Pilate, mystified, responds: "So you are a king, then?" Jesus: "King was the word you used and, rightly understood, used well. I was born for this authority and that is why I am here in the world. Truth lovers know this well enough."[1]

What 'kingship' in this paraphrase made confusing for a Roman, 'Sonship' obscures even more darkly for a Muslim. Just as the early Church in the Gentile context was willing to forego the term "Son of Man" for the sake of its proper translation, so must the Church today take creative responsibility for the phrase "Son of God". Where analogies are irretrievably distorted for or by certain listeners, they must be re-cast. The New Testament understanding of the Sonship of Jesus to God does not mean Divine paternity, nor Divine duality, nor prophetic pretension, nor *Shirk*, nor deification. Nor is it rightly understood as 'adoption'—the frequent Quranic term is *ittikhādh*[2]—meaning the exaltation of Jesus to Divine status at some point in an initially human story. It is not alternate to, nor destructive of, the role of "servant" and "Messiah", both of them Quranic titles of Jesus. As carefully as Jesus Himself before Pilate, we must abjure the hearer's attributable meanings that falsify the word's intention and, beyond the reach of these distortions, we must care for what it really affirms.

Bringing together all we have pondered within Islam about a sure anti-idolatry and the human need for an authentic relation to God wherein all other worships may be truly renounced and excluded, we understand in the person of Jesus the touchstone of such knowledge of God. Christians believe that human life in Him became the point and focus of

[1] This understanding of John 18: 33–37 is clear enough from the New English Bible translation. See also C. H. Dodd, *About the Gospels*, London, 1952, p. 33.

[2] See Surahs 17: 11; 19: 35; 19: 92; 25: 2; 39: 4, etc.

Divine self-disclosure, the Divine nature, as it were, auto-biographically given in this human history, as its revelatory drama, at once real, personal, dependable and accessible to men. They see this conviction steadily born, without compromise, in the hearts of unwavering monotheists set for the recognition of God in worship and moved, by one and the same emotion, to the inclusion of Christ within it, on the ground that He was integrally within the Divine activity and worth to which such worship is responsive. They did not thereby 'deify': they 'acknowledged'. In the order of knowing they *came* to understand and confess because they had sensed and understood what, in the order of being, ever was. Here the sign principle which the Qur'ān knows so well is, so to speak, realized in a single, inclusive, living 'Sign': the Names of God have that within humanity by which they may be reliably apprehended. God, we believe, undertakes the conditions of being humanly knowable, by taking the pre-requisites of our knowing—humanity, time, place and history—and expressing His nature therein. This grace of self-communication, though here decisive and climactic, may be seen as continuous with that Divine involvement with mankind and with human relevance which we have seen to be implicit in all Islamic convictions about creation, law and prophecy. For all these require and mean that activities, to which we can rightly refer as "of God" or as God's—will, purpose, reminder, mercy and all else—turn upon, and take shape from, human reaction and human participation. Thus law "stakes" the heavenly will upon the earthly answer: prophecy serves the Divine message through the human instrument: creation through all subjects the Divine intention to the human surrender by the very dependability of the dominion that permits men, if they will, to be idolaters. One cannot believe in the reality of idolatry and at the same time believe that God is exempt from significant engagement with His world.

It was in just this sort of context that, earlier, we arrived at the strange yet inescapable thought of the Divine vulnerability. It must be clear that any adequate concern about

Shirk has to come to terms with this mystery. If we are really to say: "Let God be God" it must be because there are, in human sinfulness, forces and passions saying: "Let not God be God". All such disavowal is the reality of sin. We may, therefore, expect to find the Divine vindication against all false worships rooted in a deep encounter with their essential enmity, and so to learn the Divine sovereignty most surely where it is most critically challenged.

This—surely a properly Islamic—logic brings us to the Christian Cross whence, in the meaning of the Resurrection, the assurance of Christ's Sonship springs. It has to do with the Christian sense of just such an encounter between a power of love worthy to be seen as God's and a qualitative expression of the world of self-centred, idol building, religious preening, God disowning, humanity to which we all belong. There is a quality about the Cross on both sides—suffering accepted in compassion and inflicted in evil—which qualifies it to be seen and received by faith as, at one and the same time, a sacrament of the Divine vulnerability to men and of the Divine glory with men.

If all that we understood above, from Islam, is true, then we should anticipate that the one revelation would be inseparable from the other, that we should experience the Divine reality precisely where it meets and masters the intrinsic human blindness to its claims. "Let God be God" is a true cry for the theologian and for the iconoclast, because the issue it concerns has a focal point of decision within creation and among men, a climax where all that is at stake has the conclusive victory—the victory by which it is seen, sacramentally and effectually, how and whereby God is God.

It is this sense of the Christ and Him crucified as "the power and wisdom of God" that is intended in the traditional doctrine of the Sonship of Jesus to God. That Sonship, in the texture of the event, is simply the filial responsiveness to the will of God in that human situation, "obedient" as the New Testament puts it, "unto the end". What we mean when we say that Jesus is the Son of God is this His ready identity in action with the perspectives and purposes of the Divine mind in His ministry and passion. "The cup which *my Father* has given me. . . . *Father*, glorify thy Name. . . ." All subsequent theological dogma is meant to define and safeguard, with concepts of status and relation, what is concretely an identity of will and deed with the Divine nature, at grips, as Islam sees it must be, with the human ungodliness whence all idolatries derive. From that actual and active achievement of the Divine victory according to the Divine mind, theology learned, in more formal terms, to say: "The Father sent the Son to be the Saviour of the world". What matters now is that Muslims, disabused of the alien interpretations of what the words intend, might come into the way of their intrinsic bearing on the common imperative: "Let God be God", and the kindred affirmative: "There is none save He". By moving from the action of Christ *for* God, they may retrace the way Christian theology itself went to Christ *as* God, and thus to God in Christ. But, in the end, the status by which Christianity sees and understands this meaning, as having the nature of eternity, takes form as faith only in its recognition in the dark concreteness of Gethsemane.

This is no idle concern, no remote dogmatic theme. It is to the meaning of the Divine engagement with men and history that contemporary pressures are summoning all theism. In that context the sovereignty for which Islam stands in God and the travail which Christianity learns in God draw into ever closer relevance the one to the other. It is that fundamental confidence which sustains the spirit against every suspicion that the still massive, credal problems are insurmountable, or tiresome, or both. It renews the will to make good for the worship Islam requires to be undivided the meaning of the love the Gospel knows to be undefeated. Does not the one assume what the other achieves?

CHAPTER SIX

CHRISTIAN SYMBOLISM AND THE AFRICAN MIND

I N his *Portrait of the Artist as a Young Man,* and elsewhere in his works, James Joyce follows a characteristic habit of borrowing the vocabulary of Christian devotion to describe and explore the attitudes of the secular temper. The flowing dressing-gown trails behind the morning ablutions like the Mass vestments of the priest "going unto the altar of God". The birth of a work of art is presented in language reminiscent of Christ's nativity. The word "eucharistic" becomes a term for a simply pagan delectation in "the fair courts of life", and the notion of a priestly 'call' is translated into a life-realization that has all the fervour an ascetic brings to the discipline of life-renunciation. Stephen Hero awaits the "epiphanies" by which the drab uneventfulness of the Dublin scene, in sudden disclosure of its essence, is irradiated with rich qualities of soul. Thus what is normally considered to be peculiar to theology or to the ecclesiastical furnishes the writer with images and themes that seem to be deliberately telling against their accepted sense. It is as if the author were aggressively intending to renounce Catholic Christianity in the very act of adopting its vocabulary.

A puzzled reaction is tempted to take it all as blasphemous. Can there be any other aim in thus aligning the chalice with the shaving-dish and the crucifix with the morning mirror? A longer patience, however, suggests that such a conclusion would be premature, or immature. For there is, clearly, a reversibility about such analogies. The fact that "epiphany" may be taken out of a prayer book and occur in the street serves to illuminate "epiphany" itself. That Christ can be known in the breaking of bread—taking the matter this time the usual way round—means that bread is known, in being so taken, as a sacramental thing. That baptism can be defined by imagery taken from death is eloquent, in reverse, of how death, too, is to be understood. The very capacity of things to yield parables returns to educate us in their own meaning. Merely to suspect blasphemy, then, in Joyce, is hasty and hollow: he could perhaps be hinting in this way at an unwonted reverence. Sometimes even secularity proves to be caring for the interests of the 'sacred'.

At all events, whatever may be true of the Irish novelist, this transposition of vocabulary has an important bearing on the whole task of missionary theology. Communication between widely differing parties may be said to hinge on a certain ambivalence of terms through which a growing equivalence may be ventured. The hope of this chapter is to develop a Christian mediation with the African mind, through a bold, if simple, employment of the latter's 'idiom' for the former's content. There are, surely, elemental features of African religion, two here in particular, in terms of which, if only in part and at risk, the Christian meanings can be expressed and embodied. The enterprise means not merely a new geographical realm for our interest, but also a different aspect of the religious complex. Our focus in chapter 4, in the discussion of Jewry, was primarily that of the Church as a corporate community and of its ecclesiastical or institutional self-awareness, in relation to the election-vocation of the precedent "people of God". In respect of Islam, we have had in view the theological and dogmatic areas of credal relationship, their intention and resolution. Inter-religious obligation, however, is much more than community and doctrine. It moves even more deeply in the spheres where symbol and sacrament have sway in the inner emotions and instincts of the soul, both tribal and personal. Africa is today the most compelling theme for this dimension of a world perspective, and no doubt its most formidable.

Duly stirred and sobered, our business here is to study the availability of African modes of religion for the African expression of Christian discipleship. "The only universal religious language", as Mircea Eliade observes, "is the language of symbols". "When a local history becomes sacred and at the same time exemplary, that is, a paradigm for the salvation of humanity, it demands expression in (this) universally understandable language."[1] Original Christianity made early borrowings not only, as we have seen, from the terminology of the Graeco-Roman mysteries, but from their initiatory imagery and action. It is part of that confidence in the universal translatability of the Gospel that we should believe its experience expressible in and through the patterns, critically and compassionately seen, of African society.

Our first need is to see that criticism and compassion begin in profound respect. There is no need to draw contrasts between Asia and Africa to the disadvantage of the latter.[2] There is doubtless an apparent frailty about African paganism and a numberedness about its days. But there are still deeps within men that they cannot deny and remain themselves; and there are dimensions of meaning which can and must persist through all seeming extinction or demise. Only superficial observation reports that "Africa has no history", and only the crudest insensitivity could fail to kindle to its mysteries and sorrows and its energies of soul. "To a certain extent", writes Kenneth Kaunda, "we in Africa have always had a gift for enjoying man for himself . . . Africa's gift to world culture must be in the realm of human relationships".[3] It would be criminal to imagine that African relevance to the rest of men is extinguished by the onset, irresistibly, of technological and 'superior' civilization. "Thou hast set our feet in a large room", continues President Kaunda, quoting the psalm.[4] It is this soul-space of the African view, the sense of nature, of man, of family and of tribe, which we must know how to appreciate and inhabit vicariously.

The sheer bigness of the 'subject', in Livingstone's sense of the adjective, must never be forgotten. Of course it makes 'African' as a denominator a massive generalization, for

[1] In *Birth and Rebirth*, The Religious Meanings of Initiation in Human Culture, trans. from the French by W. R. Trask, London, 1961, p. 119.

[2] As Bede Griffiths, for example, in *Christian Ashram*, London, 1966, p. 71. A gentle and discerning work on Hindu-Christian dialogue.

[3] In *A Humanist in Africa*, Letters to Colin M. Morris, London, 1966, p. 22.
[4] *Ibid.*, p. 28.

10 per cent. of the world's population using 25 per cent. of its languages. With Latin America, Africa is of all the continents the most malleable. The speed and fluidity of its present changes, political, social, religious and material, overrun their reasoned analysis. It represents, we may fairly say, at once the most wistful and the most disappointed arena of the West's relationships with the non-west. Laurens Van Der Post writes:

> I am old enough to remember . . . the enormous hush that fell over Africa in the wake of the coming of European man. In the African heart there was a calm and tense air of expectation of growing wonders to come, and as a result there was also the most moving and wonderful readiness of the African to serve, to imitate, to follow the European, and finally an unqualified preparedness to love and be loved.[1]

But when the spell was broken, the deep inner experience of exploitation left the sorest wounds, the more so by dint of the absence, in the story of African penetration, of the entrenchments with which Hinduism and Buddhism were equipped to despise western pretension and to counter its overtures. Also, of course, the final 'scramble' for Africa was the more formidable for having been earlier delayed or thwarted by the physical deterrents of the continent to exploration. Its coastal accessibility sufficed, however, to bring to it a tragedy surely unparalleled in length and suffering in any other territory—the Slave Trade. It has also incurred the misery of a stubbornly racialist minority-authority bastioned on its proper soil.

These are only tokens of the reasons why we must reckon with the search of the African temper for positive fulfilment, through and within the pressures of modern change and external impact, and with the urgent passion to possess a soul of one's own.

> I know the problem of Africa can be studied in a variety of ways, economically, historically, scientifically, anthropologically and sociologically. These are all perfectly valid . . . But . . . for me the one primary and elemental approach is through the

---

[1] *The Dark Eye in Africa*, London, 1956, p. 43.

being of man . . . The conflict in Africa is at heart a battle
about being and non-being . . .[1]

Here lies the genesis of the urge for *négritude* as an assertion of
identity. It is notable that it has emerged in those very areas
of *France outre Mer*, where African intellectuals went furthest
in Europeanization,[2] as if to dramatize a rejection in the very
acceptance of western necessities. The misgiving here does
not only derive from a concern for the survival of the given
self, in the sense of Jean Price Mar's words, "We have no
chance of being ourselves unless we repudiate no part of our
ancestral heritage".[3] It arises from a serious question-mark
about the integrity of Christian relationships, that goes far
beyond the sensitivities belonging to defensive instincts. It is
one thing to ponder, with Chinua Achebe, how

> . . . of late
> A strange bell
> Has been ringing a song of desolation:
> Leave your yams and cocoyams
> And come to school.
> And I must scuttle away in haste,
> Where children, in play or in earnest cry:
> Look! a Christian is on the way.[4]

It is another—though the emotions may merge imperceptibly
—to reckon with the many tragic compromises of the
Christian faith to which Africa has been exposed, at western
hands. This is not simply

> . . . the failure of the churches . . . to keep alive man's natural
> sense of religion and to sustain his urge to seek an answer to the
> riddle of life through the quality and temper of his being.

It is the other

> . . . and more sinister dimension . . . the churches . . . actually
> standing between man and this ancient respected way. This
> is what I would call "sabotage in the fourth dimension".[5]

[1] *Ibid.*, pp. 15 and 46.
[2] In contrast to the British areas where local custom was more generally
conserved.
[3] A Haitian writer, in *Ainsi Parla l'Oncle*, Port au Prince, 1928, p. 210.
[4] Chinua Achebe, *Arrow of God*, London, 1964, pp. 227–8.
[5] Van Der Post, *op. cit.*, p. 15. See in similar sense, Kenneth Kaunda, *op. cit.*,
pp. 100–1.

This "standing between" can be illustrated on many sides, not least in the invocation of 'Christian' sanction by white dominance, with bells tolling, as Ian Smith has it, "for justice, civilization and Christianity".[1] There can be no saving the Christian realities for African benediction except in their own deep quality of honest, open bearing of this African dimension of disappointment, with sorrow for its truth and imagination in its retrieval. The western Christian must be ready to move from, and amid, a widespread discredit of his associations and this ardent, positive re-possession of African identity.

This context of emotions, already broadly discussed in chapter 1, gives the right urgency here to a reflection on how Christian symbolism, with the tenderness and realism these considerations enjoin, can meet and measure the African world-view. No more than a simple essay can be attempted in a most complex theme and only that, by a wholesale neglect of a score of related problems, academic and practical. But allowing the temerity involved, there may be some value in a suggestion to ruminate on the two deepest elements in Christian symbolism—initiation by baptism and participation by Holy Communion—and their actual, or possible, bearing on the African sense of "the name" and of "community".

What follows has no claim to be taken as more than the barest effort to relate meaning to meaning and see if there is not, to revert to Joyce, a real ambivalence of concepts that may be wisely ripened into an equivalence, in something of the manner of the New Testament ventures of vocabulary argued in chapter 2. Whether successful or not, the effort may, at any rate, exemplify the sort of onus which is on the faith if it is to keep faith with the world.

THE 'NAME' AND BAPTISM

Ekwefi had suffered a good deal in her life. She had borne ten children and nine of them had died in infancy, usually before the age of three. As she buried one child after another, her

---

[1] 'Toll' seems the appropriate word.

sorrow gave way to despair and then to grim resignation. The birth of her children, which should be a woman's crowning glory, became for Ekwefi mere physical agony devoid of promise. The naming ceremony after seven market weeks, became an empty ritual. Her deepening despair found expression in the names she gave her children. One of them was a pathetic cry: Onwumbiko: 'Death, I implore you'. But death took no notice. Onwumbiko died in his fifteenth month. The next child was a girl: Ozoemena: 'May it not happen again'. She died in her eleventh month and two others after her. Ekwefi then became defiant and called her next child: Onwuma: 'Death may please himself'. And he did.[1]

Ekwefi ought not to be brought within earshot of the contrasted bliss of a Didinga mother's song to her firstborn:

> O my child, now indeed I am happy.
> Now indeed, I am a wife;
> No more a bride, but a mother of one.
> Be splendid and magnificent, child of desire. . . .
> Child, child, child, love I have had from my man,
> But now, only now, am I his wife and the mother
> Of his firstborn.
> His soul is safe in your keeping, my child,
> And it was I, I, I, who have made you.
> Therefore I am loved, therefore I am happy . . .
> You will tend his shrine when he is gone,
> With sacrifice and oblation you will recall his name
> Year by year, and he will live in your prayers,
> And there will be no more death for him,
> But everlasting life, springing from your loins.[2]

Here the tragedy and triumph of motherhood—human, elemental, universal, yet also in these pieces unmistakably African—the naming ceremony, the eloquent names, the immortality of 'seed', the maternal anticipation, the filial naming-again of the father. Our purpose, with a due haunt in our imagination for the rapture and the plaintiveness of progeny made and undone, is to explore this sense of the name, the *persona* and his inauguration into life by the family

[1] Chinua Achebe, *Things Fall Apart*, London, 1958, p. 68.
[2] Quoted from J. H. Driberg, *Initiation*, trans. from Didinga and Lango tribes.

that gives him being and meaning. For individuation is alien to African traditional society. As Placide Tempels writes in his perceptive study:

> The Bantu cannot be a lone being. It is not a good enough synonym . . . to say that he is a social being. No: he feels and knows himself to be a vital force, at this very time to be in intimate and personal relationship with other forces acting above and below him in the hierarchy of forces. He knows himself to be a vital force, even now influencing some forces and being influenced by others. The human being, apart from the ontological hierarchy and the interaction of forces, has no existence in the conceptions of the Bantu.[1]

Muntu, or vital force, binds each to all in a mutual or acceptance community, essentially integrative, in which self-hood is not separable from the inclusiveness of relationships received and treasured from the older living and from the departed, and perpetuating towards the generations yet unborn, while extending laterally to all things in their respective, but subordinate, powers, and inhering in God as the supreme and complete *muntu*.

Within this co-existence of vitality, as it might be described, the person possesses his *muntu* by being, so to speak, himself. In that sense all human life is inalienably "one's own". Yet this could never be a solipsism, or an egocentric predicament such as the cold, rational abstractions of European philosophy have debated. Solipsism, for the African view, contradicts what it states. There is no *ipse*, no man himself, that is *solus*. One cannot be, without inter-being. The 'name' in African usage, or better the 'names', are simply the expression of this relational existence, and thus of the reality of the person. In parlance everywhere, of course, names are in practice relational, in that they do not merely serve to denote their owners, but also to address them. Robinson Crusoe never hears his name in the desert island and thus no longer bears it. But for all this inter-existence of names, they can

---

[1] *Bantu Philosophy*, Eng. trans. by Colin King from the French version of the Dutch original, Paris, 1959, pp. 68–69. This is one of the most penetrating analyses of the Bantu mind. On *muntu* see also Janheinz Jahn, *Muntu: An Outline of Neo African Culture*, trans. by M. Grene, London, 1961.

still remain, for western usage, no more than labels, cour-
tesies, denoters, identifiers, in theory if not in fact, entirely
inter-changeable. John Jones can never be James Smith, but
by accidents of nomenclature he perfectly well could be.
For names, in the white world, are no more than what men
"are called". Not so in Africa where they are what men *are*.
Or to return to Father Tempels:

> If one hesitates as to the name of an European and asks him:
> "You are called Louis, are you not?" he will reply: "Yes" or
> "No". If, however, you ask a 'muntu': "Are you called Ilunga?"
> you will elicit one of the answers: "Tata" (Father) or "Bwana"
> (Master) or "I" or "Myself" or "Here I am" or "It is I":
> but he will not say: "Eyo" or "Ndio" (Yes).[1]

The reaction is not to admit a term but to pursue a relationship. It moves with the instinctive fact: "I participate and so
I am".

Hence, of course, the deep significance of the entry upon
participation which is the meaning of procreation, conception, birth, circumcision, communal appropriation, and
all the other points and rites by which the new being, the
emerging *muntu*, possesses and is possessed by its living
context. Descriptions of birth ceremonies abound in contemporary African writing and the documentation of anthro-
pologists. One, at random, may be cited from a recent
Nigerian autobiography, tracing the father's story in the son's
telling and the successive stages of the child's 'circulation'
and the mother's return to customary life. In this, an Ibo,
sequence, the newborn is laid on a plantain leaf in the open
air in the privacy of the back yard of his mother's compound.
Within eight to twelve days he is circumcised without formal
ceremonies. After three native weeks a further ritual ensues
by which the child is taken into the *Obu* and received by the
senior man with libation of palm-wine in a bell-shaped
wooden receptacle which represents the ancestor whose
reincarnation the child is believed to be. At this point the
mother is free to eat again with her husband, and with
prayers and blessings the child is presented to the ancestors.

[1] *Op. cit.*, p. 70.

Twenty-eight days from birth the newcomer is presented to the people of the village as a whole, with elaborate ceremonial and naming. The child is greeted with cheers, and the senior man in the village places a hoe and a matchet into his hands, saying, with the bestowal of these major implements of husbandry, "Live, grow and be strong". At this point the mother is free to attend the market. A further childhood ceremony is the giving of the insignia of the spiritual guardians among the ancestors, in the form of a branchlet from a sacred tree.[1]

In other variant patterns, there may be presentation to some ruling feature of the landscape, the brooding mountain, the Kenya or the Kilimanjaro, that shelters its human throng, or more prosaically, a ceremony when teeth appear, or an ear is pierced. Mugo Gatheru, in a Kikuyu autobiography, gives a graphic description of the second-birth ceremony, at two years of age, in which there is a kind of symbolic re-enactment of 'crouching' in the womb, the drama of delivery and the cutting of the umbilical cord.[2] In this case circumcision did not take place until sixteen years of age: "the day" (he calls it) "the knife bit me". There are, indeed, countless variants of this traditional scheme of life-inauguration and, at the other end of life, occasions of successive leave-taking, the ceremonial sequences by which the newly dead are reluctantly, and still possessively, yielded into the living past, where reciprocally to their own abiding is the yearning of memory in the sensible world that abide they shall. For unremembered the dead are pushed into the 'gone', into the far past, their very *muntu* failing in the lapsing of the relatedness by which it always was. In every case it is the name that holds the vital secret.

There can be no doubt that here, in this belonging with the whole, is a deep affinity with many of the intentions of Christian baptism. The African name spells relationship, not by rational option or social consent—for these imply some incomprehensible isolation of men—but by ontological

[1] Dilim Okafor Omali, *A Nigerian Childhood in Two Worlds*, London, 1965.
[2] R. Mugo Gatheru, *Child of Two Worlds*, London, 1964.

togetherness, by simply being at all. Baptism, it may be objected, is precisely choice and decision, and in that sense plainly belongs with western, perhaps we could say, Semitic, attitudes. But before we reach that problem, there is a more immediate practical consideration that makes a preface to it —a preface which has the merit of keeping us close to the 'naming' act where the double meanings lie and where their merging might begin.

It is evident on many hands that the actual ordinance of baptism, initially seen, suffers very unfavourable comparison with local lore and custom in respect of its ability, outside the committed church, to capture the communal sense. It seems, for the most part, foreign, peripheral, inconsequential, tolerable perhaps, but not moving with the pulse of the whole. Even among Christians the 'Christian' name may have more of the 'label' quality, while the 'native' name effectuates relationality.[1] This marginal quality of baptism in cultural terms—and indeed of much else in Christian usage—is a recurrent note in recent African writing and there are instances, too, when baptism, so to speak, even typifies subordination as affording that (Christian) name by which the local-born responded to the calls and dictates of white authority.[2] This disadvantage of the Christian sacrament is part of the problem arising everywhere in the contact of diverse cults. Society is occupied territory, habituated to other norms. Can the strangeness be surmounted unless its intention be set, consistently with its newness, in the context of the existing norms? Can there not be, as it were, a baptism of baptism?

If so, it must surely lie in this inner concept of incorporation, this constraining, even conferring, of *muntu*, this acceptance and shaping of the inherently social being of man. The name acknowledges and underwrites, one might almost say, the 'currency' of the person, were the phrase not so

[1] Cf. Tempels, *op. cit.*, p. 70.
[2] See, for example, N. Nwankwo: *Danda*, London, 1964, an Ibo novel about a rather ebullient character who despises as jejune the Christian ministrations he submits to. On names see also William Plomer, *Turbott Wolfe*, new edition, London, 1965.

metallic and mercenary. Each person, in his being named, is a point of receiving and being received, of acting and being acted upon. This nature the rite of traditional naming hallows and solemnizes, and in all the ensuing exchanges of life, the being-in-the-naming is enlarged or diminished, grows or decreases. There are processes of destruction or damage by which *muntu* is perverted and there are intensifications, often with bestowal of a further name, whereby quality as chief, father, doctor, is signalized, not through external acquisition but by inward cause. May it be that there is a feasible movement here into the New Testament meaning of sin and grace?

Evil, in this *muntu*-world, is that which sunders the solidarity, which disrupts relation, and so jeopardizes others' well-being. Envy, jealousy, hypocrisy, evil-thinking, and the rest, are depredations of a perverted *muntu* against the security of another's. These are not simply offences against 'principles' or infractions of abstract law. Nor are they anti-social acts made culpable by some rationale of mutual help which they defy. They are, on the contrary, elemental threats in the very constitution of humanity, a malevolence violating the participation by which life is. Endlessly diversified as they may be in the detailed formulations of anthropology, from people to people, they belong with a common African reading of human evil and lie behind the manifold protective measures which 'superstition' devises to counter their sinister effects. Man's inhumanity, by this reading, the menace of the human for the human, is far more dangerous an enemy than the calamities of external nature. Deliberate anger, meditated malice—as opposed to sudden, circumstantial exasperations—corrode or even destroy the vital force they attack. Against this quality of evil all the apparatus of force-protection has to be employed, and this in turn may become the fertile occasion of more devious actions of ill-will. This web of vital exposure and vital strife is too tangled to unravel here. But it is not rightly seen if we simply equate it, roughly, with Hobbes' dictum about life as "nasty, brutish and short", arguing the creation of Leviathan to subdue all private quarrels to an all powerful and enslaving moderator. For that would be, both in diagnosis and dubious rescue, to miss the *charisma* quality of this participant life, the gift of inter-being, and this evil antithesis of *charisma* by which counter-being wars against its soul.[1]

Are we not rightly taking its perspective if we associate its sense of a relational humanity with the kindred Christian dimension where the same exposure quality of existence is present? The New Testament diagnosis of man finds him knowing evil, both as source and subject, as something other than merely legal inculpation and beyond simply prudential criteria. From that affinity with the African, the Christian moves. Sin is seen as the corrosion of the self in the corrosion of its human relationships under God, as an inner defiance of true being socially experienced and corporately grounded. Sin is this deliberate disjuncture from the good, as constituted and demanded by participation in man. It is the depredatory thing which by self-aggrandisement spells self-distortion, and provokes to its own hurt the defensive reactions of other parties, with accentuating evil consequences. Sin, self-aggravating, is a thing of momentum, retaliation and waste, and as such, for all the contrasts of elaborated doctrine, is plainly the common theme of this paganism and Christ's Gospel.

The kinship opens up two related questions: the 'salvation' *from* the malice, and the 'salvation' *of* the evil-doer. Christian baptism, in simple terms, has to do with the patterns of a community of 'redemption' with the Cross at its heart, as sign and instrument. ("I do sign you with the sign of the Cross".) Beginning from this realism about the menace we are to ours, it goes beyond the resources of deterrence and the concerns of counter-action, to propose a transmuting 'force', both personal and social, by means of which the entail of evil can be broken and mere 'insurance' transcended. Truly the human intentions of will must be 'safe' for society. The Greeks, too, had this idea. But there is need, evil being as

[1] See more fully Tempels, *op. cit.*, chaps. iv and v. Also J. V. Taylor, *The Primal Vision*, London, 1963, chap. 12.

evil as we with Africa know it to be, for wills that are 'saving' as well as 'safe', for folk whose 'currency' in the world is not innocuous only, but redemptive. This only happens by an acceptance relationship, costly in its nature and loving in its impulse. The whole core of Christian atonement lies in a relational openness. Sin-bearing is not some arbitrary enactment or transference to satisfy a scheme. It is the readiness for the suffering relationship entails when evil strikes, or simply broods and lurks. By this suffering, taking what, via relationship, the other man's wrong means to this man's hurt, its entail is blessedly thwarted and its evil sting drawn. This alone is the 'counter-action', which, being neither insulating nor retributive, but reconciling, re-establishes community by the energy of forgiveness. There is now a new option such as evil, otherwise, ought to have forfeited, and which reciprocal enmity would certainly have excluded. These are the only terms in which evil is transmuted into good: they are inevitably sacrificial and strenuous. In any evil situation, love suffers. But therein is the material of its victory, of its efficacy, of its justification.

Africa, after all, knows much of pain, and has been one of the liveliest educators of humanity in the qualities on which the Gospel itself hinges, qualities of gaiety, of hope and of long-suffering, in the face of evils visited from the outer human world. Ought it to be difficult, then, in essence, however hard in fact, to interpret the nature of Christian community as precisely this redemptive relationality to men in evil, of which Christ crucified is the full and perfect sacrament in history and to which baptism in His Name admits and consecrates?

For the name here in its Biblical sense means the whole nature, open to experience and participation. Scriptural names, like African, are far from being labels of convenience: they are points of encounter and the very substance of meaning. The Name "mentioned", as the psalmist knew, is the Presence realized. The baptismal confession of the Triune Name means, not the bare acknowledgement of a doctrine, but an active relationship with its grace and authority. It means being participant in the reality of God, in the community of faith, and in its pattern of relation to men.

For this commitment the personal, baptismal naming is meant. Can we not say of it that it is a *muntu*, or nature, enabling the identity it describes? The African mind is familiar enough with occasions of naming to 'special' aspects of relational life, and sees them inaugurating from within what they bestow. It knows qualitative changes in men by an awakening of new being, and "an inner accession of essential life . . . indicated by the gift of a new name",[1] just as it knows that a man's *muntu* may die within himself by evil doing and the atrophy of the good will. Is there here a clue to the personal experience of grace in Christ, the working in the inward man of those forces of re-making of which Jesus spoke to Nicodemus and which St. Paul felt stirring through him in the wake of Damascus?

There are doubtless endless complexities attending any sense of fruitful ambivalence in these terms between Christian symbolism and the African view. It would be as presumptuous to discount them, as it is impossible here to assess them. But there are two considerations that cannot, even so, be ignored. What of the personal uniqueness of the 'individual' as pre-supposed in Christian faith, and what of modern changes? Is the whole suggestion already out of date? Does it fall foul of the whole notion of re-incarnation and the ancestors?

Taking the latter first and seeking, as argued in chapter 3, for the intention of beliefs, it seems feasible *not* to see in the African cult of ancestors any essential compromise of personality. The purpose of the belief is to assert the chain of indebtedness within existence, the moving bridge between past and future which the present makes. The new life is not usurped in some depriving recurrence of the dead. On the contrary, the ancestral vitality only gives itself in and through the present being. There is, or need be, here, in the broad view, no forfeiture of personality, as distinct from what the

[1] *Op. cit.*, p. 68.

cult and awareness of past generations may mean in actual
fears or superstitions attaching to its practice.

> The predeceased ancestor or spirit is not the cause of con-
> ception, any more than it is his person which is reborn in the
> proper sense of the word . . . it is not a predetermined human
> being belonging to the clan who is reborn . . . it is his individ-
> uality returning to take part in the life of the clan by means
> of the vital influences through which the deceased gives
> clan individualization to the newly born, to the living fruit of
> the womb . . . This vital influence is preserved throughout the
> whole existence, since it is inherent in the very essence of the
> being.[1]

It all has to do with continuity of being to which we must
attend in the next section.

But what of the suspicion that contemporary time has,
in any event, outmoded and quite disrupted this world view,
fragmenting society and precluding in its industrialization
and detribalizing materialism the survival of traditional
bonds? Some general review of the impact of modernity upon
folk religion, and of secularity in full cry, is reserved for
chapter 7. Even given the wholesale physical and sociological
inroads of the new day, it is well not to underestimate the
staying power of the religious culture. Moreover, as happened
with white techniques and 'powers' at the beginning of their
impact, the subtleties of the 'scientific' world are readily
digested within the prevailing scheme of *muntu*, even if it
means an unwonted effort of humility for western sophistication to believe this. There are, no doubt, innumerable
crises of personal lostness and distraughtness, "all cohesion
gone", as Donne would have said, among African intellectuals and *évolués*. Two titles of Chinua Achebe, *No Longer at
Ease* and *Things Fall Apart*, borrowed from the poems of
Eliot and Auden, are a random token of that fact. Yet,
in the last resort, we shall only be doing justice, whether as
observers or as servants, to that dissolution of meaning, if
we see that there remains, within the old tradition, a crucial
wisdom about man, without which his very competence will

[1] *Op. cit.*, p. 73–74.

break and his being perish. It is that inner truth of the African world view, by which men are men only in a due reverence, an awe of participation, a hierarchy of reality, with room, but only conditional room, for the inventive and acquisitive science of the modern age. Westerners tend instinctively to underestimate the capacity of African traditional thinking to assimilate the new perspectives of the human vitality in which it has always believed. But it is the old ones which, in measure, will seem to the Christian mind to have sensed and treasured dimensions of the human situation still urgent in their truth and appropriate to Christ.

If reflections on the name and baptism do not fully make their case, they each have their counterparts in memory and communion. We turn to the other dominical sacrament and to another elemental activity of the African soul.

THE PRESENT-PAST AND HOLY COMMUNION

"A continent ages quickly once we come", wrote Ernest Hemingway, in *The Green Hills of Africa*,[1] commenting on western inroads breaking up the 'native' directness and 'natural' awareness of the world and substituting a jaded 'maturity'. "And a people forgets quickly", he might have added, in the sense that by and large the 'civilized' preoccupations tend to shorten corporate memory and to shroud or blur the long distances of the past with the concentrations of the present and the cult of the immediate. The apparatus of modernity revolves in mathematical time, in measurable flux and movement and rarely stands outside duration. Winston Churchill, it is true, remarks, in a somewhat African quality of conviction, that "we cannot say the past is past without surrendering the future". The West, assuredly, has its sense of history. But in the ordinary human dimension it knows only seldom the intimate participation with the past that is the heart of African 'memory'.

Yet in this deficiency, if the term is fair, it stands in contrast to the inner mystery and quality of the central sacrament of its Christian religion, which could rightly be claimed as

[1] New York, 1935, p. 284.

close to the genius, in its positive expression, of African mentality. Our aim in the rest of this chapter is to ponder the potential bearing of the Christian *anamnesis*, or present-past-participation, on the traditional African sense of community-continuity, of the past and the future alike in the context of the 'here' and the 'now'.

Much of the latter is already before us in the review of name and naming. Perhaps, therefore, we may reverse the order followed in the consideration of baptism and take first the nature of Christian *memorabilia* and then ponder the African kinships involved, conceding that we only do the one by the stimulus of the other—which, we have argued, is precisely how a lively theology ought to be proceeding.

The Old Testament, where the Christian situation has its roots, is a book of expectant memory. The reality of God is a living experience, not an abstract concept. It is events which declare and disclose Him. What in Exodus and Exile, and many intervening and lesser episodes, is seen as the Divine hand is received as the shape and pledge of destiny. From generation to generation, the story and its meaning are retentively held in grateful recognition as the sure index to the nature of time. Celebrated in symbol, song and saga, they bind the participant people into one unbroken identity which they seal and hallow. "I will be there, as He whom I there will be", in the words of the promise at the burning bush, is the abiding principle of all the ethnic history. Its effect is to incorporate the whole nation in a single consciousness, an exchange of relationship between God and themselves, in the unfolding experience of life, which at the same time engages them as comrades together through all generations. It is a tradition that the covenant at Sinai was made, not merely with the contemporaries present there, but with every succeeding generation of the people to the end of time. The very telling of the history involves this mythization of its content and its actuality, in the form of a perpetual awareness by which the there-and-then remains the here-and-now. Retrospect becomes the theme of prospect.

The Christian Church is heir to this double sense of participation and incorporation as the content of history. Time, for the New Testament, is likewise the καιρος in which God is mediated, by His own initiative and grace, to men in the shape of the incarnate ministry and death of Jesus as the Christ. The sources and crises of this conviction we have already pondered in chapter 2. They find their focus in the Holy Communion, set, significantly, in the specific framework of the Passover and taken as inaugurating a new covenant as the crux of a new emancipation and leading to a new nation-hood, not now of one ethnic origin, but of plural peoples on the single condition of faith. The concentration of the sacra-ment on the suffering of Jesus includes all the antecedent teaching that had been its prelude. It is in no sense an iso-lation of the end, but the epitome of one entire self-con-sistency in the terms of its consummation. The whole event of the Christ is there, as constitutive through its historical character of a redemptive work, intending all humanity, and so, in turn, of a community of love and acceptance in its meaning.

The bread and the wine, in the poetry of their inter-pretation, are at once the sign and the binding pledge of that redeemed community. The body and the blood they signify speak from within the actual history that holds them as a climax and, so doing, they are the credentials of the corporate fellowship that derives from it. But in that fellow-ship the history is not remembered as an event in the departed past. "Do this in remembrance of me" is not a commandment concerned about oblivion. The sacrament is not a device to elude a possible forgetfulness. And if it were so, it could not succeed. It is, rather, the form of the disciple-ship in which an unbroken relationship is perpetually defined. It is a shape of recollection that steadily renews the actuality of Christ crucified, as known to faith, and thus gathers round Him, as fellows and contemporaries, all whose love and loyalty belong "in the night in which He was betrayed" as a present transaction. The sacrament could almost be taken as having had an 'African' origin. For it is not, western-wise, an effort to recall a past, but that past ensuing in its own present through the memory. When we are remembered, the usage of a continent seems to say, we are here: and in that we are here memory greets and knows us. How close this is to the New Testament meaning of Jesus' will to be remembered and to the response of the Church to it.

Here, too, lies the togetherness by which community is experienced at the same point, and this, also, tribally constituted, is of the essence of traditionally African society. The common life blood makes its people one within the circle, including the remembered dead. "The blood of the new covenant" incorporates among all peoples and moves, as we must see, in a different quality of mind as to the Lord God, the other generations and ourselves. Yet even so the parables would surely have been there to hand had Jesus walked by Lake Uganda rather than by Galilee. At the heart of Christ's passion and sacramentalized in the Holy Communion is this deep 'African' truth of a human society responsibly aware of its members. "Woman, behold your son"; "Son, behold your mother"—"member" and "remember" in such a communion are one meaning.

Their juncture may be strikingly seen in a very ordinary, even sorry, detail of St. Paul's correspondence with Corinth. When he heard of their ill-disciplined habits in the Christian sacrament, with participants giving vent to a crude form of private interest in the common meal, he chided them for "not discerning the body".[1] They vulgarized the Eucharist in that they had not sensed the community, "the body" of comrades: but in this failure they had also missed "the body" of Christ broken in redemption. In not allowing the whole, they had denied the holy. Had they had a mind for the death of Jesus, they would have waited for their brothers. "Is it not the communion of the body?" is a question which has to be answered in a double sense, or not at all.

There is, of course, here a still wider confession of participation. For Holy Communion, heir as it is *via* the person of

---

[1] In I Cor. 11: 20–29, the crucial passage, outside the Gospels, for the understanding of the Supper. It demonstrates how the 'communalizing' nature of the sacrament had to make its way against ignorance and unfamiliarity. Here we see meaning being effectuated.

Jesus with the whole Biblical understanding of creation, affirms and consecrates a conscious human relationship with the whole natural order. Thanks with and for bread, duty in and through it to men around, are fundamental elements in physical and economic life. Under forms of bread and wine, the Christian sacrament acknowledges and hallows the whole material basis of life, society and commerce as constituted by nature and skill. The loaf and the cup, with their sources in hidden ripening, growth and process, under the intelligent lordship of man, epitomize the wealth of nations and, in the 'offertory' betoken the sanctity of all matter in men's hands. The fact that the basic elements of bread and wine are consecrated for their use in the sacramental situation of communion with Christ and his Cross requires that all they symbolize in daily life should never be desecrated but infused with an essential reverence as at once the mystery and the majesty of man's domain.

All these reaches of the Christian symbol relate, however ambiguously, to characteristic aspects of the African's awareness of reality, as sacral, communal, participatory and present. The correspondence between Biblical assumptions and African, about time, people, things, nature and society, has often been remarked. The text of Christian Scripture, with some seriously opaque exceptions,[1] often comes more readily home to an African listener than to a contemporary westerner. Mugo Gatheru, in the autobiography already quoted, puts the point one way when he notes:

> If the Christians could drop their insistence on the existence of the devil and of Jesus as magnified in their religion, Christianity would not be too strange to the Kikuyu.[2]

The 'if' no doubt is a large one, and probably both its parts owe more to extraneous influences than local factors. What has been said, under baptism, about the reality of evils, and of evil, probably suffices, in this context, in respect of the first. Given Jesus' white associates, it is natural on that

[1] Of which the theme of 'shepherds' is perhaps the most important. "I am the good Chief" would be much preferred.

[2] *Op. cit.*, p. 53.

ground alone for modern Africa to resent his centrality. But that emotion, offset by far deeper considerations, only makes the more important the disembarrassment of Jesus from western monopoly with which our whole plea is concerned. Whatever its negative impediments, the African authentication of the Gospel both requires and engages deep, abiding insights of its own cultures. It is this fact, in its broad outline, that we are concerned to understand.

There is room here for only three, inter-related issues in this relation of Holy Communion and African community. These have to do with the universality studied in chapter 2, as implicit in the Messianic achievement of Jesus and critically fulfilled in the Church by the apostles; with the right sense of the presence of the generations within the presence of God; and with the due sense of contemporary man in the terms of the 'ecumenical' theme taken up in the final chapter.

By geographical and other factors, Africa, it might be said, has been the most emphatically 'tribal' of all the continents. It was this feature which facilitated its tragic victimization at the hands of the slave traders.[1] We have already noted how large its share of the world's languages compared with its proportion of world population. The community sense, vital to all our foregoing argument, has been powerfully integrative but also chronically combative. All our usage of 'African' has been in this way precarious and proximate. It is a very different denominator from 'pan-African'. The continent, thus, had, and has, a peculiarly strenuous venture in the widening of its human solidarities beyond their traditional tribal emphasis. Political incentives here tend only partially in the right direction. Nationhood in general enlarges and consolidates the units but sometimes for that very reason strains and frets the unities. Economic and social forces both sunder and detribalize, and establish new groupings and interests of their own. The Church is all too often

---

[1] See Basil Davidson, *Black Mother*, London, 1962. Enslaved captives often passed through as many as six tribes' hands, before ever seeing a white man or reaching the coastal 'barracoon' or 'warehouse' whence shipments were made.

the creature of these factors, reflecting no less than others the stresses of the current history, conserving and acquiescent. Yet the old collective sense, for all its fragmentation, persists. Kinship as a vital force gives sanction to an inter-human-ness which may reach beyond its own blood limits in discovering a blood without limits. The Church originated in just such a discovery and lives still by the resulting sacrament.

This first point belongs with today and with the living. The second concerns the relegation of the sense of the Divine to which African thought has always been prone, just because of its vivid awareness of the remembered dead. It is import-ant to realize that ancestor relationships are very rarely, if ever, 'worship', in the Divine meaning. What happens, rather, is that the dead, by the very strength and urge of their claim to remembrance and honour, tend to the upward 'exclusion' of God. Operatively, they then displace what continues to be the essential Lordship of the universe and, in these practical terms, they may be said to be 'deified', or, rather, the higher echelons that have their place in tribal origins or mythical history. Even the lesser, nearer, dead exercise in many areas of emotion, fear, 'insurance', and reliance, a role more intimate and alive than the supreme Deity whose very ultimacy means, paradoxically, either inaccessible majesty or lordly aloofness. In either case the ancestors, whether as lesser gods or erstwhile mortals and always as bestowers and creditors of life, are closer, nearer, surer foci of reverence and dependence and obligation.

This irrelevance, by sheer elevation and removed-ness, of the African God has its consequences in the intimidations and tyrannies in which ancestors may engage, with the human empire thus left, by default or exile, to themselves. The situa-tion may be deepened by the despairing idea that disdain or dudgeon has alienated God from all human approach— a fear that exists despite the African assumption on the human level that accessibility is the proper mark of power. Either way, it becomes an urgent Christian task to save all that is valid in the incorporation of man with his fellows, in life and death, from the eclipse of the Divine presence. In the

Holy Communion, it is in that real presence we may believe all other communions to be hallowed and ensured. It is in the broken bread that we are united, in the confession of God as knowing and sharing our frailties and sorrows that we are effectively together. "God with us" is spoken in the context of a birth: all that we are by birth, including the generations of our sequence, belongs there.

The edging-out of God, however, to move to our third point, takes place for modern men, not by the ousting priority of the remembered dead, but by the invading self-sufficiencies of technology. The full bearings of this theme await us in the next chapter. There is everywhere this evident growth of a practical going-it-alone in the world, partly by the drastic curtailment to the sensible and the acquisitive of what going-it involves, and partly by a deep recession of the sense of the Divine, whether blandly or wistfully expressed. All too readily this instinct of our time coincides with the other 'African' absence of the Divine just considered and may critically reinforce its consequences. Any habit of Divine exclusion makes a reasoned discipline of technology the harder and more strenuous. Here the Christian relation to the threat of an African materialism is to strain all Christian resources to a right interpretation of man's *muntu* as scientifically heightened and enlarged. The early African response to the white 'superiority' of tillage, arms, medicine and environmental control, was to take it as an enhanced vital force, with which African 'inferiority' *muntu* would have to reckon. Yet, within that categorization, technology is still obligated to community, still essentially a 'property' of man relationally involved. Thus technology cannot be rightly guided merely by reference to what is technically feasible. It must needs be subdued to the meaning of man.

It is this necessity, adequately applied, which brings us back to the Divine authority, since we cannot do justice to man on a hypothesis about the irrelevance of God. It takes the Divine dimension for man appropriately to possess his scientific dominion and to enjoy a right mastery in his works through a due submission of himself. More of this anon.

With its traditional attitudes, the African mind has an acute crisis and a deep asset, *vis-à-vis* the fascinating vistas of science, industrialization and urbanization. The asset is its sense of human-ness as the primary value and concept: the crisis lies in the deceptive newness of secular temptations and the tenuousness of the sense of the Divine. Christian faith and symbol are certainly calculated to undergird the one and retrieve the other.

But only if they are alert to their own temptations, of which the greatest is to withhold in day-to-day existence the sort of relationships with men that move out of sanctuary and scripture into current deed and word. John Taylor writes:

> So many of our Eucharists fall short of the glory of God because, while purporting to concentrate on the Real Presence of Christ, they seem to be oblivious to the real presence of men, either in the worshipping family or the world around. To present oneself to God means to expose oneself, in an intense and vulnerable awareness, not only to Him but to all that is.[1]

Then deed and word, and every presence of ours with men, return back into that Divine Presence with us all, there both to find holy communion and to seek the hallowing of all community.

Within the ventures of this chapter, we may well conclude with a double quotation from a single source—all the more telling, perhaps, in that the author is now a fallen and discredited figure in the tumult of Africa. In his autobiography, Kwame Nkrumah, formerly President of Ghana, describes the loneliness he experienced in his early sojourn in America, and in the *Shawnee*, sailing between New York and Mexico:

> There was always a most haunting feeling of loneliness, not just being without companions, but of being nobody's concern. Many times as I walked in the streets of Vera Cruz or in other foreign ports the thought struck me that anybody could have set upon and killed me and nobody would have missed me unduly. I don't suppose any steps would have been taken to discover my identity.

[1] John V. Taylor, *The Primal Vision*, London, 1963, p. 200.

167

But, in Liverpool, in the autumn of 1935:

> I heard an excited newspaper boy shouting something un-
> intelligible as he grabbed a bundle of the latest editions from a
> motor van, and on the placard I read: 'Mussolini invades
> Ethiopia'. That was all I needed. At that moment it was almost
> as if the whole of London had declared war on me personally.
> For the next few minutes I could do nothing but glare at each
> impassive face . . .[1]

Only a personal narrative, then obscure enough. Yet within
it speak the impulses of the mind we have been studying to
review: the fear of non-identity, the spectre of being nobody's
concern, the menace of a self irrelevant in a society unknow-
ing. And, by contrast, the surge of participant belonging,
politically aroused, it is true, but for just that reason vibrant
with the demand and the search for secure community.
These emotions—dread, not of the unknown, but as one
unknown, and the power of a bond remembered—reduce
our whole study into one example. They are the yearning for
a humanity which, in the person, indifference does not
threaten, and in the collective, antagonism need not alienate,
or, in that sense, define, secure as both are, person and community, in truly human reciprocity. This, at its largest, is the
African temper: but it is also deep in the symbol of baptism
and has its surest tokens in the body and the blood. Even in
the strange places—as they may seem—we may yet say, "I
will go unto the altar of God, the God of my joy and glad-
ness."

[1] *The Autobiography of Kwame Nkrumah*, London, 1957, pp. 39 and 27.

CHRISTIAN RELATIONSHIPS IN THE SECULARIZING WORLD

A GENTLE poem by a poet of Haiti, inspired by a negro dancing girl in a Casablanca cabaret, is not perhaps a likely place from which to start our present purposes.

Your slim arms
raised among the smoke
yearned to embrace
centuries of pride
and miles of landscape
while your feet
on the waxed mosaic floor
searched for the roughness
of the roads you had trodden in your childhood.[1]

Hardly, quite, the sacred and the secular. But still, in its reflective way, alive with a double perspective—aware of the immediate actuality, artificial, expert and mercenary, and at the same time sensitive to the ultimate meaning, the wistfulness of an irreducible past.

It is just this ambivalence of things which will be in the forefront of thought in the pages that follow. How do we rightly identify and relate the two aspects of existence? What is the significance for all religious faiths, and for their obligations to each other, of their great new common denominator of secularized circumstance in this time?

It was agreed in chapter 3 to seek a quality of relationship with the religions that took them sympathetically in their own seriousness and invited them to meet the Christian in a realist and radical self-awareness. The hope was that this would

[1] Roussan Camille, *Assaut à la Nuit*, Port au Prince, 1940: translated and quoted in G. R. Coulthard, *Race and Colour in Caribbean Literature*, London, 1962, p. 95.

eliminate, or at least by-pass, the barren controversies that belong only with misconception or disparagement and conduce only to assertive self-vindication. The way might then be open for authentic reckoning with essentials in a temper of constructive reverence. What was desired was a shape of Christian relationship that might evoke the deepest meanings of other faiths inwardly confessed. Such a pattern, it was urged, ought not to be dominated by a self-regarding concern on the Christian side to convert, at least until the whole nature of man's convertibility is interiorized and understood. It was, however, firmly acknowledged that such Christian relationships in their climax, being by their nature revolutionary, do constitute a crisis and propose a new humanity.

This we have attempted in three intervening chapters, though in each case only summarily, moving in the midst of deceptive generalization, remembering A. N. Whitehead's dictum: "Seek simplicity—and mistrust it". The first venture was in respect of Jewish continuity, its secret and meaning as a non-acceptance of the Christian claim that Jewry's proper election is fulfilled and perpetuated in the universal people of God without remaining benefit of 'privacy' to any part. The second, centring around credal rather than ecclesiastical aspects, took us to the Islamic disclaimer of Christian belief in a God of self-expending majesty and compassionate sovereignty. The third explored African mentality in its sympathy with Christian social sacrament, hallowing identity in 'naming' and incorporating the living past in the communal present.

The concern throughout was to discern a world-relationship of Christianity that was not merely geographical and, as it were, expansionist, but integral and expectant. We have taken the words "Into all the world" as intending much more than a physically global mobility. Rather the impulse within them is seen as a sense of relevance in, and anticipation from, all human cultures, taking the Church as that which corresponds, in all meanings of the verb, with "the desire of all nations". In intending the world, the Christian Gospel is proceeding not only upon affirmations in hand but also upon recognitions awaited. For this is the apostolic conviction in its being "worthy of all acceptation" (1 Tim. 1: 15). A whole world is needed to apprehend a whole Christ and embrace a whole Church. Mission lives by its disciples: but it lives for its absentees.

All these ventures, however, will forfeit integrity in contemporary terms if they fail to face the other great world-wideness of our time, the insistent, frontier-ignoring ubiquity of technology and applied science, with the 'secularization' they engender as currently interpreted. What by some writers is dubbed 'technocracy' has a far more massive, penetrative and effective quality than 'evangelism'. It invades and shapes the cultures and assumptions of men with an impact quite unparalleled in human history. We live in an age when humanity has more in common, both for good and ill, than any previous generation. No seclusions remain, behind which segments of mankind can secrete or secure themselves from the whole. Radio engineering has feasibly made the entire human community a single, simultaneous audience for one human speaker. If such a listening or watching congregation of the world has not yet occurred the reasons are political, not technological. World newspapers, via satellites, are at hand. There are sundry other tokens and themes of this terrestrial efficiency of man— the nuclear cloud, the supersonic plane, the space-treading cosmonaut. With this technocratic human mastery goes the whole profound revolution we know, loosely, as secularization, as a new quality of disbelief in the Divine and the sacred —new in the sense that, unlike earlier and wistful atheisms, it seems disinterested in its own persuasion. In Nietzsche's words, it assumes that "all the gods are dead and man must be mature enough to go on from there", while attitudes of mind and institutions of society are more and more shaped and determined, not by our independent beliefs, but by the pressures and demands of the techniques of production and mechanization which we have devised.

Clearly this situation radically affects the whole position

of the religions and, therefore, the form of their inter-relationship. As a new and operative worldwideness of its own, it is a force tending, or demanding, to secularize all cultures and thus to eliminate, or banish to archaic insignificance, their religious sanctions and diversities. Like the mark of Cain, it sets a seal of doom on sacred reference, whether pagan, theistic or 'spiritual'—a doom unaffected by the purely historical consideration that these dimensions of the sacred have each marked stages of progression towards 'maturity'. When full, it is a maturity that ends them all.

Are we then to conclude, as some do, that secularization being irresistible and irreversible, and altogether appropriate to man, all religious systems must prepare themselves for present extinction? In view of the universal authority and feasibility of the claim that man is left to himself in the universe, are we to decide that there is virtually no more need or place for a Christian relation to Buddhism, to Hinduism, to Islam and the rest? Do we waste our time with a solicitous and reverential attitude towards their dogmas, cults and codes? Would the energies of world Christianity be better spent on tutoring the rest of mankind in the acceptance of scientific culture and in adjustment to secularity seen as inevitable? Are we to follow some mentors in the further assurance that Christianity is uniquely suited for this tutorial role, being, on this count, itself in part the matrix of these changes? Can we comfortably see in the stature of a secular and self-sufficient humanity the proper, even the justifying, end-product of Biblical religion and the contemporary form of the Christian conception of man?

That these proposals can be seriously made is some measure of the crisis in Christian theology and the crucial debate about missionary postures towards the plural cultures of the world. What has our theology to say of this alternative thesis about the shape of our duty? How are we to estimate this confident, even brutal, supersession with Christian connivance of humanity's religions? The answer needs to be as thoroughly alive as the thesis is to the actualities of the world: it must be courageously contemporary in its awareness of cybernation and computers, its sense of this crowded, pulsating, shrinking, exploited but still sustaining earth. We shall not rightly confront the escapism to be detected in secularization if there is an escapism of our own in the criticism with which we must reject it.

SECULAR STATEHOOD NOT IN QUESTION

It will be wise to get one matter out of the way first. It is understood in what follows that there is no quarrel with the concept of 'the secular state'. Political secularity in the sense of the indifference of the political power to religious affiliation of the citizen, the equal status of all citizens before the law regardless of race, creed, colour, or cult, is not here in dispute. 'Secularism' and 'secularization' are used, it is true, with much confusion by their advocates. The former might be claimed, though we think inaccurately, for this political and legal impartiality towards the religions. By these terms, and certainly by the latter, is generally meant a human self-sufficiency which either regretfully or defiantly excludes any reference of man beyond himself, for explanation, direction, authority or salvation. Secularity, in this total and philosophic sense, is firmly distinguished here from the secular state, meaning a comprehension of religious diversity and of irreligion under the law and within the nation.

The secular state is a modern necessity: valid and proper and desirable. It need not exclude a general symbolic association of the state with the religion of the majority, provided this association is neither oppressive nor assertive. "This nation under God" is plainly not a secular phrase in the 'areligious' sense; but it can and does describe a legal secularity. There is every reason for some emotive expression of the instrumentality of the state to ends larger than itself and to purposes for which it is accountable. This subordination requires a 'religious' view and, given proper safeguards, in no way compromises the legal secularity. Such a view of the state's non-ultimacy is part of what is meant by religion, and the symbols of it are likeliest housed in terms of the cultural majority. Balancing this, however, is the other principle of the proper autonomy of the natural man. Society cannot, by assertion or imposition, be made coterminous with the kingdom of God or any other religious dominion. Crime is properly distinguishable from sin and no political order can be at best more than approximately Christian, or, indeed, Islamic or, again, 'religious': it certainly cannot enlarge its modicum of Christianableness or 'Islamicity' or 'religion' by compulsiveness. Society must be free to be recalcitrant or it can never succeed to be 'religious'. This is a principle of history made all the more evident by the contemporary irrepeatability of history's experiments to the contrary. This conclusion is a great new, and common, denominator among all religions and, as such, is the measure of the secular achievement: a measure, we might add, that limits where it gladly concedes.

THE SECULAR ACHIEVEMENT AND SOME MISGIVINGS

This elucidation made, it will be evident that if we resist secularization it is not in the name of a religious manipulation of state power, nor for the sake of an imposition of dogmatic obligations either of belief or conduct. The coast, then, is clear for a further acknowledgement relating to the temper of secularization. It can be critically welcomed on many counts as a liberation from obscurantism, a solvent of many bigotries and the exposure of much unworthy vested interest. The protest validity of what radicals are saying can be readily admitted and with it the current effects in Asia and Africa of emancipation from religious domination. Religion has been guilty of intimidation and has stayed complacently, even callously, with privilege and delusion. "God as a restrictive force on human liberty" in Sartre's words is not a phrase or a notion that can be airily dismissed. The urge to the religionless temper has its point, in that religions have exploited, or accentuated, human weakness, fear, apathy and superstition. Tyranny, division, ignorance, evil acquiescence and egoism have been waymarks of the religious story. Variously, everywhere in the world, postures of religious conservatism tend still to aggravate economic and social problems, obstructing sound ameliorative measures for the sake of scruple or perversity, letting dogma feed hunger rather than the hungry, and preserving privilege by dint of piety.

Yet there is a sense in which these proper strictures mean a different expectation. By some no doubt the case is taken for hopeless, and religion fit only for extinction. With others, however, the anathemas seem bent towards a future. In the domestic realm of Christian theology some radicals still cling to the Christian name and office. In the justice of their so desiring, and being so allowed, we may identify desperate reproach rather than utter disavowal. The very disruptiveness arises from a kind of loyalty.

There is, in this context, another important factor to be acknowledged. Engineering, medicine, irrigation, production and techniques of every kind have opened vistas of hope, of dignity, health and leisure, for vast populations. Technology may be said to be doing, macrocosmically, what Christian mission was attempting to do microcosmically, bringing to a burdened humanity new dimensions of life and fulfilment, let us say, of salvation. Through these skills and their mass application what Carey, Livingstone and Schweitzer symbolize in human 'ministry' is, on its 'efficient' side, multiplied and disseminated in every place, perhaps the more adequately for its detachment from a conversion concern. Technology, it may be said, is one whole massive, if conditional, philanthropy. As such, it can arguably be seen as effectuation of human purposes that belong closely with the Christian intention. This on the practical side. Conceptually the science within it proceeds by the Biblical assurance that nature is properly technologizable. On both counts technical achievement may be said to embody and to actualize a fully human 'responsibility' for man.

All this amounts to a large confession of the fact and the merit of secularized history in our time. It is one which few open-hearted and positive minds would wish to dispute or deny. Yet, precisely for its very worth, this secularizing of the world requires serious critical reservations. With the Haitian poet who opened this chapter, we must know that there is much else within and around the techniques. There is more than the commerce of the body: the dance and the cabaret are history and continent. The secular, by definition, cannot be the total scene and meaning. Behind and beyond the approving appetite for technological means and ends lies the whole revolt of the diversified human spirit against the mechanized efficiencies of a single hemisphere. There are guardians of humanity all the more forceful and authentic for their *not* being white, technological and sophisticated. If we are Christian and concerned for a whole world, we cannot fail to repudiate the equation between any one culture, albeit scientific, and a destiny to define and dominate humanity.

Equally, on Biblical and Christian grounds, must we reject the prevalent notion that technology proceeds only in the abeyance of the sacred or that the world has to be 'disenchanted' before it can be organized. A medley of other thoughts break in upon the temptation to march with the secularizers and dismiss inter-religious thinking as an idle anachronism. What follows is an attempt to sort out some of them, in a simple enumeration that makes no pretence at being a thorough or systematic critique of the secularizing process of thought. Our responsibility in these pages is primarily with the Christian engagement in the world. For this the secular assurance is both a new obligation and a flank attack. While receiving its own due, it must not be allowed to divert conviction from the themes between religions which it does not itself penetrate or even recognize.

There are, for present purposes, five queries that make for serious hesitation about the secularizing thesis as a displacer of religious relevance and so of inter-religious communication. An intelligent suspicion of the religionless argument has at least this fivefold count.

The first misgiving has to do with its patent over-simplification. In the hypothesis of man as beyond religion and beyond mystery, sufficient to himself in a 'secular' universe, the world appears in too tidy, too naïve, too prosaic, a guise ever long to satisfy the mind. All is too impersonal to constitute a whole story.

Maybe the surest touchstone of this incompleteness can be found—as one might expect—in assessments made by men and peoples outside the orbit of its modern origins. If their tone in some cases reflects other factors, such as racial oppression or economic injustice, not strictly within a simple evaluation of secularization *per se*, this circumstance merely reciprocates the materialist and acquisitive mood in which technology has pursued its world self-exportation. The situation confirms the over-simplification we are alleging. Appetite and aversion, together, have been evoked in humanity by the western invasion of science, and both must be weighed.

"Pity for our conquerors, omniscient and naïve".[1] Thus Aimé Césaire in the poem earlier cited. He goes on to aver that it is the non-exploiters who are truly the "adults" or "elder sons" of the world. The temptation to deliberate primitivism in such writers should not obscure their point. The wildness it gives to their criticism of technology is the measure of how they are at once fascinated and appalled. It is the more revealing for this paradox. Their reaction cannot be scouted if a *whole* human verdict is being honestly sought.[2] To dismiss as irrelevant the psychological questions that undoubtedly underlie such protests is to be cruelly 'escapist'. It is to be blithely ignorant of the true range of human meaning, all the more culpable for the fact that 'escapism' is so often the charge of secularizing thinkers against the rest of men. There are, plainly, many human situations in which it looks to be the technocrat rather than the worshipper who is running away from reality. It is hardly the man who diagnoses a volcano who appreciates Sinai and the covenant, or a tempter who offers only bread who knows the full crises of a Christ. The very urgencies of the secular revolt have blinded it to the correctives required by its own

[1] In Coulthard, *op. cit.*, p. 59.
[2] But see below in chapter 8 the no less passionate but frankly receptive attitudes of, e.g., Ezekiel Mphahlele in *The African Image*.

Mc   177

confidence. It has sometimes and properly employed the device of the caricature and then improperly forgotten that it had not drawn a portrait.

There is, further, about the secularization theme a roundly assertive, even truculent tone, a temptation to be generally magisterial. These are no doubt the hazards of a right impatience, of a need to disturb static attitudes and assault traditional strongholds. But when this has been conceded there still remains a sharpness of assurance that rides rough-shod over valid susceptibilities and ignores what it finds uncongenial. In so far as it purports to belong with some 'election' to world tutorship in charge of one segment of humanity for all the rest, such confidence is heard declaring, "Pupils of the west, attend! you have nothing to lose but your souls". As such it is a posture of spiritual imperialism, quite lacking in gentle deference towards a whole humanity.

It is right in this connection to recall that western domin-ance in the history of science belongs only to its most recent centuries. The late near monopoly of technology by the white races *is* late. A proper perspective remembers that there have been monuments of engineering in China and Egypt and that the much vaunted European leadership in modern times has been in part due to purely circumstantial assets and advantages. When these are recognized they put into truer focus the sometimes extravagant claims about genius or uniqueness—philosophical or doctrinal.

The same kind of better modesty is fostered, too, by the recollection of the degree to which our western, scientific advantage has been so largely depredatory, arrogant and unimaginative, *vis-à-vis* other peoples, in the day of its power. There must surely be an insistent pause in the current thesis that we in the West have achieved the right to assume some universal reproduction of ourselves.

Secularization, further, arouses scepticism for its evasive-ness. Its advocates seem to be afflicted with a blind-eye mentality in respect of whole areas of human experience. In some it takes the dark form of screening out all nobility and hope. In others a facile optimism is negligent of the creaturely realms of human frailty. We will note the despairers anon. A single instance of the optimism is no doubt risky: but it is not arbitrary. Writing in *Radical Theology and the Death of God*, William Hamilton observes: "I am interested in the search for a language that does not depend upon need or problem"[1] and defines religion as "any system of thought or action in which God or the gods serve as fulfiller of needs or solver of problems". As such, the religious *a priori* has broken down: "there is no God-shaped blank within man". In so far as this is reaching out for a disinterested interest in God in order to cry, "God, my exceeding joy", as the psalmist does, it is authentic and eloquent. But can or need the desire to understand what "delighting in God" might mean be divorced from the weary and the heavy-laden? 'Depend' is the confusing word. One could equally well desire a definition of bread that did not depend upon hunger. It is agreed, both by secularists and Christians, that God is properly no convenience in human troubles. Intelligent theism has never stood for a *deus ex machina* idea. But is *homo cum machina* the right or the real alternative?

From what are these writers immunizing themselves? Do they not have to die? Or perhaps one should rather ask: Do they not have to live? Is there not a sense in which life itself persists in casting up needs? Is it not, in any real world, haunted with problems? As Dag Hammarskjöld has written:

> Instinctively we try to eliminate a person (or a problem?) from our sphere of responsibility as soon as the outcome of this particular experiment by life appears, in our eyes, to be a failure. But life pursues her experiment far beyond the limitations of our judgement. This is the reason why at times it seems so much more difficult to live than to die.[2]

And this, too, is why it is evasive to think God has died. Contrary to frequent supposition, ignoring God in any situation is always the easier option. Affirming His demise is simply making that ignoring habitual.

Truly the theology of the crutch, and worship as a solution

[1] *Op. cit.* with T. J. J. Altizer, New York, 1966, pp. 40–41.
[2] In *Markings*, trans. from the Swedish, New York, 1964, p. 32.

to difficulties, a psychology of adjustment, are rightly to be forsworn. But in denying the theology of the crutch, shall we repudiate the theology of the oil and the wine, of the two pence and the innkeeper, the theology of energetic action within the problems and for the needs of men? Can Christology make any sense, if there is no neighbour-shaped blank within man? For this is the corollary of the place where God is. Can there ever be the man for others, if the 'others' represent no needs and constitute no problem? Could the Cross ever occur in a world that generated no ultimate questions and awaited no tragic answers?

There is here, surely, an unhappy confusion of mind between pity and self-pity. The writer seems at pains to exclude the latter from his thinking with rigorous insistence: there is much that is deeply Christian about such a repudiation. But in avoiding self-pity, it would appear that he has forgotten pity itself. William Blake had a better perspective and no easy or traditional ally, he, of the Divine:

> To Mercy, Pity, Peace and Love
> All pray in their distress:
> And to these virtues of delight
> Return their thankfulness.

The exclusion of the realm, as distinct from the appeal, of weakness makes a dubious point of departure, either for humanism or theology. It is one thing to suspect, or even reject, the sort of belief that takes, or is taken by, men in their frailty. By all means let us address their strength; but forthwith remember that the quality of the strong is that they "bear the infirmities of the weak". Many radical secularizers, doubtless, will do this. There has been heroism among them, as well as academic immunity. But in the end, it is neither true nor strong to impose a pattern of forced lightheartedness upon the world in order to eliminate God and the needfulness of life at one stroke and by one repudiation. Both will return—not because they are in league for mutual advantage but, among other reasons, in order that men might become strong and compassionate and thus mature in their humanity.

Other dubious aspects of the mood of secularization are implicit in this core of the matter. We give God no proper due if our belief in Him is parasitical: rather we deny while we profess to believe. But this truth in no way sustains the assertion that there is no dependence *from strength* and no counterpart, at once inviting and answering such reliance. Rather they corroborate each other—which was Blake's point:

> Where Mercy, Love and Pity dwell,
> There God is dwelling too.

In the end the surest way to human adequacy lies in the awareness of frailty, even as courage, in the end, is only present for the fearful. The war poet, Wilfred Owen, once described himself as "a conscientious objector with a very seared conscience". He would not enforce his categorical reproach of the human condition, as war disclosed it, by opting out of its tragedies. His humanity was at once a participation and a disengagement. For us, too, there is no truth and no salvation in the sort of 'strong' autonomy that holds off the tragic dimension of one's fellows as a means to independence of the Divine. Unless, of course, we mean to resemble that fictitious character in D. H. Lawrence who "thanks his stars he needn't have a mission any more".[1] This is hardly the conclusion most radical theologians intend. Nor does it fit the situation into which technology propels the human family, with ever greater demands on our capacities of discipline, imagination and compassion.

These impressions of *naïveté*, assertiveness and over-sanguine temper in current rejection of the religious dimension are frequently confirmed by a tendency to dogmatic foreclosure of discussion characterizing the secular school. Much of it is less than candid about the depth, integrity and staying power of religious belief. It all too readily mistakes the avid appetite for technological amenities as an equal submission to secularity. It tends to a certain intoxication about human omnicompetence and mistakes the resilience in

---

[1] The *Collected Letters of D. H. Lawrence*, edited by H. T. Moore, London, 1962, p. 975. Lawrence writing to Earl Brewster about *The Man Who Died*.

the sense of the transcendent and the awesome. It inclines to take its undisputed external ascendancy as evidence of a total authority.

In these and other ways, it is liable to state its confidence in terms too sweeping and dogmatic. It delights in questions which expect the answer, No! "Can you still believe?", "Has religion really any future?", "Does the language of theology make any sense today?" The other party is clearly at a disadvantage; any refusal of the implied negatives emerges as archaism or obscurantism. The legend of a forlorn cause is thus placed around conviction about God. Discourse has given way to categorical insistence. "All those concepts by which we speak about God are either meaningless or appear as the relics of a religious era",[1] and there's an end. "To the extent that one insists on giving it (belief in the existence of God) the status of a true proposition, it is an empty proposition."[2] This is conclusive. Yet since for some at least the 'status' abides, it is also inconclusive, at least in that form.

This situation—odd enough in view of the current exhortations to honesty—can best be clinched by dint of Sartre's familiar concept of "bad faith". By this, of course, he does not mean calculated duplicity as in Neville Chamberlain's use of the phrase in his 1939 point-of-war broadcast.[3] Sartre means any deliberate retention of a creed or an idea inwardly known to be untenable. He is reproaching, as Wells did in another vein, the act of clinging to belief, against or without conviction, out of fear, vested interest or inertia.[4] We need not follow Sartre into all the implications of his argument in accepting that there are many such

[1] Richard Shaull, *Union Seminary Quarterly Review*, Vol. 21, 4, May, 1966, p. 424.

[2] D. G. Brown in *Conflicting Images of Man*, edited by William Nicholls, New York, 1965, p. 99.

[3] "It is the evil things we shall be fighting against—brute force, bad faith, njustice, oppression and persecution . . ." (Sept. 3, 1939).

[4] See *Nausea* and other works. 'Nausea' is the sequel to the foregoing of illusion, the awakening to what has always slipped before past one's intellectual guard. If all is so empty, it may be wondered whether the 'deception' needs such reproach.

situations in which men confuse 'names' for 'things' and lack the courage to insist on 'validity'. But this can only hold if there is a contrasted reality in "good faith", an integrity of mind and the will to cherish no delusions. What if such an honesty finds no ground at all for grimly reducing life into

> a ripple of behaviour, a sense of nausea. . . . a broken relation-ship . . . a meaningless journey completed to nowhere.[1]

It has, therefore, to be asked: Is all positive faith inherently "bad faith"? If one says with Altizer, "Those who refuse the death of God do so in bad faith",[2] one has made a categorical exclusion from integrity of any case other than this negative. What then if, awkwardly for this ruling, there continue to be the good-faith kind of believers 'still' around? Do we not first need to explore whether there might still be a theology coming from a whole heart, and a "refusal of the death of God" be, for such thinkers, a necessity of good faith? At all events, the possibility ought not to be one-sidedly excluded, nor the charge of bad faith given so total and unilateral a form.

Arousing the same sense of misgiving about the seculariza-tion theme—aside from a tendency to state all issues with a maximum possibility of misunderstanding—is the diffi-culty inherent in its negativity. Hamilton, for example, wishes to underscore the new character of contemporary rejection of the Divine as entire. With this concern he writes, "We are not talking about the absence of the experience of God, but about the experience of the absence of God".[3] Reflection, however, makes it clear that the distinction is meaningless. The two absences are in fact identical. One may say that one is not merely talking about "a capacity that has dried up within us" (Hamilton's phrase). But one cannot contrast this God-absentness with "an experience of His absence" in some ontological sense. The situation resolves itself into a single "absence of experience". All that can be

[1] *The Existential Imagination*, edited F. R. Karl and L. Hamalian, New York, 1965, p. 17.
[2] In "Theology and Contemporary Sensibility". Paper circulated at a Con-ference in Atlanta, Georgia, U.S.A. in November, 1965.
[3] *Op. cit.*, p. 28.

said is that "God is now without effective force". For we could not "experience His absence" if His being a presence was essentially negated. Thought can hardly go beyond "absence of experience", whether Hamilton's or any other. This inability demolishes the sting of the case. "Experience of His absence" and "absence of the experience" being the same, in the sense of the second, the experience is capable of recovery and, better, the Absent of return.

This is only the other side of the point that one needs God in order to deny Him, as noted in chapter 5 and the Islamic relevance of idolatry. There is a similar situation in Van Buren's familiar use of the parable of the "garden" where "the gardener" could never be detected, cornered or substantiated, despite the device of an electrified fence to 'catch' Him. The whole passage, of course, 'catches' itself, by sustaining, yet not noticing, its own admission that it is, throughout, discussing a "garden". So long as the entity in question is a garden there need be no artificial devices to get the gardener proven or disproven. Despite its misfortunes, the ontological argument has always suspected that there was some such relationship between reality and God, between human experience and the Divine presence.[1]

Our present concern is not with any final position in the debate but simply with the foreclosures that secularization, in certain hands, imposes. We must at all costs avoid a sort of negative positivism, analogous in the realm of philosophy to absolutist claims in politics.[2] In the essay already cited, D. G. Brown argues that "the believer misconceives the status of his own doctrine", in that he "substantializes" what might have meaning as poetry and myth into a metaphysical affirmative about "a fact".[3] It might well be asked what is the concept of 'fact' thus essentially separated from the poetic and the mythical, and, in the same sense, whether the

[1] Paul Van Buren, *The Secular Meaning of the Gospel*, London, 1963, chapter 1.
[2] Cf. a report in the *Guardian*, May 25, 1961, quoted in Brian Wicker, *Culture and Theology*, London, 1966, p. 157, about a visit to China: "We once began a conversation with: 'Suppose a person wishes to change his job...?' and got the answer: 'Which man?' 'In what factory?' There is in fact no answer to anything not now, here and expedient."
[3] *Op. cit.*, p. 99.

unbeliever has not misconstrued the status of his own objection. In that sort of contention it is by no means certain that the nod ought to go to the timid rather than the bold. Browning has the point, provokingly, when he jests:

> The rest may reason—and welcome!
> 'Tis we musicians know.

Faith and discourse must surely be more than a contest of positivisms. Perhaps it is this realization to which we are all alike summoned by our present stresses. If however, unhappily, the position has to be left so, it must remain an open question whose assertiveness is valid, that of the hallowers under God or the secularizers without Him. As long as that question is open, all religions will have their significance for Christian relation. It is fair to ask, meanwhile, why some should be so impatient in wanting the question closed, and closed in their favour?

Secularization, then, tends to be a very partial thing in its sense of humanity. In its worst forms it treats whole areas of reality with a lofty negligence, caring neither to seek nor to find. In its tormented moods it fails to find because it fears to lose. "The lie, the lie, to lying thoughts" is then its formula,[1] a stance which could, with equal force, be a counsel of faith as well as of despair. In bewaring of the hopes of dupes need we settle for the fears of liars?

Deserving of incidental note, in this connection, is the fact that some of the secularizing pleas for human 'maturity' against the allegedly enervating malaise of religiousness arise, historically, as in Camus and Sartre, from the abnormal circumstances of War and Resistance movements. For all the heroism, these are hardly a balanced index to the human condition. They need the corrective of a sense of dependence and society as positive elements in being human. Though sanctified by martyrdom, we need not take the insights of Bonhoeffer, even when rightly interpreted, as the ultimate position of a noble mind.

Where, by contrast with such a thinker, the secular temper

[1] Samuel Beckett, *Three Novels, Molloy, Malone Dies, The Unnamable*, New York, 1965 edition, p. 28.

is sanguine, it is imperative to insist on the human priority over against the technological colossus. An immense struggle is at stake for what might be called the contemporary viability of a genuine humanity. The crux lies in the tenacity of the conviction that science was made for man. He must assert a mastery of his own mastery. Sheer technological feasibility is no criterion in itself. The works of science, despite their inner quality of self-generating progression and their character as unbidden re-makers of culture, require to be subdued and harnessed to considerations beyond and above them, if we are not to be defeated and destroyed by the works of our hands. Is there not about secularization what Weizsäcker has called a "progressive amnesia" as to the setting where technology performs and achieves its instrumentalities?[1] If it is to 'remember' itself properly, there will be for science a perpetual reckoning with obligation—a relation that makes the idea of religionlessness one that has no meaning, least of all for science. Technology is, in fact, the sharpest current focus of the abiding truth of things, namely, that as man secularizes nature in his empirical freedom to conquer, so nature hallows man, in obligating him by those very works to sanity, discernment, discipline, society and love—in a word, to religion.

Science, in this way, leads into, and belongs with, a context in which more than merely scientific criteria must be acknowledged and 'revered'. 'Desacralization', as the unhappy phrase goes, has been necessary to admit of scientific action: thereby we live in a world liberated from gods and demons. Yet other demons lurk in the very human empire so attained: unwittingly we 'organize' the unmaking of our humanity. Our only health is in a sacramentalizing of all our experience, as belonging in a due framework of reference and accountability. Otherwise, as Weizsäcker observes, scientific planning designed to avoid chaos will spell servitude and technological means intended to serve dignity will conspire to degradation.[2] It is for this reason that seculari-

---

[1] C. F. von Weizsäcker, *The Relevance of Science*, New York, 1965, pp. 178–80.
[2] *Ibid.*, p. 93.

zation cannot be had humanly except in a structure of worship within which it ceases to be secularization. In such a structure both its 'secular' liberties and its 'sacred' meanings are assured.

Of one piece with this conclusion is the observation that science and technology themselves proceed upon a religious quality of devotion, of trust-in-truth, of confidence in explicability, of self-oblation. Science lives in perpetual self-correction and there is a deep moral aspect in all its activities. All hypothecation must be strictly subordinated to evidence: data are its stock in trade—their givenness the objectivity to which it must be loyal. All these are religious dimensions. We need to scout the notion, frequently vocal among us, that science only begins when the sacred ends. Admittedly, some theological attitudes in history militated against research. Yet the very ambitions of medieval theology were a prolonged education in that sense of order which is the matrix of science. Properly seen, empirical science does not evaporate wonder, save for the mercenary and the unpoetic: it rather intensifies it. 'Disenchantment' is, therefore, a pretentious word, often taken for more than it can rightly say. Is there any real reason why the heavens should be wonderful to shepherds and not also to astronauts? Are we only religious when we follow the plough?

Too much is heard of the alleged servitude of religious man. There is, or was, a will to mastery in the pagan's magic no less than in the scientist's techniques. Nature, in either case, was to be manipulated. 'Magic', as Frazer noted long ago in *The Golden Bough*, was "a kind of primitive and erroneous science . . . The analogy between the magical and the scientific concepts of the world is close".[1] Both have to do with sovereignty over the natural world, as does Biblical religion. It is well to explode the fallacy that before we can have an experimenting and exploiting relation to our environment we must abjure the thought of its sanctity. In another realm, too, it is salutary to remember about historical 'growing up', that, in Kierkegaard's words

[1] See S. E. Hyman, *The Tangled Bank*, New York, 1959, p. 235.

Whatever one generation may learn from the other, the genuinely humane no generation learns from the foregoing. In this respect every generation begins primitively, has no different task from that of every previous generation nor does it get any further.[1]

The claim made by some secularizers that technology has produced a qualitatively new humanity misunderstands both man and technology.

ALL MEN'S HALLOWING: THE CRISIS OF RELIGIONS

"The midwife of every society pregnant with a new one" was how Marx saw the role of force in history and justified it for his dialectic. The description belongs equally well to science as the shaper of all power. But what is being brought forth? The midwife is not the child.

This is the question that returns us to the faiths of men, standing as they do, though confusedly, beyond the incompleteness of the secular account of man, as now reviewed. The "depth in the mind" that leads us back to religion is no petulant reproof of scientific success, nor a vulgar alliance against human competence. It is a response to reading in the original both the promise and the prejudice of the secular achievement. It is not *against* technology that religions are to be consulted anew, but *for* its hallowing as an ever more urgent condition of its own prosperity.

In the sweet song of the servant in Isaiah 42, the prophet tells in vivid images the character and pattern of the servant's task. He does not quench the smoking flax or break the bruised reed: he is not raucous, contentious and aggressive. Yet he is unfailing, in so handling every critical situation as to let truth prevail (v. 3b). Can we envisage this quality of ministry, this likeness of realism and hope, undertaking our present cares for the secular and the religious?

Before all else, there is with the servant no shirking of the onus to care. If we share his temper it is clear that for us there

[1] *Fear and Trembling*, trans. by Walter Lowrie, Princeton, 1941, p. 190.

can be no abatement of Christian obligation to men in their faiths, on the ground that technological civilization has sounded the death-knell of them all. "Bruised", they are, painfully, and the Church with them, by contemporary changes and much chastened or bludgeoned by modern developments. Yet, for the perceptive Christian, a music remains: the reed may still speak. The patience to discern this must not be deceived by the claim that only the Christian has in his Gospel the 'eschatology' of science, or the charge that the Hindu warning against unreality, the Muslim injunction to worship, and the African delight in human-ness, have no place in the correction and discipline that technology needs.

This care for a will in men to wonder and to worship is no abstraction of their mosques and temples from the rigours of the time. Nor is it simply a psychological consideration arguing a purely emotional necessity for belief. Nor, again, is it a refusal of the irreversible processes of history whereby man is detribalized, urbanized, industrialized and computerized, as if the sense of a fundamental awe belonged only in the bush and under the stars. The servant in Isaiah's song is not some spiritual Luddite clinging to the antiquated or striving to destroy what an old order cannot face. On the contrary: the prophet makes the very point that "he does not strive"; he is not riotous in the streets of the new technopolis. Nor does he fear, like Galileo's adversaries, the reality the telescope discloses. This we know from the fact that his temper is itself steeled in exile.

But he is, nevertheless, a sort of conservationist who aims to restore, not to discard, whose criteria do not depend first upon efficiency but upon hope, and who has lived long enough with history to know and yet refuse its profound discouragements. The same temper suggests that he stir rather than foreclose the questions and let the answers have their due proportions, stunted neither by haste nor by despair. In our context it is not hard to perceive what the questions are.

Is scientific feasibility the only condition of what man

should do to man, or, rather, man's science to man's humanity? Are there human considerations that over-ride technological inventiveness? If there are, how shall they be surely asserted against technocratic pride? Is there only a self-shaped space within man's being? Is his competence also his salvation?

It is out of such issues as these that the faiths of the world deserve a ministry of Christian 'servanthood' in Isaiah's sense. This is the more imperative in that the crises with which they are beset through modern pressures, come 'telescoped' into a few decades where Europe had some two centuries.[1] They come, complicated still further by the psychological tensions of their alien origin. It is this which makes it callous as well as pretentious to dismiss Buddhism, Hinduism and Islam, as Van Leeuwen seems to suggest, as "no more than a misguided attempt to cure the ills of the technocratic era with the medicines of the Neolithic".[2] In this view lies a total capitulation to the idea that secularization is all and a consequent attempt to divest the Christian faith of any religious meanings or affinities. Thus he continues, "The idea that proclaiming the Gospel (in the non-western world) primarily and necessarily entails a meeting with the non-Christian religions" must be "shaken off".[3]

This provincialism and partiality of mind do scant justice to what the author himself sees as "the glory and the desperation, the greatness and the wretchedness of . . . technocracy." It is a thesis deceived by the frustrating dogmatism for which

. . . the spell of a divine universe is broken: upon every temple there falls the devastating judgement that it has been made by man. Modern science has to do simply with a man-made universe. It moves among the stars and probes the inmost secrets of the atom: and in all this man comes face to face with himself.[4]

"Face to face with himself"—truly—is where we all are. But why talk of "the spell" as if God-relatedness were no

[1] Kenneth Kaunda, *A Humanist in Africa*, London, 1966, p. 20, writes, "There has been a kind of telescoping of time on the African continent".
[2] A. Van Leeuwen, *Christianity in World History*, trans. H. H. Hoskins, London, 964, p. 408.
[3] *Ibid.*, p. 410.   [4] *Ibid.*, p. 417.

more than superstition? The man-made-ness of the "universe", in the limited sense of the phrase, is not a God-eliding sort. Nor is it disfigured and deceived by man-made temples, if these are seen as God-evoked. The whole enterprise of man in the making of civilization proceeds in the givenness that is man-received. It issues into obligations that are man-entrusted and, thence, into consequences that are man-achieving or man-denying. In the reception, the entrustment and the destiny, other faiths may be our allies. For they too belong with man and with the same "great and wretched" world. They are not to be dismissed from the discernment of the human future nor the crises of the human present. There is in the Christian doctrine of the Holy Spirit every reason not to consign them impatiently to a limbo of futility, nor to hold them hopeless and obtuse in the face of modern change, however catastrophic to their traditional societies. It is no true relationship in the Christ of the Incarnation to find in the Christian Gospel a secular competence from which other faiths are pathetically disqualified *in toto*. There is no loyalty in these terms to "the light which lighteneth every man", nor to a Christian understanding of revelation that is duly open to nature and humanity. Are we ever "face to face with man" if we reject him in our multitudinous fellows? We cannot tolerate, if we are "in Christ", any secular dictatorship of the range, the terms and the hopes of our religious neighbourliness.

Only in the acknowledgement of every kinship and a firm rejection of western monopolies of the human mystery shall we come "face to face with man" as technology requires we do—all of us. Let the technocratic revolutions be used to confront man the more urgently with the truths of his nature. Admit and interpret the bruising of the reeds of human wistfulness, the smoking of the flax of the religious lamps of life. But do not annihilate the poetry in their souls.[1] We need not suppose that current secularization is a wholly irreversible process. There are resources and capacities in the human

[1] Echoing the impressive, if inadequate, definition of religion by George Santayana in *Interpretations of Poetry and Religion*, London, 1900, p. 26: "Our religion is the poetry in which we believe".

spirit, which the great faiths explore and recruit, however brokenly, able to rise against the deprivations of secularity and rediscover man's stature in his lowliness. "What a colossal world . . . for a religion to assimilate" wrote Teilhard de Chardin;[1] but not so colossal as to warrant the strident secularizers forbidding the attempt. In doing so, they reckon without man.

There will be, then, for all of us, for years to come, a long, strenuous and patient task of renewing the religious quality of the human situation, in mastering the strong temptation to self-deification by men in their nations, in their techniques and in their conquests. For Christians it is a task which discerns by the criterion of Christ and the Cross the crisis of every religious system and, in discerning, serves by a relationship at once honest, realist, gentle and free.

Such a posture excludes the condemnation that extinguishes light. It does not connive impatiently with the forces that destroy. It creates an atmosphere in which doctrines are retrieved for a true survival or redeemed both from and for their thwarted meaning. It bears with a situation the impetuous would dissolve and the strong despise. In all this, it incurs what, but for one circumstance, its many discouragements would find too great to sustain. That circumstance is the conviction, often dim but always real, that this is the way of the servant "in whom the Lord delights".

[1] *Letters from a Traveller*, London, 1962, p. 124.

CHAPTER EIGHT

IDENTITY AND DIVERSITY:
THE CONTEMPORARY CHURCH

It may be that death is your ultimate gift to life: it must not
be an act of treachery against it.[1]

So Dag Hammarskjöld, writing almost in the mood of
Eliot's Thomas of Canterbury, detected in the temptation by which it becomes easier, not to say, more
rewarding, to die than to live. The logic of all our preceding
chapters is that Christianity in the world must be ready to
die to the possessiveness of western forms in order to live
authentically within the fullness of human cultures. Yet so to
die as not to elude or betray the obligations of that history and
the real onus of modernity. The hope of this present chapter
is to take stock of the shape of the Church in that vocation,
of its rightly diversified identity and its loyal universality. The
conviction is that, seen in the sequences and changes of
history, a true identity means the sort of variety demanded
by the plural world and the present setting.

These are the two themes—identity in respect of its own
past and in openness to the life of all. For "the body of
Christ" in the world is recognizable by its own recognition of
humanity. Its identity, in the sense of character and meaning,
is found by identity, in the sense of participation, with mankind. "For us men" states with simple inclusiveness what
Christianity believes about the Divine enterprise, and so, in
turn, about the open dimension of the reach of the Church.
Both the doctrine and the society of Christ take and embrace
humanity in an undifferentiated unity. Christian faith about
man is also a faithfulness towards him. Its vocation is to be as
much 'for' men as its Gospel declares God to be—men, that
is, not churchmen. All things here are manward, the range

[1] In *Markings*, trans. from the Swedish, London, 1964, p. 86.

of the Divine love reproducing its pattern in its sons, "from faith to faith" as St. Paul told the Romans—from the conviction to the fidelity. "You see your calling brethren", he said. It is that we are "involved in mankind".

Involved with them, however, not simply in death and in being mortal, but in being alive, in being each with all. "Do not send to know . . ." said Donne in his passionate way, at the sound of the passing bell, "it tolls for thee". Yet "sending to know" is precisely what we must do, if being "involved in mankind" is to mean more than the distant sense of common mortality. It is easy enough dying in the diminution of the other man's death, if the antecedents of his demise I can ignore. That all are "a part of the main" is not a truth that comes to be only when a piece falls off into the grave, or when there is a tolling bell announcing some one's end. Before the graveyard, in the real world, belongs our partaking with our fellows. What tolls for us is not merely the reminder of a future summons so certain that is chides our curiosity, but rather the sound of a humanity so insistent as to startle our neglect. Beyond the immunities of distance, birth, privilege or circumstance which can exempt me if I will, it calls to be known. Sobered by my own mortality I may mourn the unidentified. But, unidentified, I cannot save him and his passing diminishes me only in what, thus, it is no grief to lose. Merely to note that death awaits us all is not to be "involved in mankind". "Therefore, send to know for whom the living wait: it is for thee." Only then is it discovered that "no man is an island". In truly knowing men, we are ourselves known.

This is the 'ecumenical' vocation in its fullest implication. *Oikumenikos*, in Greek, is that which belongs to the *oikumene*, or whole, inhabited world, though its English derivative, invoked by Christian vocabulary, has tended to the much more limited meaning of Christian inclusions. Its fortunes, in that way, are a parable. Ecclesiastical interests, so to speak predominate in its usage. We have Ecumenical Councils and Patriarchs, for example, but somehow the word rarely finds currency in such global spheres as the United Nations and dependent agencies, which have resonable claims to what it denotes. More rarely still does it emerge as a genuine adjective of human inclusiveness. Ezekiel Mphahlele writes in that sense:

> The Church as an ecumenical force in South Africa has been on the retreat since before the Union in 1910 . . . It fixed its gaze on Calvary . . . and kept up an aloofness from political realities.[1]

He is thinking, clearly, of the Church's failure to make good its true social and political obligations in the grim world of *apartheid*. The compromises of racial conspiracy made it 'non-ecumenical'. In general employment, however, to be 'ecumenical' is to be alert for Christian 'togetherness' rather than to be truly world-aware. One can, of course, be world-wide in an association of chess players. The geographical is always the easiest of 'ecumenical' demands. Living related-ness to a whole humanity is much more exacting than moving fraternally among the churches. The ecumenical impulse in the limited sense is doubtless a necessary condition of the larger obligation. The reconciling of the churches may set them more truly and surely in the field, and certainly reduces the disqualification of their Gospel. But the faith is not fulfilled unless the *oikumene*, with its cultures and claims, is both the measure and test of their trust.

As the Christ of Galilee and Jerusalem in New Testament times became the Christ of the Mediterranean, of Athens and Rome, so the Christ of the West must be more evidently the Christ of the world. It is the conviction of Christian faith that He is only known anywhere in His fullness, when the whole world, in its cultural diversity, takes possession of Him and in freedom, in thought and in form, tells of Him what it learns and loves. As we saw in the survey of chapter 1, the churches planted as the fruit of nineteenth-century mission were shaped by the assumptions with which their foreign nurture came. Circumstances in that *diaspora* made for a generally self-reliant manner in the commendation of Christ. They were heavily weighted towards dependent,

---

[1] *Down Second Avenue*, London, 1959, p. 221.

acquiescent postures in the receiving of the Gospel and assured, proprietary dispositions in the preaching of it. The
ruling metaphors of mind tended to be military rather than
ambassadorial. The local faiths were regarded, in the main,
as hostile or perverse. The needs their worlds so tragically
disclosed were to be met by wholly missionary solutions of
compassion, conversion and transferred allegiance. The
missionary Church hoped to substantiate its own answers as
far as resources would allow. Her courage might have been
appalled by the magnitude of the task but not, broadly
speaking, her theological adequacy. The entrenched religions
reacted to the Christian intrusion in terms reciprocal to the
missionary reproach with which they were regarded. In
its general nineteenth-century form, the whole encounter
allowed, indeed encouraged, the Christian theology involved to cherish its inner assurances with a quite insufficient
attention to what its 'embassy' ought to have meant. Those
convictions revolved in a circle of authority that had few
tangents into intellectual wistfulness or perplexity, as these
were felt by the systems in possession. In confronting the
stranger, mission naturally assumed its own familiarities and
did so in a temper ill-attuned, for the most part, to the natural
prides and prejudices of the rest of men. In the pursuit of its
nobly 'ecumenical' ambition, the Church was notably
partial to itself, and all too readily forgot that it was itself as
odd and foreign to receiving cultures as it took them to be.

In some senses, it may be fair to reflect, this instinctive
domesticity of Christian theology was not unique to the
nineteenth century. Creeds anyway "possess their possessions" possessively and too readily tend to present themselves,
not as areas of hospitality to be explored even by tentative
inhabitants, but rather as strongholds to be vigilantly
guarded with strictly conditional admission. History surely
sustains the general reflection that Christian doctrine,
through most of its history, has busied itself with themes of its
own choosing and has preferred to set them within its own
premises rather than in the broad context of the outsider's
misgivings. It has not been aware of strangers with the sort of

urgency St. Paul intended in his metaphor of the "ambassa-dor" for Christ, beseeching men to be reconciled (2 Cor. 5: 20 and Eph. 6: 20). For 'embassy' if taken seriously enjoins a studiousness to commend as well as an authority to represent. Such a duty to persuade supposes a courteous deference to the thoughts and emotions it meets in the world. The mind of an ambassador must be served by an ear as well as by a voice. He must be able for alert theological residence in all the territories of his mission, human and religious, as well as geographical.

After the early creative days of Christian faith, the history of definitive Christology, both before and after Chalcedon, displays this tendency to defensive introversion and the preoccupation with heresy. The world of Greek philosophy, it is true, supplies the forms and serves the vocabulary. There are apologists, like Justin, Clement and Origen, sure of their kinship with Athens as well as Jerusalem. There grows, nevertheless, a habit of priority for right custody rather than ready embassy. To define and defend are the dominant impulses, in line with internal criteria, seen almost as ends in themselves.

A similar appraisal might be honestly made in respect of whole stretches of medieval Christianity. It is idle, of course, to apply to those centuries judgements based on modern conditions. The feasible contacts of Christendom with faiths other than its own were very different from those of our time. Yet Christendom, as a concept, means in a sense that all theology is 'domestic'. It would be foolish to accuse it of insulation from secularity in anything like the contemporary force of that term. The medieval Church bore powerfully on every aspect of its own society. Yet, by the same token, its theology was all the more liable to be related to the world within the notion of heresy and not of embassy. Unbelief evokes the vindication of dogma far more than the sense of adventure for truth. When we move to the Reformation, we find that by and large its legacies were to excite the Churches to battle within its internal stresses rather than to over-riding dialogue with the Renaissance. As a crisis of conscience and of conviction, the concerns of the Protestant and Catholic reformers were to dictate for three centuries the general themes and criteria of doctrine—authority, Scripture, tradition, faith and works, grace and justification, ministry and sacraments; while the instinctive authoritarianism of both parties delayed for long years that capacity to see an autonomous world deserving to be addressed in its own right which might reasonably have been expected as a theological corollary of the logic within the Renaissance itself. "Contention for the faith", mainly with its other exponents, and the fear of heresy continued to dominate, so that dogma was in the main internally combative, not externally alert. Some minds, it is true, strove to hold in one the faith of the Church and the attractions of the classic world. Pico Della Mirandola wore the Dominican habit but stayed wistful for Apollo's lute. But centuries, not decades, were needed before the Church had, as it were, a world in which to 'go', apostolically, as the New Testament had done, a world which it could the better occupy on behalf of Christ for the very reason of not claiming to rule or to possess it.

If we return then from this excursus to the nineteenth-century theology of mission, or better, theology in mission, we find not only a new confrontation with a world plainly non-amenable in that other faiths and cultures inform it, but also a tradition or habit of mind by which Christianity thinks and speaks with a strongly domestic accent and proceeds upon dogmatic criteria of what witness requires and owes. In the long, ensuing experience we must read a vocation to a much more total, and willing, acceptance of a world perspective, and that, not merely in the sense of geographical extension (now easy enough), but of continuing cultural pluralism, of proper autonomy over against the realities of grace, and so, in turn, of genuine theological and spiritual 'embassy', representing Christ but in full residential capacity, with credentials that, for all their authority, are subject to local presentation. This is the real 'ecumenicity' for which all our changing circumstances press, as well, surely, as the mind of the Spirit. This is the meaning and the fact of the Christian *diaspora*—not a scattered "people of God" preoccupied with aloofness, either practical or cultural, from the society around them, but minorities ready for creative engagement with it in every area of its need, its aspiration or its despair. The eternal dimension makes us all "strangers and pilgrims in the earth". But we can hold that status, as Christ intends it to be ours, with a resolute refusal to be anywhere alien and a firm will to transcend all impeding foreign-ness whether arising from birth, or sloth, or fear, or dullness of mind or slowness of heart.

What follows, then, is meant as a brief and simple exploration of some of the implications of this resolve in the present context. It seems properly to divide itself into two kindred themes which might be described as the Church, responsive to universality and responsible to unity.

THE CHURCH: RESPONSIVE TO UNIVERSALITY

The physical equation is not here in mind, though it is, of course, the condition of all else. Our concern is for the possession by the faith of the cultural expression that every pattern of human culture affords and for the ever-present issue of the compatibilities, or otherwise, of the one with the other.

It is necessary to be on our guard at the outset against a possible distortion of this intention. The urge to the cultural embodiment of Christian faith in every local scene must have no truck with some inverted, or perverted, notions of spiritual *apartheid*. To yearn that the Church be truly housed in each particular 'nativeness', to seek for Bantu symbol or Yoruba music, to covet for Tamil lyrics or Dravidian art and the resources of every place in its own place, is not at all to imply that only the English are good enough for Gothic cathedrals, or Shakespearean language, or Bach's Chorales. It is not to mean that only the west is fit to possess Handel's *Messiah* or the *Missa Solemnis*. It is not to insist that churches be built in African thatch or wattle because nothing more pretentious would be appropriate to African intelligence.

Such notions, latent or inferred, would be utterly unworthy. Yet such are the legitimate suspicions the West has incurred, that they might easily suggest themselves to sensitive spirits reacting to some crudely condescending western recommendation of native styles and norms.[1] To give the lie to this cynical temptation—since there is no good that cannot be evil spoken of—every care for local culture in the Church must be corroborated by a deliberate and energetic mediation of western Christian treasures. This is the reason, despite every persuasive argument to the contrary, why there must continue to be a patient, unstinted, unobtrusive service of the churches in the world by western personnel and avenues of close liaison with western heritage in Christ. All that the Christianity of Europe and America holds in its long and rich tradition must be accessible to the rest of men as truly part of Christ, always with lowliness of mind as a mediation arising only out of debt. To think otherwise would be criminally to handicap and impoverish the churches of Asia and Africa, as well as to indulge in irresponsibility to the real facts of history and to the trust of community in faith. Universality, clearly, is not served either by unilateral dominance or by unilateral reservation.

The ready mediation of those western treasures of the churches, however, for all to make their own as far as will and wisdom enjoin, must be in the sort of modest temper and sensitive discernment that leave every culture its legitimate dignity in discriminating and absorbing as it may. The theologians, the hymnologists, the music-makers, the classic figures, of western Christian history must be so shared with the nations that the craftsmen of the Spirit in every people are free to breathe, free to kindle their own creative genius. Only in these terms is the western presence truly a mediation, and not an incubus. Such a criterion of relationship will help to obviate the infliction longer on other Christians of 'accidents' of the western Christian story whose consequences tend to be perpetuated beyond all deserving. It will serve to ensure, for example, that the universally valid quality of the

---

[1] Something of this danger is present, of course, in the word 'native' itself, whose history is a silent parable of the dilemma we are discussing. It is used here in the proper and entirely inoffensive sense. We are all natives.

Wesleys' life and legacy be distilled in every Christian expression, without giving a perpetuity they in no wise merit to the sociological factors at work in Methodist schism in eighteenth-century England. The discrimination that liberates the truly ecumenical possessions in the particular histories and that welcomes only these elsewhere, demands a truly servant-role on the one side and an independent stature on the other. The tasks awaiting such discernment, in the adjustments of the world churches to their histories, longer and shorter, are still great.

True universality, then, does not wilfully repudiate historical relationships, yet sees them only rightly sustained in freedom and originality. There is room for indebtedness, but none for dominance. With this firmly stated, what of the trans-cultural diversities and their obligations to universal norms? How are the latter to be properly identified in due distinction from particular custodianships in history, however prolonged or familiar? How is the Church to be recognizably itself in the many patterns of cultural habitation and habituation? How is it to be validly one in the midst of its manifold variety?

These questions do not necessarily admit of the same answer at every point in the sequences of time. Missionary theology, as we saw, was frequently utterly intolerant of traditional religions and their social mores, in the nineteenth century. Whatever the abstract merits of the case, it cannot be denied that near ruthlessness has had proper times and seasons at the genesis of the Church. There is an important truth in the dictum that a man's foes in Christ are those of his own household. The fears in which paganism captivates and enthralls the heathen mind may well only be shattered in the first generation by radical rejection and denunciation of all its ways and works, as the price of a spiritual surgery indispensable to liberty of will and spirit. Only so is the bad bush demonstrably cleansed and husbanded: only so is the burden of ancestral phobias and envies, inhibiting the present world with the enmities of buried generations, truly lifted and dispelled: only so are the apathy of entrenched systems, the "lie in the right hand", as Isaiah called it, "the feeding on ashes" disclosed in their true character and brought to a decisive end, representatively, in the persons of the first liberated liberators. It has to be remembered that heathen societies and ancient faiths, by and large, presented their most ugly image, their most depraved forms, to the first generation of modern mission. There was often no option save that of radical displacement, and with it a vigorous quarrel with the *status quo* in all its aspects. Inevitably in that proceeding values were ignored or never discerned, for which, however, there could be no safe or legitimate survival until the crisis required by their perversity had been duly accomplished in emancipation.

By the same token, the thoroughgoing abruptness of that first contention plainly awaits correction, of some at least of its attitudes and consequences, once its incisiveness has achieved the redeeming newness of life. There comes the time when the invaded culture must properly retaliate, within the new dimensions of its own continuity, chastened as these are by the discontinuity through which Christ has authentically come into its experience. For that coming is not only unto judgement, not ultimately for destruction, but for health and salvation. The mature church in every place need not lose its first love in learning to do more than imitate its first converts. These, in their very proximity to the critical encounter, in their own persons, may have been disqualified for an adequate baptism of their proper culture in the waters of their own. In the love and wisdom of the Spirit, the season arrives when the personal baptism must be followed by the cultural, when things as well as people, feasts, places, songs, dances and traditions as well as converts, find an inclusion in Christ. Otherwise, the faith fails not only in its duty of regeneration but of fulfilment, and betrays its own source in the meaning of the Incarnation as this is realized in its being everywhere at home.

It needs to be remembered in this context that the faith and the Church, in their initial, radical impact, are not innocent of cultural form. Cultural neutrality is manifestly impossible.

As we have insisted throughout, the cultural forms of the bringing of the faith have no enduring right to become the permanent forms of its accepting. On the contrary, its secret is not truly known and shared save in self-abnegation on the one side and self-expression on the other. The point has surely been reached, indeed in many places is long overdue, when the churches of western missionary planting[1] must rightly seek out and make good the hidden resources of their own world and give Christian release to the potentialities which the circumstances of their origin excluded from their emotions or forbade to their desires. Music is not irretrievably entangled with tribal warfare or sensual passion, nor vocabulary, rite and usage irredeemably profaned. Conversion does not mean that a man finds grace only by foregoing the use of his legs[2] or the chords of his fingers. Were it to be so interpreted he would only be delivered over, awkwardly and passively, to the ways and idiom, the tunes and postures, of an alien imitation.

The deep, inner need is to transcend the idea that, whatever may have been the original validity of sharp disruption, the only loyalty lies in its perpetuation. For the fullness of Christ demands the enlisting of the wealth of nations to contain and serve it and for that reason is at odds with imperial assumptions in whatever guise. The fact that this necessity coincides with the contemporary politics of independence is merely incidental, though the latter may clarify and accelerate its purpose. Its sources lie at the heart of the nature of the Gospel itself as calculated to employ in its expression all that human diversity presents, freed from the accidents of mission, and gathered into active discipleship.

[1] This discussion does not overlook the significance of the long history of local Christianities in Asia and Africa, e.g. in Kerala, Ethiopia, Egypt and elsewhere, but its primary concern is with the entail of western mission. These ancient churches provide many lessons in cultural issues but precisely through their isolation and/or their minority-status, do not exemplify historically the full measure of our contemporary problem. See a useful documentation in *Christianity in the Non-Western World*, edited by C. W. Forman, New Jersey, 1967.

[2] Echoing the remark of a Patagonian who observed that since his becoming a Christian, the dances being ended, it had seemed to him as if he no longer owned his legs.

Then poets, singers, builders, writers, as well as theologians, bring their arts to worship.

It is only when we are firmly committed to this principle that it becomes clear how strenuous its tasks in practice are. Having made the point that in the wake of modern mission the conservation of cultures is more urgent and difficult, by reason of the earlier superiority and assurance of its western auspices, it is well to turn to a few concrete examples and to start from a more tolerant and permissive introduction of Christianity, where, however, the core of the dilemma can be seen.

When Augustine, later first Archbishop of Canterbury, came to Kent in 597, he found a territory not devoid of remnants of Christianity surviving from the Roman occupation and sheltered by the Christian queen, Bertha, but still predominantly pagan and dotted with heathen temples. These soon took their place as a crucial theme of his many inquiries to Pope Gregory, who in reply set down a policy which serves admirably to focus the issues. He wrote:

> Tell our brother that I have long been considering with myself about the case of the English: to wit that the temples of idols in that nation should not be destroyed, but that the idols themselves that are in them should be. Let blessed water be prepared and sprinkled in the temples and altars constructed and relics deposited: since, if these temples are well built, it is needful that they should be transferred from the worship of idols to the true God: that when the people themselves see that these temples are not destroyed, they may put away error from their heart and, knowing and adoring the true God may have recourse with the more familiarity to the place they have been accustomed to. And since they are wont to kill many oxen in sacrifice to demons, they should also have some solemnity of this kind in a changed form, so that on the day of dedication or on the anniversaries of the holy martyrs whose relics are deposited there, they may make for themselves tents of the branches of the trees around these temples that have been made into churches and celebrate the solemnity with religious feasts.
>
> Nor let them any longer sacrifice animals to the devils but slay animals to the praise of God . . . and return thanks to the Giver of all: so that while some joys are reserved for them

outwardly they may be able the more easily to incline their minds to inward joys.

Justifying this perhaps over-sanguine prescription of procedures, Gregory observed:

> It is undoubtedly impossible to cut away everything at once from hard hearts, since one who strives to ascend to the highest place must needs rise by steps or paces, not by leaps.[1]

He went on to invoke Old Testament precedent to sustain his case. All the issues at stake for trans-cultural Christianity, whether in Sarawak or Sierra Leone, are here. Is it enough, this gradualism, this recognition of popular frailties, this modest iconoclasm, this progress by substitution, this faith in sacramental exorcism, this compassion for the external joys of the common world? Or does the policy lack the cleansing that holy waters cannot effectuate? Do dangerous errors elude this easy insurance and stay to bedevil the new order? Is the resulting Christianity superficialized by the very lack of the heroic dimension and an earnest severity? Will Gregory square with St. Paul? At all events, his instinct for treating of temples not already derelict shows a healthy practicality of mind, and he warned Augustine later that no church-usage was to be idly imported among the uncouth English merely because of the repute of its church of origin.

> For things are not to be loved for the sake of places, but places for the sake of things good. Choose, therefore, from each church those things that are pious, religious and seemly, and when you have as it were, incorporated them, let the minds of the English be accustomed thereto.[2]

The mediation here was all in the hands of the mission. It was hierarchical. Augustine took his counsel with Rome rather than with Kent. Given his ecclesiastical temper and the newness of his situation, there was perhaps no other course. The recipients, in the mission's view, were still "uncouth". "Let their minds be accustomed . . ."—there lay the question.

[1] See B. J. Kidd, *Documents illustrative of the History of the Church*, Vol. 3, London, 1941, pp. 42–43, and also Margaret Deanesly, *The Pre-Conquest Church in England*, London, 1961, p. 54.
[2] See H. Bettenson, *Documents of the Christian Church*, London, 1943, p. 213.

How were faith and liturgy, word and symbol, to become the familiar thing, and were they to take, or not to take, partnership with existent familiars, to harness or combat them?

That crucial question is everywhere transferable. Ceremonies of harvest, of betrothal or of burial in every society; patterns of solidarity against the lawless and the depredatory; the sacramental recognition of territory or of the past as in the practice of libation; forms of awareness of the hinterland of ancestors around the living; protective devices in the threat or presence of disease and calamity; seasons and festivals of the human or the natural cycle with their recurrent and "external joys"—all these shape perennial themes of Christian decision *pro* or *con* and make the pastoral life of every church a perpetual theology of culture.

Nor are the problems only one-directional, namely how the Church is to translate, through, or despite, the local mores. No less important is how its ways and words are digested in the receiving context. There is no *tabula rasa* situation either of the mind or of the will. The Church is not merely interpreting: it is being interpreted. Thus baptism may be sought, or shunned, on the ground that it is some magic formula, advantageous or risky. Christian conformity may be taken, or mistaken, as an alternative insurance against adversity, a prudent acquisition of status, or "my people's way of splitting risks".[1] The both/and mentality is all too likely in the stresses and bewilderments of a world in flux. The Bible itself, with its Old Testament liabilities, is far from being the unifying moral source-book which some theologies have assumed. Not a few excesses in the churches have, in fact, been justified by subjective, yet persuasive, invocation of Biblical precedent—a situation reflected, for example, in the marked tendency to sectarian vagaries within Roman Catholic Christianity in Asia and Africa since its more liberal policy about Biblical access and exegesis among ordinary Christians. That David was "after God's own heart" may in certain circumstances constitute a very confusing dictum. These cultural accommodations, especially in their

[1] W. Conton, *The African*, New York, 1960, p. 17.

pronounced sectarian forms, have the further attraction of success—a success sharpened in many cases by the implicit avoidance, if not the explicit disowning, of the western tutelage to which a sophistication with the Bible is likely to be tied.

Many elements of our whole discussion, prefaced by Augustine and Gregory, find a curious focus in the activities of C. L. Coolen in the Surabaja region of East Java in the forties of last century.[1] As a random example, it becomes more telling by the useful foil of staunch orthodoxy provided by W. H. Medhurst, of the London Missionary Society, his contemporary in the same region. Coolen was the son of a Dutch mercenary soldier in the employ of the Dutch East India Company and of a Javanese mother from whom he inherited a princely bearing, a deep kinship with the local ways, and a ready facility in traditional song and society. After a varied career, he became an important landowner and engaged in ardent evangelism in his locality. He delighted in Javanese orchestration, performing with great skill, and translating the Dutch Bible extemporaneously, with hymns and prayers in Javanese style. He attracted a wide following and gathered an impressive 'church' on the basis, without baptism, of acceptance of the Lord's Prayer and the Apostles' Creed. He barred baptism on the ground that it would imply the loss of local identity and the adoption of Dutch custom. He likewise excluded the Holy Communion but taught, with vigorous practice, the hallowing of daily toil and the active restitution into an 'accepting' community of wrongdoers and criminals. Coolen himself had a wife and family from whom he was separated and lived with a Javanese woman by whom he had several children.

This last circumstance, apart from all else, sufficed to ensure the antipathy of W. H. Medhurst when he encountered Coolen and his 'church', in 1841. His censure contained all the instincts of the rigorist mind, yet Coolen had the argument of achievement. He asked Medhurst why his

[1] See a summary presentation in David Bentley Taylor, *The Weathercock's Reward*, Christian Progress in Muslim Java, London, 1967, pp. 58–78.

twenty years of utter probity of conduct and purity of evangelism had reaped little or no success, whereas a measurable impact had been made by his own poor, 'compromised' efforts. Medhurst held doggedly to his reproachful brief, dismissed the visions by which Coolen had been emboldened to disturb the traditions of his simple neighbours in Christ's name,[1] questioned Coolen's own converted state and, of course, his second marriage, took a dim view of the "low, sing-song drawl" of his music for the Creed, and objected to Coolen's practice of repeating, in Muslim formula, the refrain, "There is no god but God and Jesus Christ is the Spirit of God". After pointing out the distinction between 'Spirit' and 'Son', Medhurst went on, in a reporting letter:

> In the course of his sermon he (Coolen) stated that what the ancient Javanese used to say of Krishna is the same as Europeans say of Jesus Christ. After the sermon he was asked what he meant by this statement, to which he replied that Krishna was one of the ancient heroes of Javanese fable and many things said of him were also true of Jesus Christ. Here he was cautioned against such comparisons. He said that in the Holy Scriptures Christ was compared to Melchisedec and why might we not trace such resemblances as we could find between our Saviour and the fabulous heroes of antiquity, in order to catch the minds of the natives with a bait so pleasing and familiar? That Christ used similitudes . . . He, of course, was told that we were only warranted in exhibiting those as types of Christ which were set forth as such in the Scripture of truth, and that the project of mixing truth with error in order to captivate the minds of men was one of the wildest as it was one of the wickedest that had ever been conceived.[2]

It is intriguing to reflect how this single, and indeed obscure, instance epitomizes all the queries belonging to universality. Is there an indispensable role for persons who by their birth combine two races and cultures? Can venturesome adaptation be made, relying, if need be, on correction

---

[1] *Ibid.*, p. 67. This is perhaps the most fascinating detail of all, indicating as it does a certain, healthy, missionary disquiet, whatever may be said of Noah's reassuring role.

[2] *Ibid.*, p. 70.

in a later generation? If so, do we abandon the immediacy of human convertibility on which the New Testament itself proceeds? How are baptism and alien naturalization to be distinguished? Are tactical rephrasings of creed and liturgy valid and viable? If meaning is not exclusively wedded to particular formulation how is its fullness ensured in the alternatives? Is the Old Testament solely a source book of types or also an exemplification of their feasible multiplication out of other sources? Is there a loyalty to the Scriptures that belongs with their imitation rather than only with their enforcement? Can the evangelist freely parabolize by his own lights? And perhaps more immediate than all these, is the Medhurst cast of mind too impatient and too rigid? Is there a place for suspension of judgement, for dangerous freedom, for a larger, because less anchored, reliance on the Word? Was Medhurst inhibited, by his role as a custodian of truth and a guardian of morals, from a creative sense of the Holy Spirit? If so, what becomes of the principle of orthodoxy and, without it, what becomes of the faith? Furthermore, while we are wrestling with these issues, how do we keep "the unity of the Spirit in the bond of peace", liable as they are to sharp contentions of view and of temper? These are the truly 'ecumenical' questions.

Their incidence in every quarter of the globe is legion. Yet, if they are not being raised, suffered and solved, there is no loyal response to universality. It is well to be aware of what we incur if genuinely we seek a trans-cultural Church. Do western Christians who enthuse at that call appreciate the diversity it must be ready to embrace? But the only alternative is, in the end, to assume a faith and a Church fixed in the likeness of our own familiars. Or should we rather say, what our familiars have made of the Scriptural norms and the primitive faith, remembering, as we must, that these are "of no private interpretation", but exist to be possessed by all generations and by all lands? To be the norm of Christ is a duty no heirs can arrogate from them and which, indeed, they only possess, in *their* cultural particularity, by virtue of the unresting activity of the Holy Spirit.

THE CHURCH: RESPONSIBLE TO UNITY

To say that the one is properly many is to mean that also the many are to be truly one. To be responsive to universality is to be responsible to unity. The latter theme has all the time been implicit in our reflections on the former. Archbishop William Temple, preaching in Canterbury Cathedral in 1942, spoke of "a Christian fellowship which now extends into almost every nation", as "the great new fact of our era", adding how it made itself "apparent from time to time in World Conferences . . ."[1] But the sad further fact is that, while relationships between that Protestant fellowship (as it was in 1942) and the great Roman and Orthodox wings of Christianity have developed beyond all but the most ardent dreams, there has occurred a parallel proliferation of divergent sects and sectaries, some of the wildest order, confusing and distracting the entire Christian presence among the nations. In Japan, for example, there has arisen in recent years a daunting number of groups holding heterogeneous elements from a variety of sources in a bizarre amalgam of ideas and emotions. Africa, west and east, blossoms novel and strange versions of Christianity with a seemingly endless fecundity, marrying elements of pagan or Muslim practice with Old Testament vestiges oddly interpreted and features of Christian liturgy or dogma often only remotely recognizable as such. Such fertile progeny derives, no doubt, from an equal variety of inter-acting causes—the sense of independence of white church tradition and authority, the assertion of local genius and mood, the ingenuity of imaginative minds, the perversities of human nature and personal ambition, and the sheer, restless exuberance of the native spirit. They constitute a salutary reminder to the older churches of the revenge that neglected culture takes on institutions and patterns of emotional adherence that ignore its quality and scout its needs. The extent to which they deviate from the norms of the faith and so confound the religious picture is probably in direct proportion to the

[1] *The Church Looks Forward*, London, 1944, p. 2.

failure elsewhere to do justice to the impulses and energies they release and satisfy. It is this reflection which must give pause to the likely temptation of traditional or tidy minds to avoid all cultural adaptation like the plague. For in that way of timidity lies no respite from duty, no escape from burdens, but only, in the long run, an unwanted provocation of precisely the thing it fears.

All this is not to refer to the heavy, even bitter, complexities introduced by sects of western origin and white deviationism and propagated in the world at large with ample resources of finance and personnel. Drawing both their strength and their disruptiveness from excessive or disproportionate emphasis, they distort the wholeness of Christian meaning and sanity and sadly jeopardize and bedevil the transcultural obligations of the churches, whether by intransigence, confusion or ill-will. There is no place here to attempt even a summary documentation of this melancholy picture. There are times when a realistic observer of 'Christian' propagation in the world might be tempted to conclude that it is in fact drowned in the very spate of ambiguity and shamed into silence by its own contradictions.

But this would be an unduly despairing verdict. Tragic as the distortions and stridencies of sectarianism are, there is peril for the churches which fail to reckon with the fascination 'sectaries' feel and exercise. Their vivid personalism and immediacy of experience, the exhilaration of their certainties, the thrill of their protests or their non-conformity, hold abiding relevance for institutionalism, authority and the sense of disciplined orthodoxy. These latter, as church history demonstrates, can so readily miss, or disarm, the ultimate significance of the Holy Spirit. The Church, or the churches, readily lose what Albert Mirgeler calls their "transcendental permeability", by dint of "a massive self-sufficiency"[1] out of keeping with their real vocation. Though it is a deep and authentic Christian conviction that

---

[1] *Mutations of Western Christianity, op. cit.*, p. 128. The quotation is taken from a most perceptive summary of the medieval problem of 'sect' and 'establishment'.

the activity of the Spirit in the world is ever within the self-consistency of God as given in Christ, we can never safely erect that truth into a secure disregard or disdain for the deviations, however lamentable, of the -isms that compete around us. It is not only neglected pagan customs which avenge themselves on the churches but also forgotten, or scouted, aspects of the Holy Spirit. There is need, therefore, for courage, humour and undauntedness in the face of contemporary diversity besetting the search for the unity of Christ. The fear, and the real menace, of syncretism must not be allowed to deflect us from the will to the human fullness in Christ, while it properly sobers us to the risks and stresses that attend its pursuit. There is here no neutrality. If we seek refuge from the pain or distaste of sectarian distortion and contumacy, we shall by the same token abandon, for an authoritarian retreat, the true and creative labours of Christian unity across the cultures.

That unity, happily, can be discerned by different criteria of intensity. The recognition of the frailer ones need not deter the will for the stronger. The deepest factors of integration belong with the Scriptures, the Creeds and the structure of the Christian society historically received. The mind to unity already activated in the ecumenical movement and intention has been powerfully reinforced by recent developments within the Roman Catholic Church and by the participation of 'Eastern' Orthodoxy, in significant measure, in the World Council of Churches, no longer a solely Protestant aegis. Its principle of mutual church recognition throughout its membership—though the church status of all is not explicitly approved by each—gives a strong practical impetus to common understanding and sustained theological incentive to self-awareness within a larger whole.

But these formal patterns and occasions of ecumenical enterprise need not constitute its limits. There are other less tangible, more indefined, integrative forces which we must allow to their full potential. Communities, naming the name of Christ, however divisively, must be patiently

regarded in the open effort to reduce their will to fragmentation, to separate their sometimes right reasons from wrong
postures, to take their legitimate if ill-balanced criticism of
ourselves and the checks to equanimity that are implicit,
however crudely, in their prejudice. A constraining sense of
the bewildering tensions of the time within which we all
serve, or disserve, the faith will foster the needed realism.
Our calling is to a robust confidence in the indestructibility
of the faith and a proper perspective of the vicissitudes it
has already survived. The identity of the Church, for all its
historical obscuring and confounding, remains as the
incorporated counterpart of the authenticity of Christ
and the indefectibility of the Spirit. As such we must hold to
it, as not only the touchstone of our incompleteness, but the
shape of our joy and judgement, in Christ. This means that in
the service of its trans-cultural, inter-human, expression, our
confidence must be set towards the future to which Christ
summons us, rather than to the past of our compromise. The
very definition of the Church means prospect as well as
retrospect, and there is no surer context for its attainment
than the exactions of a truly world-wide residence among
men.

The sum of the matter is implicit in the relation of the
three adjectives, 'holy', 'catholic' and 'apostolic' by which
the unity of the Church is credally described: "I believe in
One, Holy, Catholic and Apostolic Church". 'Catholic' and
'apostolic' may be readily related as the goal and the
means, the same character in concept and in pursuit,
having inclusiveness as a quality and as a policy. But there is
a potential paradox between 'holy' and 'catholic', in that this
embrace is also a distinctiveness. It has to do with the inclusion that separates. 'Holiness' means, not so much an
actual piety of behaviour (for which the New Testament
uses ὅσιος rather than ἅγιος), but denotes the hallowedness
by which the whole created order is bounded, but which is
intensively realized in the society of redemption whose
calling disqualifies human self-centredness. Yet its consequent 'apartness' is neither aloof nor censorious. For it holds

the sign and instrument by which the whole of life is meant to read its secret and find its meaning. The vocation to 'holiness' does not abstract or 'aristocricize': it does not establish a caste or an *élite*. For that would be unholy, in exempting from its meaning what it did not want to embrace. It only remains its distinctive self when it lives to communicate, to baptize, to greet and to include. Yet in doing so, it perpetually risks its own identity in order to retain it truly. This is its catholicity, addressing not only the profane and the secular, but also the schismatic and the divergent, responsibly reaching to men everywhere, in their religion or their irreligion and to the cultures, which are the marriage of their material with their conceptual worlds, the homes they make for their spirits out of their landscapes and ecology, their circumstance and genius, the achievement of their particular humanity.

It is here we return to our initial paraphrase of John Donne and to the ultimate sense of the 'ecumenical'. The calling of the Church to unity must mean its will to union with men in the setting of the day-to-day world and of historical time. Have we traditionally conceived of mission with too heavy an accent on doctrinal terms and communal allegiance, seeing our duty as an invitation to others to join themselves with our 'institution' on the basis of an acceptance of an alternative creed to their own, and with differing symbols? This pattern of address to the world presupposes the intelligibility in all contexts of the faith we proclaim and, with that assumption, our own credibility—the thing we have so often forfeited or strained. It also expects a readiness in men for what might be called doctrinal, or even metaphysical, migration and a detachability of persons from familiarity for a venture in identifying truth. It also assumes that our time and place genuinely await and admit what have been described as the 'be' questions: *Is* God? Who *is* man? What *is* truth? and related, theological queries. Can we rely on the broad, relevant, vital answerability of these questions in the contemporary mood, either of western or of eastern man? There is around us a scepticism of mood, rather than of logic, which is not pervious to persuasions that begin from assurance, however justified. May it not be, then, that the interrogatives in which faith and mission must first participate are the 'do' questions: What are we to do about population? about poverty, about social evils, about revolution? what does faith do? what use does religion have? how does love act in the racial conflict? does anything 'do' in our predicament?

It is not that the doctrine and the allegiance are ever dispensable. On the contrary. It is, rather, that their meaning is to be discovered, not in specific, still less abstract, commendation, but in the context of companionship and identity, within the perplexed crises and stresses of the human neighbourhood. At least in our time, whatever may have earlier been true, relevance is not, first, to be realized by dint of proposition, but only of participation—ours with men. Is it finally the Incarnation to which we hope to recruit a confessing faith? It will only be as the Divine solidarity with men is exemplified in the God-with-us quality they may experience in the persons whose belief in such Divinity joins them to human distress. Is it with the centrality of the Cross, as index to the being of God, that our doctrine has to do? Then its authenticity will be accessible first in the dimension of sacrifice which it plainly sustains in the believer's dealings with his fellows. Are we concerned that other faiths enter into the knowledge of these Christian apprehensions of truth? Then will it not be as concrete situations within their own societies are seen to require for their saving men made in this image of the Divine?

We put the point in another way if we say that we are arguing for a revision of our understanding of conversion. The characteristic picture, with all its simple attraction, might well be seen in the Ethiopian chancellor in the closing scene of Acts 8: a Scriptural perusal, an exegetical inquiry, a doctrinal confession and an initiating rite. One may suspect that even here there is much else besides, unspoken. But the narrative condenses it in those classic terms. In the no less familiar passage in Acts 16, however, about the Philippian gaoler, there is apparently no premeditated search, no persuasive reading, no studious catechism. Only the baptism is there, and this follows the use of water the other way round. Was the man perhaps baptized in water from the laver of his own ministering hands? His conversion, at all events, responds to how the apostles act in his own crisis, not to what they preached in the city. When Jesus said to Simon Peter: "When you are converted, strengthen your brethren" (St. Luke 22: 32), the word means "when you have come back to life" or "when you have rallied". (The adjacent clause "that thy faith fail not" uses a medical term about a pulse that ceases.) This 'conversion', post-dating long months of intimate doctrinal tutelage already acknowledged, has to do with the discovery of meaning in and beyond the concrete dilemma of what to do about the suffering Messiah who could not be rescued, and so called into practical question all the lights by which Peter's discipleship moved.

There are, then, in the New Testament ample precedents for what we are pondering, without devalidating, where it may be viable, the traditional pattern of intellectual credence and creed. When we invite to conversion we mean first a re-orientation of personality into the Christ dimension in practical terms. The question we have to ask ourselves is whether this may not come to pass apart from the formal recognition of Christian dogma—the sort of recognition for which we have mostly sought hitherto. Can it not arise within the existing traditions of social and religious community? May it perhaps suffice that the doctrinal home and sanction of this newness of life is secured, if need be vicariously, for all men, within the convictions of the Christian community, finding there the intensive dogmatic formulation other men fail to share? Is it indispensable that they should first accede?

This is in no way to make that house of doctrinal faith a closed society. For that would be a conclusion utterly intolerable. The creed and community that have in trust the universally human secret of God in Christ must be ever accessible to belief and hospitable to discipleship. Baptism is an inalienable right of all men and the freedom for it remains the deepest tribute to their dignity and stature. Admissibility to the faith of Christ is the ecumenical birthright of mankind, never to be suspended or curtailed.

But, given this fact, the Church is called, nevertheless, to seek identification with men before, without, or even against, such credal discipleship, in the trust for which the doctrinal theme exists, namely the living incidence through all the world of the quality of human relationship which has the supremely worthy and Divine prototype in Jesus as the Christ through the Cross. We need to see this human presence of the Church, not first as bearing a dogma for adherence but rather a life for experience, in a Christ for imitation. We should not regard the active compassion of mission, in medicine and pastoral care, as ancillary to the corroboration or propagation of belief, but rather as token of that humanity all men, with us, are invited to be. And in this carefreeness about its own security and acceptance the doctrine will take care of itself. Thus the identity of the Church will be known and its diversity fulfilled.

When "the servant of the Lord" is described in the passage from Isaiah 42, quoted at the close of the previous chapter, he is said "not to fail or be discouraged" in the patience that does "not quench the smoking flax or break the bruised reed". It is notable that there is used of him here a kindred pair of words with those employed for the flax and the reed. He too will not be quenched or dimmed, nor will he break before his service is achieved. Can we then infer that in the end the ground of hopefulness in Christian mission is one with the ground of hope in men? The ministry takes upon itself precisely those qualities which are apt to the reality with which it deals. In effect, the faith's future is one with the flickering capacities of humanity in whom and for whom it burns and the Church's destiny moves with and for the precarious responsiveness of mankind.

St. Paul has it, forcefully, in his characteristic fashion. "For we preach, not ourselves"—the institutional non-priority, "but Christ Jesus the Lord"—the Christ-reality,

217

central and entire; "and ourselves"—the relevant community only in the prior context; "your servants for Jesus' sake"—and given to men in the capacity proper to the Gospel. In that service, we need have no fear to lose the Christ of faith, if we will be loyal to the Christ of the world.

INDEX

BIBLICAL PASSAGES